PRAISE FOR *"SHORTCUTS TO A HAPPIER LIFE"*

"What a gift to the world! Sean brings his keen insight and vast experience to every essay. Read them in order or skip around. I plan to use this book for myself and as a training tool for my staff."

Diana Gasperoni, Founder & CEO BeWELL Psychotherapy

"Shortcuts to a Happier Life" captivates readers. Sean's essays will challenge you to think differently, laugh a little, and reflect on your life."

Liz Morrison, Psychotherapist

"Distilled from his years as a psychotherapist, Sean documents how changing one's perspective can transform a life and capture the creative magic between patient and therapist."

Dr. Julie Low, Psychiatrist, NYU Faculty

"Shortcuts to a Happier Life" offers self-healing work on every page."

Dr. Leonard Rosenblum, Union Square Spine

"Sean Grover's essays are a joy to read. His care and thoughtfulness leap from the page."

Jonathan Curelop, author of *Tanker 10*

"Wit and wisdom on every other page. Kidding! On every page. I'll be keeping it handy. You should, too."

Bill Santiago, Comedian and author of *"Pardon My Spanglish"*

"Sean's essays are accessible, clarifying, motivating— a perfect starting place for those needing a change."

Ari Brand, Broadway actor, writer and parent

"Mr. Grover's writing cuts right to the heart of America."

Suzanna Bowling, Times Square Chronicles

SHORTCUTS
TO A
HAPPIER LIFE

Essays on Life, Love, and Parenting

SEAN GROVER

Author of *When Kids Call The Shots*

Shortcuts to a Happier Life

Essays on Life, Love, and Parenting

Sean Grover

ISBN (Print Edition): 979-8-35093-914-9

ISBN (eBook Edition): 979-8-35093-915-6

To my beautiful wife and best friend, Yuko.

INTRODUCTION

Almost ten years ago, when I was asked to write a blog for *Psychology Today*, I had no idea what a blog was. I thought, *"What an ugly word! Sounds more like a skin infection."*

Since then, and one hundred sixty posts later, the *When Kids Call The Shots* blog has gathered over ten million reads. And no one is more surprised than me.

I've received dozens of letters of thanks from folks who drew inspiration and encouragement from the posts:

- A US Air Force pilot who discovered the upside of growing up without a dad in *Boys Without Fathers: 3 Myths, 3 Miracles.*
- A grieving widow who drew strength from *Death Shock: How to Recover When a Loved One Dies Suddenly.*
- A woman in London who found answers for her vocal problems in *Where Do You Store Stress in Your Body? Top 10 Secret Areas.*
- A devastated father struggling with his son's suicide found comfort in *How to Recover When Life Crushes You.*
- A stressed-out mother in Russia, struggling with defiant twin boys, applauded the practical solutions in the *Bullied Parent* posts.

It moves me deeply that so many took the time to write letters. My writing goal has always been guiding people toward hope in moments of despair. As Buddhist peace activist Daisaku Ikeda writes:

"Life is filled with all sorts of struggles and sufferings. Problems are unavoidable. They are an inescapable reality of life. Our only alternative is to become strong."

Many of these articles grew from my struggles and discoveries in therapy. I wrote some of them in the middle of sleepless nights or during solitary walks by the Hudson River. Others were inspired by the courage and resilience demonstrated every week by the folks in my therapy groups.

I hope you find some strength and clarity in the pages that follow. Until then, I'll keep blogging. (*Is that really a word?*)

TABLE OF CONTENTS

CHAPTER 1:
ADDICTION

When Someone You Love Becomes an Addict

3 Ways to Care For Yourself and Find Help.

Addiction is a disease like no other. It doesn't appear on X-rays, nor is it an injury or allergy with a simple cure. It's a phantom that travels through families, crossing decades, and suddenly reappears in new generations. It destroys marriages and devastates relationships. Today, with the outbreak of prescription drug abuse, it can be even harder to recognize signs of addiction.

Whether the person is a sibling, parent, friend, son, or daughter, your world falls apart when someone you love destroys themselves with substances. You'd willingly sacrifice all you have for that person to be right again.

Desperate for relief, you may lie to yourself:

- *"She's doing better."*
- *"I can trust him again."*
- *"I should be optimistic."*

You may try to talk sense to them, but your efforts to help are met with callous anger.

- *"I'm fine. Leave me alone."*

- *"Stop worrying! You're making me feel worse."*
- *"Why don't you believe me?"*

Perhaps the person you love stands before you, wild-eyed, body trembling for a fix. In such unforgettable moments, you feel your heartbreak.

Sooner or later, hopelessness wears you down. Everything is tested: your faith, relationships, and even trust in yourself. You may wander down the path of self-blame:

- *This is my fault.*
- *I should have seen the signs.*
- *What was I thinking?*

There are no easy answers when dealing with addiction. You want your love to be enough -- unfortunately, it isn't. But you can take action to strengthen yourself and weaken its spell.

Care for the Caregiver

When you're tending to someone in crisis, a rare friend asks, *"How are you doing?"* The addicted person takes up so much time and space it's common to neglect themselves. Here's how best to help yourself and those you love.

1. **Seek Out Support**

   Find a group, hire a professional, and attend a meeting. The internet is full of free support programs for families and individuals. Addiction is one of the most complex and complicated diagnoses. Talking out your feelings and sharing your experience will help more than you think. If you're hesitant, bring a friend. Nothing is more powerful than being in the presence of people who share your experience and come out whole again. Bottom line: Don't go it alone.

2. **Practice Self Care**

   Stress can have a profoundly negative effect on your physical and emotional health. That's why you must take care of yourself even more. Long walks are excellent for clearing your head. Surround yourself with nurturing friends. See a movie, visit a gallery, go to a concert. Such tasks may seem mundane, but they will raise your spirits and give your mind a break from the stress it desperately needs.

3. Pace Yourself

Sometimes, no matter what you do, someone won't listen. Another person's will is ultimately beyond our power. Until they are ready to get help or "hit bottom," do your best to stay firm. You're not giving up on them; you're remaining supportive. Hopefully, the moment will arrive, they will turn to you for help and accept your support. Remember: recovery is a long journey that can't be rushed.

A New Beginning: A Story

A family reunited with their daughter, who had nearly died of an overdose. She had spent two months in a girls' wilderness program deep in the mountains of Georgia, far from the urban life she knew. When they last saw her, her thin body was marked with cuts, her face bruised from hitting herself.

Sending her there, without a doubt, was the most excruciating decision they had ever made as parents. She said she would never speak to them again—ever.

The visiting day arrives. The mother and father drive their rented car up the gravel road and park. They look like frightened children, out of place in the overgrown forest, unsure of what to expect.

Seconds later, their daughter is running breathlessly down a hill toward them, waving, hair wild and unkempt, clothes stained with the muck of the woods.

"Mom! Dad!"

They almost don't recognize her. How long had it been since she called them that?

They fall into each other's arms, wrapped in a single, timeless embrace, their bodies shaking with emotion. In the distance, the addiction counselors, like mountain angels, watch, tend to open fire, and exchange smiles. No one notices the light rain trickling through the pines.

After a long while, their daughter attempts to speak, her face wet with tears, words caught in her throat, then finally she whispers:

"Thank you...for...not giving up...on me."

And in a single magical moment—everything changed. Much work was still needed, but hope returned and was gaining momentum. True healing could now begin.

What You Can Do Today

Caring for someone who is addicted is a test of love. Seek support. Reach out to friends, talk to professionals, re-engage your spiritual practice, or start one. An enormous community of people in recovery, everyday heroes, waiting to help you. Such actions will give you hope, even when your situation feels hopeless.

When Someone You Love Relapses

And 3 Steps to Get Help Today.

You trusted him. He promised you that he'd changed and convinced you that he'd learned his lesson, that his days of using drugs and alcohol were over. He finished a rehab program and celebrated the anniversary of his abstinence with you. He hugged and thanked you for being there and for not abandoning him.

And you felt relief in your soul. The dark cloud that hung over and overshadowed everything finally lifted. You could breathe again and sleep again. You told yourself, "I grew from this pain. I am a better person for it. More humane, more compassionate, more understanding." You congratulated yourself on staying strong. You didn't give up on him. You made it through the worst life could throw at you. Now you could finally get back to enjoying your time together. You don't have to hide your prescription drugs anymore.

Then, one day, you notice that dark clouds are gathering again. Things don't seem right. You have a sense that the lies are back. You push the thought away. You tell yourself, "It's not true. I'm just being paranoid." You engage in reckless optimism, ignoring the signs in front of you. Maybe it's because you don't think your heart could recover again; you don't think you could survive another relapse.

How many times can a heartbreak before it can't be mended?

Slowly, it dawns on you: the old behaviors have returned. He looks different, talks differently. Something in his manner seems false and calculated.

When you dare to talk to him, tell yourself, "Be gentle. Talk from a place of love." You even practice what to say. After all, you want to be mindful.

When you express your concerns, he becomes enraged. "Why can't you believe in me?" he yells, "You're the problem. You're the cause of this — not me."

You feel ashamed. You feel embarrassed. You apologize. But, deep down, you know something is wrong again. Something is broken. You can't ignore it anymore.

Who do you turn to? Who do you tell?

Your Recovery

It's impossible to describe your pain when someone you love relapses. Your world turns upside down. You discover so many lies and falsehoods you don't know what's real anymore.

Your recovery starts when you step away from trying to help the one you love and focus on helping yourself. Here are three critical steps toward feeling whole again:

1. Find a Support Group

In over twenty years of working as a therapist, I've found nothing more powerful than a group of people struggling together. The empathy of peers and the love and support of individuals who share your experience are healing. Look online, call an 800 number, find a group, and go.

2. Avoid Isolation

There will be the impulse to withdraw, isolate yourself, and hide from others. Please don't do it. Isolate breeds depression, anxiety, and fear. It makes problems feel insurmountable. Force yourself out, go for walks, go to the gym, and go to the theater. Keep seeing friends, keep being active—keep living.

3. Stop Enabling

Addicts thrive on empty promises. You may want to believe that they can stop using drugs and alcohol on their own. The reality is it's rare for someone to recover without professional support. Unless they are willing to get help, there's very little you can do.

One Day at a Time

Gather support. Find the angels in your life and reach out to them. Renew your faith, turn to loved ones, and keep striving. You can't control addiction but can take charge of your own life.

The Inner Voice of a Teenager Addicted to Marijuana

"Nothing is coming between me and smoking. Nothing."

I had my first hit in middle school, in a park near my house, hanging out, basically doing nothing. My friend took out a joint his brother gave him for his thirteenth birthday. Sounds sketchy, right? But his brother is a straight-A student. He wasn't a drug dealer.

To be honest, I wasn't into it. I coughed so much it burned my throat. But I had this euphoric feeling that I never had before—total freedom. Everything I worried about went away, like thinking I was too short, nerdy, or worrying about my acne. It all disappeared.

I decided right then and there, "I need to get more."

Before you judge me, I'm not a loser with a sad story. No one in my family does drugs, and my parents aren't abusive. I'm not from a poor neighborhood. I love my mom and dad; my brother and I are best friends. On winter breaks, when I was little, we visited Disney World and my grandparents in Florida.

I guess you could say we're an all-American family.

But smoking weed just feels so good. That's all I think about now. When I'm not high, I'm thinking about getting high. When my supply is low, I think about buying more weed or bumming some off a friend. I can't imagine not having weed on me. Man, that would so suck.

Even when my parents caught me smoking in my room, and I promised I wouldn't do it again, I knew I was lying. I smoked later that night. My mom cries, and my dad has this defeated look. They're so dramatic. They need to chill out. Even my brother is dumping on me, saying that I've changed, that I'm hurting Mom and Dad.

Honesty, I don't care what he says. Nothing is coming between me and smoking. Nothing.

I get high alone now. I don't need friends. I smoke before school, in the stairwell during lunch, behind the gym after school. I don't need a reason to get high. Honestly, I forget what it feels like not to be high.

Most days, I can't stand my parents. They're always sniffing around my room. Judging me. They make me want to smoke more. I can't wait to move out. I tell them that weed isn't addictive, but they won't listen.

There are so many ways to get high, too. You can roll or bake; they even have weed gummy bears. My friend's parents smoke with him. How cool is that? They even taught him how to make weed butter.

Last week, I got a vape pen. I traded my guitar for it. Now, I can smoke anywhere. Sometimes, I even take a few hits in the back of my English class. The other kids stare and shake their heads like they're better than me. But I don't care. That's why I quit sports and band. They're all uptight and stupid.

The truth is, weed just makes everything better. If I watch a movie, I watch it high. If I skateboard, I ride high. I even ate dinner with my family high. They can't even tell anymore.

I owe everything to weed. Weed is a part of my identity. I don't know who I would be without it."

"I Tried to Cut Back"

"Honestly, I've tried to smoke less. But I just can't. Seriously. Last year, I went two or three days without smoking, and I had a wicked panic attack. My hands were sweating; my heart was racing. Thank God my friend let me hit his pipe after school. I took a few puffs, and I calmed right down.

Weed is good for me. It helps me. It helps a lot of people. Even doctors describe it. Is that the word? Described?

Whatever.

Now, all the kids at school are obsessed with college applications. What a joke! Spending all that money. Stressing about grades—for what? Honestly, I feel sorry for them. I stopped worrying about my grades a long time ago.

Most days, you'll find me chillin' in my bedroom. Watching YouTube videos or playing Fortnite. And smoking, of course.

I'm not an addict. Seriously, I'm not. I'm a good person. And if you think that I'm addicted to weed, well, whatever. Get over yourself."

Teens Sharing Drugs Can Be Convicted As "Drug Dealers"

Parents beware, your kid could end up in jail.

It's a situation that happens daily throughout the country. Teens meet in local parks, homes, or parties after school to get high together. Obtaining illegal substances has never been easier thanks to technological advances, such as cell phones, the Internet, and social media. Many teens report having drugs delivered right to their front door while their parents are home. Others order drugs on the dark web and receive them in the mail.

Before we explore the impact of the law, let's examine substance abuse use among teenagers.

What Drugs Are Teens Using?

According to Addiction Resource, the United States is the second largest consumer of marijuana in the world. A recent CNN report notes that 24 percent of high school teenagers polled admitted to using marijuana in the last year.

Though marijuana and alcohol remain the dominant drugs teens use, prescription drugs, which are far more powerful and addictive, are gaining popularity. According to The Foundation for a Drug-Free World, 90 percent of prescription drug addicts reported using prescription drugs in middle school or high school. This is supported by a National Institute on Drug Abuse report, which notes that 25 percent of prescription drug abusers started using prescription drugs before they were 13 years old.

How Can Teens Afford to Buy Drugs?

Honest Marijuana suggests that the average price for medium-quality marijuana is $9-15 a gram, which should produce 1.5 joints. However, vaping and cannabis "oil pens" are gaining in popularity because they're virtually odor-free and can be quickly hidden, which makes them ideal for smoking in school or other public places.

You can track the current street prices for prescription drugs on StreetRx. Here's a sample of the going rates for prescription drugs in major cities:

- **New York:** 30 mg of Adderall sells for $10.
- **Connecticut:** 15 mg morphine ER pill sells for $10.
- **Nevada:** 5 mg of Valium sells $5.

The site notes that Adderall is the most famous street drug.

How Do Teens Get Access to Drugs?

The three most common ways teenagers obtain drugs are:

- *They pool their money to buy drugs.*
- *A teen with access to drugs uses, sells, or shares them.*

- *Prescription drugs are stolen or taken from parents'/grandparents' medicine cabinets.*

Now that we've covered the cost of drugs and how teenagers get them, let's look at how new drug laws make these situations particularly difficult for everyone involved.

Drug Laws

If your child shares drugs with a friend, regardless of how they were obtained, they can be charged as a drug dealer, even if they give the pills away.

Moreover, if an accidental overdose occurs, homicide charges can be brought against the teen who distributed the drug. Teenagers no longer have to sell drugs to be charged and held responsible.

According to a report by the New York Times, Not a Drug Dealer? Here's Why the Law Might Say Otherwise charges in overdose cases can be brought against nearly anyone who was a party to the crime, including the victim's friends, siblings, or parents. For example, the report notes a 17-year-old and two classmates faced murder charges after the LSD they gave to a friend resulted in a fatal overdose. It also mentions a 21-year-old in Minnesota sentenced to over nine years in prison after his best friend fatally overdosed due to a drug he shared with him at a party.

Unfortunately, the National Institute on Drug Abuse for Teens reports that teen overdose deaths are increasing, which means harsh punishments are likely to grow and become more frequent. According to another NY Times report, They Shared Drugs. Someone Died. That Makes Them Killers? The number of prosecutions in accidental overdose deaths doubled between 2015 and 2017, totaling more than 1,000 cases in 36 states with charges from manslaughter to first-degree murder.

If you're a parent of a teen who is using or sharing drugs, here are five steps you can take today:

1. **Share this information.**

   Discuss drug sharing and the new legal consequences with your child.

2. **Involve Others**

   Get a family member or friend with recovery experience to speak with your kids.

3. **Talk to School Officials**

   Visit your kid's principal or guidance counselor and discuss starting a drug awareness program at your school.

4. **Find a Teen Drug Prevention Program**

   Talk to your local law enforcement and find out what drug prevention organizations are available.

5. **Drug Test Your Kid**

   Consider adding a drug test to your child's annual physical. You can buy a home kit or have your doctor perform the test.

———————

5 Warning Signs Your Teenager May Be Using Drugs

The earlier a teen is exposed, the higher the risk of addiction.

Figuring out whether or not your teenager is using drugs can be a challenge. I sat down with Holly Holloway from MedMark Treatment Centers to discuss what concerned parents can do. Holly works to help spread awareness and end the stigma of addiction. Here's what she had to say:

Young adults deal with many physical and emotional changes throughout their teen years, making it difficult to pinpoint whether their symptoms are drug-related or puberty-related. With the rising awareness of mental health in teens, it's also something to consider when approaching the subject. However, there are specific signs to look out for and precautions to take if you are concerned about their well-being.

Behavioral Changes

If your teen has recently begun acting differently to the point where it's affecting previously stable relationships with family members, it could be a sign of substance misuse. Arguing with siblings, extreme moodiness, or lashing out in anger can be related to being under the influence. Staying out past curfew and blatantly defying ground rules are classic teenage behaviors. Still, if your teen is using drugs, these behaviors may also coincide with staying out all night, driving recklessly, constantly asking for money, and disappearing for long periods. There can also be more physical signs that include incessant sniffling, eye redness, manic behavior, drastic appetite changes, very fast or slow speech, and poor coordination. Depending on the substance they are using, their behaviors will vary. Staying in tune with your child as they approach teen ages and are most prone to experimentation is essential.

Emotional Changes

Teens are notorious for mood swings and emotional stability shifts. Coupled with drug use, adolescence's familiar peaks and valleys can be magnified. A teen who is acting withdrawn and depressed may be dealing with mental health issues, and it's essential to also look for deceitfulness or secretive behavior. Those are both signs they may be involved in drug-related activities. Sudden excitability or restless behavior can also indicate being under the influence. Drugs can counteract normal hormonal development in teens especially. Hormones can significantly affect a child's behavior and growth, and development. While it's hard to gauge the reasoning behind a teenager's behavior sometimes, it's still important to observe their moods and personality shifts if other signs of possible drug use are present.

Health and Hygiene

Young adults are in the process of figuring out how life works as their bodies change. While rapid growth and changing hormones can take their toll on a teenager, there are specific signs that could be related to drug use. Other than noticeable track marks on arms from injecting drugs, frequent contusions and abrasions could also indicate injuries sustained while intoxicated. Frequent lethargy, headaches, and periods of very little sleep, followed by several days of non-stop slumber, are common in young adults who misuse drugs, including prescription medication. If your child has drastically changed how much they mind their appearance, their focus may be shifted towards other things. A messy exterior and lack of regard towards their hygiene could also be signs of degrading mental health and drug use.

Changes at Home and School

If you've noticed a drastic decline in your teen's grades and an increase in them skipping school, drug use could be involved. If a teacher has reached out about behavior in the classroom or reports of possible intoxication during school hours, those are red flags not to be ignored. Be looking for concealed drug paraphernalia around the house or car, including cellophane wrappers, aluminum foil, rolling papers, small pipes, and small bags or containers. If teens can't obtain jobs, they will often steal items from their homes to sell for money, including prescription medication. It's essential to check and ensure any alcohol cabinets and refrigerators are monitored, as alcoholic beverages can also be used as currency for underage teens.

Other Risk Factors

Teenage behavior can be unpredictable and vague, but external factors can influence them negatively and drive them toward drug use.

- **Family History:** If there is a genetic trend of addiction on either side of a child's family, they are more susceptible to following that path. This can include issues with alcohol, nicotine addiction, prescription drugs, or illicit substances. Studies have shown that first-degree relatives of those with addiction issues are eight times more likely to develop addiction disease.

- **Surroundings:** Areas that have a high rate of drug and alcohol use can be a harmful environment for growing young adults. Living in an atmosphere where drugs are used recreationally can normalize exposure to certain substances. In homes where parents and siblings frequently misuse drugs and alcohol, children are prone to a higher rate of experimentation that can lead to addiction.

- **Age:** Teenagers are bound to experiment as their growing brains become curious about the world surrounding them. However, the earlier a teen is exposed to drugs and alcohol, the higher the risk of addiction because the human brain does not finish primary development until one's mid-twenties, the damage that drug use can cause can be irreversible.

Being a teenager has never been easy, but there are ways for parents to create healthy relationships with their children to help guide them toward good decision-making. Being genuinely interested in your child's life is a great way to be proactive and engaged. Asking simple questions about their school and social life is an excellent opportunity to gather information to know what they are up to daily.

While shifts in social circles, activities, and interests are expected, keeping up with them is a supportive and non-intrusive way to know what is happening. Keeping a teen's home life and surroundings safe, clean, and comfortable is also crucial in guiding them to stay on the right track. Most importantly, discussing aspects of their teen life and relating to their problems is far more productive than interrogation and accusation. It will create open communication if your child feels they can trust you and come to you with fears, thoughts, and troubles. This will help them feel safe and more stable, thus less likely to turn to drugs to help them deal with their emotions.

---

3 Health Risks Caused by Marijuana Edibles

Emergency room visits skyrocket with legalization.

Marijuana is enjoying a surge in popularity. Legalization has increased and spread to over 25 states as medical studies continue to show the benefits of weed for treating conditions including anorexia, chronic pain, PTSD, and some forms of cancer.

But before you embrace your inner stoner, there's increasing evidence that the abuse of weed edibles could land you in the hospital. A recent report in the *New York Times* outlines the startling health risks caused by using edibles. In states where marijuana has been legalized, hospitalizations and emergency room visits due to edible abuse have skyrocketed.

A study of thousands of emergency room visits in Denver reveals that over-consuming edibles can result in three serious health risks:

1. **Acute Psychiatric Symptoms.**

    Overindulging in edibles may trigger psychotic symptoms such as auditory or visual hallucinations or extreme paranoia. Individuals abusing edibles are at high risk of provoking psychotic episodes, mainly if there is a family history of mental illness.

2. Severe Intoxication.

When you inhale marijuana, the effect is felt almost immediately, which allows you to regulate your intake. With edibles, the product may not hit you entirely for up to two hours or more, and absorption varies depending on the person and the fat content of the food. As a result, people consume beyond the recommended amount, which puts teenagers and college students at an exceptionally high risk of edible abuse as they are prone to impulsivity, peer pressure, and poor judgment. What's more, the effects of ingested marijuana last far longer than when marijuana is inhaled.

3. Cardiovascular Problems.

Overusing edibles can cause spikes in anxiety, panic attacks, and racing or irregular heartbeats. Cardiovascular problems are nearly three times more likely with edible users than smokers or vapers. In addition to potential health risks, state officials who oppose legalization cite concerns about impaired driving and accidents, increased addiction, and the harmful impact marijuana has on brain development in youth.

If you're considering edibles, remember that although those pot brownies and gummy bears may look harmless when overconsumed, the side effects are much more severe than the munchies or the giggles.

CHAPTER 2:
ANXIETY

The Voice of Panic Attacks

And seven things you can do today to reduce their occurrence.

"It just happened again. I was having a good day. Work went well; I had lunch with an old friend, and my commute home was smooth. After dinner, I decided to take a hot shower and watch a movie. After all, it was Friday night. Why not unwind and enjoy a quiet evening?

When I stepped out of the shower, my chest felt tight, my breathing became harder, and my fingers and hands went numb. "No!" I said as I wrapped myself in a towel and ran to my bedroom.

I had another panic attack.

If you've never had one, let me tell you, it feels like you're dying. Your heart beats so fast you think it's going to burst. Your body betrays you. Then, the negative thoughts start. You feel like you're going crazy. You begin to think your whole life is a lie. Everyone is phony. No one loves or cares about you. Why would they? You're worthless.

Sometimes, my panic attacks last a few minutes, sometimes longer. But each one feels like an eternity. And here's the worst part: They can happen anywhere. Most of the time, they hit me without any notice. Recently, I was at a friend's wedding, and I had to lock myself in the bathroom until a panic attack passed. When I came out, everyone kept saying, "Are you alright?" I went home early. I wish I could have stayed.

I lie about my panic attacks.

Sometimes, I say that I have the flu or an upset stomach. What else can I do? The few times that I've told people, they'd reacted severely. Like they didn't believe me. Or they give me lame advice. My gym-obsessed friends ask me to work out. As if cardio cures everything. They don't mean to be insensitive, but sometimes their advice feels cruel. They've never had a panic attack. They don't know how bad it can be.

Lately, my panic attacks are getting worse. Sometimes, just worrying about having a panic attack can trigger one. The other day, I was waiting in line at my grocery store. Suddenly, my hands start to tingle. I got dizzy. I had chest pains and felt like everyone was staring at me. I left the line and walked out of the store. On my way out, the store manager yelled, "Please don't leave your shopping cart there!" I ignored him, kept walking, and hid in my car until the panic attack passed. Now I'm afraid to go back to the store. It was so humiliating.

Panic attacks are shrinking my life.

I'm starting to isolate myself. I travel less, fear family gatherings and work events, and I've stopped dating. I'm afraid if I don't do something, my fear of panic attacks will ruin my life.

What if I start to have panic attacks at work? What if I lose my job? What will I do then?

I can't keep pretending my panic attacks will get better. I've got to get professional help.

Here are seven things I started to do to reduce my panic attacks:

1. *I made a list of foods to avoid, like caffeinated food or drinks.*
2. *I started a journal to record when I have panic attacks and under what conditions.*
3. *I found a support group for panic attacks.*

4. *I called a psychotherapist who specializes in panic disorders.*
   I made an appointment and asked a friend to go with me.

5. *I bought a panic attack workbook.*

6. *I slowly started exercising again with a friend.*

7. *I started listening to relaxation podcasts.*

I know it sounds like a lot, but I've concluded that defeating panic attacks is a battle that I'm determined to win."

_____

Social Anxiety? Acting Class Can Help

Acting teacher Terry Knickerbocker explains how actor training can lower anxiety.

Social anxiety negatively affects every area of people's lives. It can hurt them professionally, limit them romantically, and damage their friendships. While group therapy is an effective treatment for reducing social anxiety, acting class is another invention that can deliver astonishing transformations.

I sat down with Terry Knickerbocker, Director of Terry Knickerbocker Studio, an acclaimed acting school in New York City. Terry has coached actors on over 300 films, television, and theater projects, both on and off-Broadway and regionally, in addition to consulting with playwrights and screenwriters and coaching Oscar-winning actor Sam Rockwell.

Can you explain how acting classes benefit someone with social anxiety?

In my experience, being too self-involved often triggers social anxiety. Not that people who feel anxious in social situations are narcissists — but they tend to have their attention turned inward rather than outward. When your attention is on yourself, you get anxious. However, when your attention is focused on another person or an activity, your anxiety usually dissipates.

As humans, we are hardwired to connect. The problem is, when we're worried about connecting, we're inherently making ourselves unavailable to do so. People with social anxiety are worried about the future rather than the now — *"What should I say next? What if I say something that makes me look dumb/silly?" "What if they don't like me?"*

Learning to be present and a better listener is a big part of our actor training. Being in the moment and building an experience organically — be it a conversation or scene — is the quickest and simplest way to catapult yourself out of an anxious headspace and into contact with another human being.

The Sanford Meisner approach to acting, which we teach at the studio, also draws on the idea of play. Acting is a form of playing with someone else. It's hard to be anxious under those circumstances. (Think small children fully engaged in play- not a lot of anxiety for the most part.)

What tools would they gain from an acting class that they can apply in life?

Students at the studio learn to be extremely good listeners. They become more self-aware and in touch with their feelings, thoughts, and attitudes. They learn how to improvise from moment to moment and to be present rather than dwelling on the past or worrying about the future.

Our students learn to identify and vocalize their thoughts and feelings in real-time. They learn how to read intonation and body language. We urge them to foster curiosity and hold space for their effect on others. Good acting training encourages humanity, empathy, and self-awareness.

This training is a very personal and individual journey of self-discovery. For example, our students might explore something that excites them, makes them mad, or feel romantic. With greater self-knowledge comes greater self-confidence.

Do you need acting experience to take classes at your school?

We seek diverse, generous, curious, collaborative, open-hearted, spirited, uncompromising, and real students. The work we do at the Terry Knickerbocker Studio exemplifies impeccable integrity, joyous practice, bold choices, and a lively sense of play.

This technique is unique in that it gives actors a blueprint by which to expand their understanding of themselves as artists and human beings. It celebrates the fact that we are each individual with our own unique life experiences. Unlike other Conservatory Programs, TKS aims to mold non-cookie-cutter artists who can play any role they're handed.

Many of our students come to us with significant previous training and impressive resumes, but another group has no experience. In fact, here's a blog article which is written by a current student about this very topic: How Can I Get Into Acting With No Experience? We have a beginner class, a summer class, and a two-year intensive class.

What do you recommend for someone who is interested in taking classes at Knickerbocker Studios?

All admission is done by an in-person or Skype interview. We'd love to meet you and hear about your goals, even if you're anxious. Please visit us at terryknickerbockerstudio.com for more information!

---

5 Simple Ways to Relieve Stress and Anxiety
Try these simple stress-relieving techniques.

Everyone experiences stress and anxiety from time to time. Stress often occurs when you encounter a frustrating situation or a dilemma. Social pressures, heavy workloads, and financial instabilities also cause stress, which can reduce productivity, cause health problems, or lead to chronic symptoms of anxiety or depression.

I sat down with Ayesha Khan, a certified yoga therapist who has spent multiple years coaching people in the healing tradition of classical yoga and meditation. Here's what she had to say:

Stress attacks your hope and willpower and makes you feel vulnerable. You get annoyed easily and react to petty issues. You may suffer mood swings, and your behavior becomes unpredictable. Escaping stress might seem difficult or impossible, but you can eventually fight back. Try these simple stress-relieving techniques.

1. Exercise

Exercise has unlimited benefits for the human body, and fighting stress is one of them. Research has shown that people who exercise daily are less likely to experience anxiety. Exercise causes the following effects:

Reduced stress hormones: Regular exercise lowers your stress hormones and releases the endorphins that amplify your mood.

Improved Sleep: Exercise improves the quality of sleep. If you get enough sleep, you will automatically start to feel better.

Increased Self-Confidence: You will feel more self-assured and think positively after a good workout.

You can go for a morning walk, jog, climb and do yoga. Meditations, such as circular breathing, are also beneficial in combating stress. If you are physically active, your mind will stay healthy and assertive, too. Exercise is good for your mental well-being and boosts your immune system.

2. Lower Your Caffeine Intake

You might think coffee keeps you going in the morning, but a significant increase in stress levels has been linked to excessive caffeine use. Coffee stimulates adrenaline in your body, which might give you a boost temporarily, but later, you will feel increased fatigue and possible disturbances in your sleep cycle. On average, less than 3 cups per day is a moderate consumption level of caffeine. However, cutting coffee entirely is the best solution for people sensitive to caffeine.

3. Proper Diet

Stress negatively impacts blood flow and blood pressure. A healthy diet is necessary to overcome chronic stress. Substitute fruits and green leafy vegetables instead of eating starchy or sugary foods. Fruits have vitamin E, and vegetables have carotenoids, improving brain blood flow. Fish has a particular substance called omega-3 fatty acid, which lowers stress hormones. Nutritious foods like blueberries and fibrous fruits have positive effects on brain functioning.

4. Chewing Gum

Another interesting way of reducing stress is having a piece of chewing gum. The brain of a person who chews gum generates specific types of waves. These waves resemble those produced by the brain of a happy person. In addition, chewing gum improves blood flow, naturally reducing anxiety.

5. Spend Time With Loved Ones

There is no substitute for the quality time you spend with loved ones. Social support helps you get through stressful times. You feel very weak and vulnerable in stressful conditions; healthy friendships help at such times and lift your spirits.

You feel important and heard when you spend time with your close friends and family members. You may express your opinions and feelings more freely. When you speak from your heart, you feel lighter. As a result, you will not overthink an issue or engage in self-harming thoughts.

The Negative Voices of an Anxiety Disorder

These five self-care tips can lower anxiety.

I don't know why I worry so much. I don't want to. Seriously, I don't.

But negative thoughts jab at me and invade my head. Fears and anxieties that may sound ridiculous to you torture me daily.

For example, I'm afraid that everyone secretly hates me. I find evidence everywhere. Friends don't return my messages or take days to get back to me. Even when we make plans, they cancel or stand me up at the last minute.

I stalk them on social media. I shouldn't do it, but I can't help it. I look at their photos and say, "Look how much fun they're having without me."

I know what you're thinking: practice meditation, take a yoga class. Blah, blah, blah. I have heard it all before. If only it were that easy!

Most days, I don't want to leave the house. The one time I took a class, I kept imagining people looking at me and thinking, *"Why are you here?"* In my head, I could hear them snicker as I left the room.

Believe it or not, I can fake it at work. No one knows how I struggle. I keep to myself or make small talk. If they only knew!

I rush home, crawl into bed, and binge-watch movies or stupid videos at night. I eat unhealthy food or drink too much—anything to distract me from my nervousness.

Eventually, I try to sleep -- that's when the bad memories come. Old disappointments or criticisms flood my head. Hurtful words become fresh wounds, reopened by my despair.

Next, self-criticism kicks in.

> *"You're such an idiot!"*
>
> *"What's wrong with you!"*
>
> *"Why can't you be normal?"*

I wake tired, ignore the dirty clothes and dishes, and wait until the last moment to leave. I'm late so often I wonder if, deep down, I want to be fired.

At times, fear grips me. My stomach tightens. I get a headache or have a panic attack. I can't breathe, my heart races, and I feel like I will pass out or disappear.

That's what worries me the most. That I will disappear and no one will care.

I think about hurting myself. When I am using a knife in my kitchen. My heart rises when crossing a busy intersection or standing near an open window on a high floor. Sometimes I hear a voice say, *"Get it over with. Jump."*

Sometimes I wish I could.

Don't get me wrong -- I want help. Seriously, I do. I wish someone could rescue me from myself and ditch those negative voices.

I make so many resolutions. But this time, I want to stick to them. Here are my top five.

1. **Get off social media**

   I will delete the apps from my phone and close my accounts. Maybe call a social media addiction hotline.

2. **Join a therapy group**

   I need to find people like me. I need to know I'm not alone. Maybe we can help each other.

3. **Find a Therapist**

   Self-help books aren't enough. I need professional help.

4. **Exercise**

   Staying cooped up in my house only makes me worse. I feel so disconnected from my body. I can start with long walks and work my way up to jogging.

5. **Talk to my doctor**

   I hate the idea of medication, but it's worth it if it can lower my anxiety, even just a little. Maybe I'll have more energy to start doing things I enjoy.

   I guess I'm not giving up on myself. Maybe underneath all this anxiety is a healthy person. A person who isn't afraid of taking chances. A person who has hope.

Where Do You Store Stress in Your Body? Top 10 Secret Areas

Stiff neck or back? It means more than you think.

Our language is filled with negative psychosomatic references to stress:

> *"My boss is a pain in the neck."*

> *"My coworker gives me a headache."*

> *"My ex-boyfriend makes me sick to my stomach."*

Often, we attempt to push unwanted feelings—such as irritation, fear, and sadness—out of our awareness. We associate such feelings with hopelessness or powerlessness. So, to blot them, we forcefully engage in denial or repression. We drive them out of our consciousness and deny our emotions. Instead of acknowledging, processing, and releasing these unwanted feelings, we bottle them up.

Nathaniel Branden, the founder of The Psychology of Self-Esteem, insists that we must accept all our feelings without censorship; we should never disown, deny, or repress any part of our experience. He points out that to deny our feelings is to keep ourselves in a perpetual state of internal conflict. The more you distance yourself from your feelings, the more disempowered and out of touch with your true self.

But where do these unwanted feelings go?

Mysterious Aches and Pains

For years, I've studied where people store unwanted emotions. Indeed, not all body aches or illnesses are psychosomatic. However, recurring patterns emerged as I looked at people's bodily reactions to stress.

Healthy vs. Unhealthy Repression

Fear is the driving force behind repression and is frequently rooted in your past. Repression is often necessary, particularly when you feel overwhelmed or experience trauma. However, over-dependence on repression fuels psychosomatic symptoms and self-destructive patterns. As a therapist, I challenge my clients to come up with new responses to fear instead of repeating old behaviors.

I've made a list of these patterns below. You may recognize some of them. I can identify with all of them. Remember, psychosomatic reactions are not neatly organized; some overlap, and some converge. It all depends on your character and interpersonal style. The list below is best used as a general introduction to psychosomatic symptoms, a jumping-off point for personal exploration.

As you review the list, ask yourself: Do any of these symptoms sound familiar?

Top 10 Tension Areas for Unwanted Feelings

1. Lower Back: Anger

If you sit in frustration, the lower back is a common place for storing repressed anger. For relief, learn to articulate frustration constructively and address conflicts with others. Sounds simple? It's not. Learning to harness the power of anger and turn it into a creative force is vital to living an active and rewarding life. Strive to convert anger into assertion; express it constructively, not destructively. You'll be rewarded with a surge in confidence, energy, and healthier relationships.

2. Stomach & Intestines: Fear

When you're afraid, you tend to tense your stomach and intestines. Sayings such as, "I'm sick to my stomach," are usually bodily responses to conflict. The more you deny or repress fears, the more physical reactions will manifest. Begin by acknowledging your trepidation and talking it through with someone you trust. Consider all your choices and outcomes. The more you can express the fear in words, the less of a hold it will have on your body.

3. Heart & Chest: Hurt

I recently worked with a woman complaining of chest pains. A series of medical work-ups found no physical cause for her symptoms. Was she supposed to live with chronic discomfort? Reluctantly, she turned to therapy. When I asked if someone she loved had hurt her, she guffawed and brushed my question off as psychobabble. A few sessions later, as she spoke about the demise of her last relationship, she began to cry uncontrollably. For too long, she ignored her broken heart. She needed to mourn the relationship and honor her sadness. After this release, the tension in her chest finally lifted.

4. Headache: Loss of Control

If you're a major or minor control freak, you're in for a real challenge. No matter how strong-willed you might be, an emphasis on control will eventually lead to burnout–and splitting headaches. Not all difficulties in life can be solved by intellect or trying to control everything. Controlling tendencies exacerbate many problems. Letting go, accepting what you can and can't control, and developing a mindfulness practice are the steps you need to take to cure your headache habit.

5. Neck /Shoulder Tension: Burdens and Responsibilities

Shouldering too many responsibilities is a pain in the neck. You're likely overly burdened if you suffer from neck and shoulder tension. Rather than ask for help from others, you'll probably do everything yourself. This most often leads to neck and shoulder tightness. Learn to delegate, ask for support, decide what is worth taking on, and for goodness' sake, share responsibilities with others.

6. Fatigue: Resentments

Resentment stresses your entire body and does more damage to you than the people you resent. Blaming others, playing the victim, reliving the events–these are the empty calories of self-expression. Resentments keep you from living in the moment and experiencing the benefits of being present. When you focus on those who wronged you, you are giving them free real estate in your head. Instead, try to focus on forgiveness or, at the very least, moving on. Strive for more fulfilling relationships, add a healthy dose of self-care, and you'll feel years younger.

7. Numbness: Trauma

When overwhelmed by an event, we tend to numb our feelings. This is our psyche's way of disassociating from overpowering pain or danger. Traumatic events are not always life-threatening—they can result from a brush with real or imagined threats or a history of childhood abuse or neglect. Over time, if you don't process the trauma, the memory of it gets lodged in your body. As a result, you deaden your feelings when vulnerable; trusting others is impossible, and true intimacy is lost. Any situation that makes you feel unsafe causes great confusion; you freeze up or go blank. The first step toward freeing yourself from trauma is recognizing its power over you and asking for help.

8. Breathing Difficulties: Anxiety

Breathing difficulties, a panic attack that leaves you gasping for air and a suffocating feeling when anxious. These are the symptoms I've noticed in folks who are repressing great sadness. They don't want to cry and avoid tragic mourning events. Instead, they hide sadness, move on, and focus on something else. But restricting tears is a lot like holding your breath. When you finally cry, it comes gushing out; equal parts pain and relief. Freeing bottled-up sadness is like sucking in a dose of fresh oxygen. It's refreshing and liberating!

9. Voice & Throat Problems: Oppression

Oppressed people are not allowed to have a voice. If you grew up in an oppressive atmosphere, speaking your mind or expressing your needs was dangerous. You also carry around a harsh inner critic. As a result, as an adult, you tend to withhold feelings. When you have the impulse to speak up, you resort to your childhood tendency to silence and repress your voice. This clash between the urge to speak and withhold causes tension and often manifests in throat and voice problems. In therapy, I've found that journal writing is a great way to expose your inner critic and start talking back to it. Also, reading poetry out loud (poetry has a profound connection to the unconscious) is a way of gaining confidence in your voice. Hopefully, you will soon realize you have the right to be heard.

10. Insomnia: Loss of Self

People tend to lose sleep during life-changing events–good or bad. You experience anxiety when your life circumstances are in flux. This can happen during times of stress or times of significant personal growth. For me, sleeplessness is most often associated with the fear of the unknown. Please write down your worries or, better yet, talk them out with a close friend. Learn to work with change rather than repress your fear of it. Working with it, you can hit the pillow and have sweet dreams.

Toward a More Rewarding Way of Being

Releasing bottled-up feelings is fundamental to psychotherapy; it offers respite from the psychic stress of repression. People always feel relieved when the weight of repression lifts. Soon after, they report a surge of confidence, a product of a stronger emotional core. Group therapy is also an excellent tool for building stronger and healthier relationships.

When you take better care of your feelings, you take better care of yourself and those you love. You come to appreciate and value your relationships more. Could you take the time to consider how you manage your feelings and what your psychosomatic pain is trying to tell you? Not only will you feel happier, but many studies also show you might live longer.

How Perfectionism Increases Anxiety and Procrastination

7 negative outcomes of perfectionism.

An artist who struggled with perfectionism contacted me for a consultation. He explained that he had been creating sculptures and paintings in his studio for many years. On rare occasions when he allowed others to see his work, they were amazed by the beauty of his creations. Still, he refused to share his art in public.

"It's not perfect!" he explained, his bloodshot eyes wide with exasperation. "If something isn't perfect, I simply cannot let the world see it."

Why was he in my psychotherapy office? He had crippling anxiety, trouble sleeping, headaches, backaches, obsessive thoughts, and rages. He had recently taken a sledgehammer and destroyed a sculpture he had lovingly labored over for more than six months.

The artist's struggle illustrates the potentially devastating effects of perfectionism.

The Adverse Effects of Perfectionism

Perfection may seem noble, but it can do more damage than good when pursued obsessively. Let's take a look at seven possible tragic outcomes of perfectionism.

1. **Stress:** Striving for perfection creates enormous psychic pressure that can trigger psychosomatic symptoms such as chronic fatigue, anxiety, and restlessness.

2. **Procrastination:** Deadlines come and go; nothing ever feels good enough. You fail to complete projects; you're never content with your work. Eventually, if satisfaction remains elusive, you may abandon your efforts entirely.

3. **Disappointment:** Your self-esteem takes a big hit with so many incomplete tasks and critical thoughts. You rarely experience the esteem-boosting burst of satisfaction and pride that comes with a well-done job.

4. **Self-critical thoughts:** You fault yourself relentlessly. Chronic self-criticism fuels anxiety and hopelessness.

5. **Compare and despair:** You negatively compare yourself to others. In your mind, you're always the outlier or underdog who never gets acknowledged. You long for praise and attention yet remain in the shadows.

6. **Less creativity:** It's difficult, if not impossible, to be creative in a hostile environment— especially if the prime source of negativity comes from your internal critics. Over time, creativity is avoided because it feels unrewarding and too painful to pursue.

7. **Lower ambition:** Completed tasks and accomplishments fuel ambition, passion, and inspiration. Unfortunately, perfectionism drains such aspirations.

Breaking Free of Perfectionism

The essence of perfectionism is the illusion that nothing has value unless it's perfect. Try these simple steps to break free of the chains of perfectionism and the illusion that perfection is your only goal.

- **Unplug:** Consuming media can fill your head with unrealistic expectations of how you should look, how wealthy you should be, where you should live, etc. A whole world of "shoulds" will negatively impact your body image, mood, and integrity.

- **Hold fast to deadlines:** Skipping deadlines can have a devastating effect on your sense of self. Once you set a realistic deadline, do your best to meet it.

- **Reward yourself:** Go ahead, celebrate your wins, and treat yourself to something special.

- **Embrace imperfection:** Mistakes are frequently better than our original intent. Give yourself the flexibility and freedom to explore without the goal of perfection.

- **Read biographies:** Many biographies tell the story of highly successful people who experienced rejection, criticism, and failure for many years. Bottom line: Mistakes and failures are part of the process of success.

CHAPTER 3:
BULLIED PARENT

How Pushover Parents Raise Bullies

... and 4 ways to take back control.

When I wrote *When Kids Call the Shots,* I thought I was writing about a small group of children and teens I was seeing in my psychotherapy practice. Since the book was published, I've received hundreds of calls, emails, and letters from parents. My workshops about undoing bullying behaviors at home are in demand, and the book has been translated into Chinese, Korean, and Russian.

I've written at length here about bullying behaviors in children that occur at home. And I've explored the complex reasons parents fail to provide structure, set limits, and teach boundaries.

Now I want to examine what happens when these bullying behaviors in childhood go unchecked, look at who pays the price, and discuss what to do about them.

The Consequences of Unaddressed Bullying at Home

When parents fail to resolve bullying behaviors at home, the negative consequences spill out into the world. A child who bullies his or her parents brings these negative traits into all of their relationships:

- An excessive hunger for instant gratification.

- Poor frustration tolerance.
- Lack of impulse control.
- Ingrained narcissism.
- Little empathy or compassion for others.
- No interest in altruistic or charitable activities.
- Impaired social relationships.
- Potentially violent and abusive behaviors toward peers.

These negative imprints from their childhood or teen years extend into adulthood. As adults, they are more likely to

- Verbally, emotionally, or physically abuse a spouse.
- Suffer from addiction or alcoholism.
- Develop obesity-related health problems.
- Engage in erratic or poor finances.
- Manipulate and lie to get what they want.
- Promote the scapegoating or villainizing of others.

The Consequences for Parents

Parents who allow their children to bully them may suffer the most long-term effects. As adults, bullying children are more likely to:

- Fail to provide care for elderly parents.
- Remain financially dependent on parents.
- Steal from or mismanage their parents' finances.
- Promote conflict between siblings and relatives.
- Continue to emotionally, physically, or verbally abuse their parents.

I've witnessed many children who bully their parents become bullying adults who wreak havoc in families or grow into abusive parents or spouses. Sadly, they never learned better ways of expressing frustration, self-soothing, or engaging in mature communication. Without intervention, they continue having temper tantrums and blaming others.

If You're Being Bullied By Your Child

The longer these behaviors are in place, the harder they are to undo. To reverse bullying, you'll need to gather the right support. Yes, I'm asking you to break the silence on your situation, ask for help, and begin to share your parenting struggles with others. Here's why: Being bullied by your kid is always accompanied by feelings of shame. Time and again, parents try to hide their situation. They put on a good face in public while suffering silently in private. The reality is that bullying must be handled directly. It won't end until you have the courage to stop it.

These four tips can help you address the young bully in your home:

1. Unite with your spouse or partner.

United parenting is crucial to reestablishing trust and respect with your kids. If your child bullies you and not your partner, it's likely that you have contrasting parenting styles. Nothing is worse for a child's emotional health than to be caught in the crossfire between bickering parents.

When parents are divided in their parenting, the imbalance throws off the family dynamic. The split can disrupt a kid's sense of well-being and create a split in his feelings toward each parent. Trying to make sense of parents' contradictory and inconsistent communications causes mental stress and a mess of internal conflicts. And poor modeling by parents normalizes negative or aggressive behaviors. Kids who witness their parents' poor modeling may decide:

- It's okay to bully someone you love.
- It's okay to yell at or belittle someone you care for.
- Name-calling or verbal attacks are acceptable when frustrated.

This is why it's crucial for parents to never stop working on their relationship. Whether married, separated, or divorced, they must strive to work as a team and collaborate for the well-being of their children. When conflicts arise, parents should model how to work through them effectively—without resorting to combat or bullying.

This doesn't mean you and your spouse have to agree on everything; that would be unrealistic (and just plain weird). Parenting is full of complications and changing circumstances, so disagreements will always exist. You can still disagree and stay united in your parenting choices.

2. Enlist your friends and family.

Bullied parents are everywhere. These days, everybody knows one. So there's no need to feel embarrassed about your situation. Chances are, your friends and family already sense your struggle, no matter how secretive you have tried to be. You'll be surprised how eager they are to help and how much better you'll feel after enlisting their support.

3. Involve school officials.

I spent more than 10 years working with struggling parents in the New York City public school system. During that time, I discovered that the parents who needed the most help rarely stepped forward. In fact, the more trouble they had at home, the less likely they were to ask for help.

Maybe they felt embarrassed, weary, or distrustful of school officials. Maybe they suffered from anxiety or depression. One thing's for sure: Remaining isolated only made their difficulties worse.

Asking for help is never easy. But being a good parent requires the willingness to put up with personal discomfort for your child's benefit.

You may fear what other parents will say; you may worry about family members or neighbors judging you. But when you put aside such fears and ask for help, you become stronger—the kind of parent a bullying kid needs.

Guidance counselors, school psychologists, and other school officials have access to support services in the school in addition to neighborhood resources such as counseling and tutoring centers. But first, you have to break your silence.

4. Seek professional help.

Never has there been so much professional care and support for parents. The internet is full of parenting sites, podcasts, and videos. Libraries, bookstores, and community centers host discussions with experts. Psychotherapists and social workers in schools and private practices specialize in parenting. If you decide to consult with a therapist, here are a few things to keep in mind.

- **Contact your child's school guidance counselor:** Experienced school counselors understand local child/adolescent therapists. They can provide you with reliable referrals to professionals who specialize in children and parents.

- **Attend parenting workshops or lectures:** Schools, therapy institutes, parenting organizations, and youth centers offer free lectures and workshops for parents. Listening to therapists discuss their work and explain the therapeutic process can serve as a wonderful introduction to the world of therapy. You'll also benefit from the questions other parents ask. If you appreciate a particular therapist's presentation, contact him or her for a consultation.

- **Get a referral from a trusted friend:** A friend who has had a positive experience with a therapist may be your most reliable source for a referral. Find out how the process unfolded. Investigating your friend's experience will save you a lot of time and energy, and will point you in the right direction.

Don't Wait: Get Help

For more than 20 years, bullied parents have been visiting my office seeking advice and guidance. Those who are proactive about getting help for themselves and their kids always win in the end.

————————

3 Reasons Why Parents Let Their Kids Bully Them

Patterns formed in childhood that are especially hard to break.

The parents most likely to be bullied by their kids are:

1. Parents who were bullied by their own parents.

2. Parents who had absent or neglectful parents.

3. Narcissistic parents.

1. Parents Who Were Bullied By Their Own Parents

When I examined the personal histories of parents whose children bully them, I discovered that these parents tended to have been bullied by their parents as well. The culture of bullying is often passed on from one generation to the next. Parents who were bullied as children remain victims of bullying, only now their children are the perpetrators.

Parents who were bullied by their parents may overcompensate with their own children by being too permissive. For example, adults who grow up in homes with overly strict parents tend to be very liberal with their kids. They set out to undo their own history by giving their children the freedom that they were denied. These parents often vow in their youth, "When I grow up, I won't treat my kids the way I was treated."

However, this backlash against the authoritarian parenting of the past, however, is fueling the bullied-parent dilemma many parents find themselves in today. For example:

- If your parents were dominating, you might overcompensate by being too accommodating and permissive.
- If your parents were critical, you might strive to be more of a friend than a parent to your child.
- If your parents were inattentive, you might smother your kid with attention and become overly involved in his life.

Don't fret: Bullied parents' hearts are in the right place. They want their kids to have a better childhood than they did, but their overreaching effort to undo the pain of their own history prevents them from providing the leadership their kids need for healthy social and emotional development.

These parents tend to avoid decisions that may anger or disappoint their children. They begin to fear their child's temper, just as they feared their parents. Soon, they stop thinking with their adult mind and start acting more like their childhood selves. As a result, parents who were bullied by their parents experience waves of personal anxiety and indecisiveness. The pattern of trauma from their childhood is reawakened, and the emotional abuse they suffered as children impacts the choices they make as mothers or fathers.

2. Parents Who Had Absent or Neglectful Parents

Adults who grow up with absent or neglectful parents have a particularly difficult time being parents because they have no parental model to internalize. Even if they had a mother or father, they felt parentless.

Unsurprisingly, such parents find it hard to parent. With no parenting model to follow, or oppose, they are lost and overwhelmed in their new role. Desperate, they defer decisions and avoid making unpopular choices. They may even shift the burden of parenting onto the shoulders of their own kids, letting them make decisions for themselves. While kids naturally jump at the chance to seize leadership from their parents, they are usually completely unprepared to manage themselves. They can't structure their day, set a schedule, or plan for their future. Without the guiding hand of a confident parent, it's only a matter of time before they grow frustrated and abusive; *no kid wants to parent himself.*

3. Narcissistic Parents

Narcissistic parents are often hard to spot. They attend school events and parent-teacher conferences. They throw birthday parties. From a distance, they seem ideal parents. So why are they bullied by their children?

Take a closer look, and you'll see the problem hiding in plain sight: They are terrible listeners and conversation monopolizers. Incessantly self-referential, rather than respecting and promoting their kids' individuality, they try to make their children mini-versions of themselves. Nothing is more enraging for kids than not being recognized by a parent.

Children of narcissists frequently turn to bullying in an effort to break through a parent's self-absorption. But narcissistic parents are too wrapped up in themselves to identify with their kids. They steer conversations back to themselves, fixate on their childhoods, tell endless stories about the past, or force their children to endure tiresome yarns about their achievements.

Narcissistic parents don't live in the moment, which creates a profound sense of emotional deprivation in children that fuels bullying. Every child has three basic emotional needs—to be listened to, recognized, and validated. Narcissistic parents are too self-absorbed to meet any of these needs.

When adolescence hits, and kids begin to claim their own separate ideas and identities, narcissistic parents often see this as a betrayal. Conflicts begin to escalate the moment their children try to define themselves as separate and different.

Sadly, most relationships between a narcissistic parent and a bullying kid end in estrangement. Unless the parent changes his or her ways, the relationship is doomed.

Breaking the Pattern

These three broad categories—parents who were bullied by their own parents, parents who had absent or neglectful parents, and narcissistic parents—are presented as a way to process and examine your own upbringing. Parents are much more complex than the snapshot histories presented here. But if you find yourself nodding in recognition, identifying with the parent types, or recalling unhappy events from your past, it's time to consider how your childhood history may shape the parenting choices you make today.

---

3 Mistakes Parents Make When Their Kids Bully Them

Never Surrender.

It's the end of a long day. You've just arrived home from work, completely exhausted. You flip on the TV, collapse on the sofa, and catch the end of your favorite program. You savor this quiet time.

Just then, your child begins to whine and carry on. He wants a slice of chocolate cake before dinner. You tell him no.

"You promised!" he demands. "You said I could have it when you got home."

You tell him to wait until after dinner. He stands in front of the TV. "I want it now. Right now!"

You close your eyes and take a breath. Maybe you count to 10. But your kid turns up the volume: "You lied to me! I waited all day for you! I hate you! You're stupid!"

Okay, freeze-frame: This *testing* moment has just tipped into a *bullying* moment. You're being verbally assaulted and degraded by your own child.

What do you do?

3 Common Tactics That Backfire

Typically, parents choose one of three responses in such moments: surrender, punish, or negotiate.

1. Surrender.

Not every battle is worth fighting; surrendering and giving your kid what he wants is sometimes a good option—especially if you're looking to buy yourself a bit of peace. But when testing turns into bullying? Never give in to a child's demands. To do so would be tantamount to rewarding abusive behavior. That's a teaching moment that delivers the wrong lesson!

Every time you surrender to your child's bullying, you send this simple message: *Bullying works.* So the next time she's frustrated by your restrictions, she will bully to get what she wants. After all, you have taught her that if she pushes hard enough, you'll surrender.

2. Punish.

When your kid bullies you, it's difficult not to become reactive and bully back. Possessing the strength of character to resist mirroring a child's aggressive behavior is not a skill that rarely comes naturally. As with any form of self-mastery, you must cultivate it.

Losing your cool, hollering, and coming down on your child with harsh punishments are forms of counter-bullying that create a culture of bullying in the family. Parents who win battles with their kids by leaning heavily on punishment achieve a bitter victory: There's a winner and a loser. Someone's happy—and someone isn't.

Children who receive constant punishment become contemptuous and resentful—and then more serious behavior problems may emerge. For example, kids may:

- Become defiant and oppositional, directly or through silent resistance.
- Turn their frustration inward and fall victim to depression or anxiety.
- Bully more intensely, escalating conflicts and disrupting the entire family.

3. Negotiate.

Okay, your kid is having a meltdown. Being a mindful parent, you take a moment and consider your options. You try to understand his perspective: He waited all day for you (and for his cake). Then, when you finally got home, instead of greeting him, you collapsed on the couch, turned on the TV, and ignored him.

You get it: He's upset and has a right to be. So you decide to cut a deal: You offer half a slice of cake now and the other half after dinner. Now consider:

- Is negotiation the best choice at this moment?
- What if he makes a counteroffer?
- Suppose he continues to bully and demands the whole slice?

Negotiation is a popular choice in modern parenting. And the notion of finding common ground with your child during conflicts is not a bad idea. You give a little, he gives a little, and everyone is happy. Right?

Yes and no.

When testing turns to bullying, negotiation is off the table. When you negotiate with a bully, you set the stage for ongoing conflicts. Like surrendering, it rewards bullying and trains your child that bullying works. The next time your kid is frustrated by your restrictions, he will return to bullying because bullying leads to negotiation, and negotiation leans toward getting what he wants.

Another flaw with negotiation: Kids might begin to think that everything, even good behavior, is negotiable. Rather than doing something for themselves and the good feelings it produces, they may only do it to get a reward. For example:

- Your daughter demands to get paid for making her bed.
- Your son expects a reward for doing his homework.
- Your kids ask for cash for good grades.

Good behavior should never be a bartering point. Negotiating for rewards replaces personal achievement—and kids miss out on self-esteem. Rather than developing self-reliance and autonomy, they remain immature and tethered to their parents for gratification.

3 Immediate Steps You Can Take

You just learned that surrendering, punishing, and negotiating all fall short in the long run. These tactics offer some short-term relief by managing the symptoms of bullying, but don't address its causes.

Before we look at the deeper issues, let's consider the three most important steps you can take in bullying moments: de-escalate the conflict, validate feelings, and praise strengths.

1. De-escalate.

In bullying moments, parents too often react impulsively and escalate conflicts. They yell or punish, which increases the tension and worsens the bullying. It's vital to maintain composure and leadership in such moments. Don't become reactive or fall back on knee-jerk responses. Stand your ground without drama.

If the conflict escalates, hit the pause button: Take a time out and give everyone a chance to cool off. When kids are in a state of intense frustration, you can't reason with them. If you try, you'll only increase their frustration.

You and your child will benefit greatly from a quiet moment to gather your thoughts and regain equilibrium. If you can, leave the room or take a quiet walk. Get some fresh air. It will give you both time to calm down. Find peace in yourself before you try to make peace with your child. Once things have quieted down, you can mindfully consider what action to take.

2. Validate Feelings.

You can never go wrong by validating your kid's feelings:

- "I understand that you're frustrated. I am, too."

- "I can see you're upset. Give me 10 minutes of quiet to think about this."

- "Let's have something to eat first. We'll both feel better."

Kids respond positively when you acknowledge their feelings. They immediately start to calm down.

During the break, ask yourself: "What could be causing my kid's bullying? Is he tired? Hungry? Feeling neglected? Has it been a long day for everyone? Maybe he's spent too long playing a computer game or surfing the Net?"

Bullying is an *effect*; there's always an underlying *cause*. Consider what could be making your child so irritable. Help him speak his mind, then validate his feelings.

- "I understand that you're angry; you have a right to be."

- "Your feelings are hurt. You're mad that I won't give you what you want."

- "Instead of fighting, let's try something new: Tell me why you're so mad."

Encourage more mature communication. Feeling understood by you will defuse his frustration and reframe the moment.

Remember: Give kids what they *need*, not what they *want*. Learning to communicate effectively while frustrated is more important than anything your kid craves at the moment. Surrendering, punishing, or negotiating robs kids of the opportunity to wrestle with their frustration and master it.

Make it clear that bullying never works:

- "I'm not going to respond as long as you're yelling at me."
- "Bullying is not going to get you what you want."
- "You can do better than this. You're too smart to be a bully."

3. Praise Progress.

Once you both reach a decision, stand your ground. Don't revisit it lest your child tests you and pushes for more. Along the way, be sure to praise your kid's strengths:

- "I appreciate how you are talking to me right now."
- "I know this was hard for you. I'm proud of the way you expressed yourself."
- "You're doing a great job. You're really maturing."

Reinforcing your kid's strengths will boost his confidence and make mature communication more rewarding than fighting.

The 3 Types of Children That Bully Their Parents

The good and bad news about dealing with each.

All children have unique personalities and temperaments, but kids who bully their parents have very particular traits and three most prevalent styles:

1. The Defiant Bully

- *Is your kid always opposing you?*
- *Does your kid blackmail you?*
- *Are you afraid of your kid's anger?*

The most challenging of the bullying personality types, these in-your-face kids are exceedingly confrontational and oppositional. If you say, "Go right," they will go left. If you say, "Sit still," they will run. Impulsive, impatient, reckless, defiant bullies want to live on their own terms. They reject every attempt parents make to manage their behavior. If you're a single parent, defiant kids can be particularly aggressive: With only one parent to focus on, you'll likely get a double dose of defiance.

Self-righteous and puffed up with false confidence, such kids delight in debate—and are determined to win every argument. For them, being "right" takes priority over being respectful or getting along. When you try to stand up to their bullying, they may turn obsessive and harass you until you give in. Determined to get their way, they'll stop at nothing.

Good News and Bad News

Defiance is not necessarily a problematic trait. Many artists, inventors, designers, and original thinkers have a healthy defiant streak. They pioneer new ways of thinking because they oppose conventions. They use their defiance as a creative force for inspiration and vision. In other words, when defiance is fused with ambition and channeled into creativity, it is *progressive*. Defiant kids have a lot of unbridled and unfocused energy. The challenge is to help them channel it into a positive outlet.

But in fact, every well-adjusted kid has a healthy dose of defiance. If children are too cooperative or accommodating, they lack definition and leave no lasting imprint on others. You don't *want* your kid to agree with you all the time. You want her to have her own opinions and views.

Now, here's the bad news about defiance: It takes a lot of effort to help a kid with a defiant bullying style see any relationship as a two-way street—and the longer the pattern has been in place, the more difficult it is to reverse. It takes energy and commitment to help a defiant kid break old habits and foster new ones.

What Drives the Defiant Kid?

Underneath the bravado of defiance is a kid who, for some reason, feels unrecognized and undervalued. She lives with a fear of others forgetting her or leaving her out. No matter how much attention she gets, positive or negative, it's rarely enough.

You'd never know how vulnerable defiant kids feel because they conceal their insecurities so well. And yet, ultimately, defiance is a form of *dependency*.

45

Here's why: In order to feel whole, defiant kids must have something to defy. Pushing against someone or something gives them a false sense of strength. For example, imagine a kid leaning against a wall. He may appear secure, but what happens when you take the wall away? He falls down. Defiance works in the same way: Without someone or something to defy, defiant kids can't keep their stance.

What do defiant kids gain from their defiance? Defiance forms a protective barrier against interpersonal insecurities, providing a temporary identity for kids who feel uncertain about their individuality. Kids with a defiant bullying style are easily misinterpreted: Their defiance creates the illusion that they are strong and secure, when actually it's just the opposite. Spend enough time with defiant kids, and you'll sense their insecurities just below the surface.

2. The Anxious Bully

- *Is your kid continually on the verge of a breakdown?*
- *Does she need constant comforting and reassuring?*
- *Are his angst-filled monologues wearing you down?*

Anxious children tend to oscillate between clinging to their parents and pushing them away. Of course, it's natural for kids to turn to their parents for comfort, but an anxious kid's fretfulness is exhausting. Anxious children have little or no self-soothing skills. The moment they feel threatened or frightened, they run to their parents for reassurance. Once they receive comfort, they reject their parents again—and so the cycle repeats itself.

In their heart, anxious kids don't want to be dependent on their parents, but they can't break free of their reliance on them. They appear less outwardly aggressive than defiant kids, but their bullying—powered by constant neediness—is no less intense. Here's the worst part: If anxious kids don't learn to be self-reliant, their parents will become *enablers*. When this happens, the kids rarely leave home or find their own way in the world: *Love that enables, ultimately disempowers.*

Good News and Bad News

The good news: Unlike defiant kids who outwardly rebel, anxious kids are too fearful to put themselves in dangerous situations, so they rarely engage in risky behaviors. Parents are more likely to beg them to leave their rooms and venture into the world. But the more parents try to push them out the door, the more anxious kids will dig in. Hunkering in a bedroom is far more satisfying than the unknowns beyond it. For anxious kids, the familiar always wins over the unknown.

The bad news: Anxious children have trouble growing up. Anything chancy, anything that involves risk, increases their anxiety. As a result, they miss out on many opportunities for growth.

What Drives the Anxious Kid to Bully?

Parents of anxious kids often wonder:

- *Was my kid born anxious?*
- *Am I doing something wrong?*
- *Is there something that I don't know about causing him anxiety?*

These are great questions, but rather than getting caught in the old dilemma of nature *vs.* nurture, consider nature *and* nurture to get a clear diagnostic picture. For example, let's consider your child's age, temperament, and family history:

- *Is there a history of anxiety in your family?*
- *Have you had difficulties with anxiety?*
- *Has your kid always been anxious, or did it come on suddenly?*

If your family has a history of anxiety, it's more likely that your child inherited this trait. Also, keep in mind that anxiety is *contagious*: Parents who are anxious or families that are filled with conflict and angst are more likely to produce anxious children.

But even if your child seems wired for anxiety, you can do plenty of things to break the cycle. First, let's look for changes in his or her environment that could be generating anxiety:

- *Have there been any modifications in family routines, such as moving, changing schools, or starting a new class?*
- *Are your child's social insecurities ongoing or recent?*
- *Did he or she experience a traumatic event?*

Sudden changes in mood or temperament usually have clear precipitating events, which are easy to spot and typically affect the whole family. *However, many will overlook developmental shifts*: For example, it's common for many kids to develop off-the-wall anxiety as they enter adolescence. This stage, with its surge of hormones, massive psychological shifts, and physiological maturation triggers enormous insecurities in preteens and teens. Many kids who were calm, cool, and collected in elementary school suddenly turned turbulent in middle and high school. We refer to these responses to adolescence as *normative developmental crises*.

3. The Manipulative Bully

- *Is your kid an excellent liar?*
- *Does he know how to exploit your fears?*
- *Are you blackmailed with threats of self-harm?*

If you suffer fears and insecurities about your parenting, it won't take long for a manipulative bullying child to home in on them, particularly if you are an anxious or guilty parent. Phony illness or injuries, elaborate plots, extortion, blackmail—these are the tools the manipulative bully uses to extort his wants and needs from his parents by preying on their anxieties and generating self-doubt.

This can make the manipulative bully sound like a monster destined to ruin a family. Of course, that's not true: Just as with the defiant and anxious bullying styles, the manipulative bully is trying to manage his fears and insecurities, in this case by controlling his environment and everyone in it. Getting to the root of his fears and helping him put them into words is key to helping a manipulative bully develop better ways of relating.

From Conflict to Cooperation

Naturally, children's personalities are too complex to fit into such tidy little categories. The bullying styles discussed here offer a lens through which to view your child's behavior. With a clearer understanding of his or her bullying style, you will better understand the child's inner life and be better prepared to steer your relationship in a new direction. Keep in mind that beneath the tough exterior of every bully is a scared child, constantly wrestling with insecurities and worries. Bullying is an expression of this internal unrest. By understanding what makes your bully tick, you will gain insight into the nature of her fears, better understand the forces that fuel her bullying, and become poised to take action to restore balance.

Signs That You're An Abused Parent

Who's to Blame?

It happens all the time. Parents arrive in my office in a state of shock, wondering how their sweet, adorable child morphed into a domestic tyrant.

This raises an important question: *Is kids abusing their parents normal?*

Let's look at basic child psychology and see how developmental phases come with built-in power struggles that put children and their parents on a collision course.

Little Monster Psych. 101

In each developmental phase, children wrestle with new skills and abilities, such as learning to walk, use language, or write. If a phase goes well, after a period of intense struggle and sustained effort, a breakthrough occurs; a personal victory that feels so good that it triggers a leap in maturity.

Suddenly, in an amazingly short period of time, kids discard their old way of doing things and reject help. For example:

- The baby who has just fed herself with a spoon no longer wants to be fed.

- The wobbly child who just learned to walk no longer wants to hold your hand.
- The teenager who has just gotten his driver's license doesn't want his parents in the car.

Each time kids master new skills, they experience a rush of joy and confidence. Here's when things start to get complicated.

The Drive for Independence Promotes Conflict

Mastery triggers a wish for greater independence. The problem is children don't know their limits. Whether they like it or not, they need adult supervision.

Now the battle begins. All parents eventually have to stand In the way of their kid's will. It's impossible to be a good parent without making unpopular decisions.

How Frustration Gives Way to Abuse

Children don't like hearing the word no. The moment their parents prevent them from getting what they want, they grow irritated.

> Why are my parents ruining my fun?
>
> Can't they see I'm enjoying myself?
>
> Why are they getting in my way?

It's human nature to rebel against restrictions. Kids don't understand that their parents are protecting them. Parental restraint feels like oppression – and who likes that? That's why, eventually, all healthy children must enter into battle with their parents.

This fight is natural -- and necessary. It's how children can begin to define themselves. If kids are too accommodating or too compliant with their parents, they will lack confidence and self-definition later in life.

Testing Moments

After parents set restrictions, kids test how far they can push back without consequences.

If I scream for it, will Dad give in?

If I cry, will I get my way?

If I make a scene, will Mom surrender?

When Testing Turns to Abuse

From preschool to high school, test periods are the prime clashing points in all parent–child relationships. They are trying times when kids flex their young muscles and test their parents' tenacity.

Okay, let's pause here and take a moment to remember that parents are human. They have good days and bad days. On good days, they are good-humored and flexible and have boundless or at least enough patience. On bad days, they are grumpy; they lose their temper and sometimes act like children themselves.

During test periods:

1. **Stand Your Ground:** Once you limit is set, don't back down or renegotiate. Giving in teaches children that abuse works.

2. **Abuse is Never Acceptable:** Make it clear that name-calling, cursing, and physical abuse are never tolerated. Mutual respect is the standard. Be sure to model the behavior you want from your child and don't sink to his or her level.

3. **Don't Threaten or Bully Back:** If your kid is bullying, don't respond with counter threats or bullying. Remember, you're the parent. Maintain your authority and keep your cool.

4. **Take a Time Out:** When possible, step away and give yourself and your kid time to calm down. Self-reflection fosters greater maturity. Mindfulness de-escalates conflicts.

5. **Stay United with Your Spouse:** Kids always practice "divide and conquer" with their parents. Don't be pulled

into debates about decisions. Stand strong together in parenting decisions and work out disagreements in private.

Parents Set Behavioral Standards

While it's natural for kids to rebel against their parents, when rebelling turns into abuse, it's vital for parents to take a stand. Structure, limits and boundaries are not organic-- they must be taught to children. Remember, parent abuse only thrives when authority is weak.

CHAPTER 4:
DEPRESSION

Do You Have Depression or "Lifestyle Fatigue"?

Take this "Lifestyle Fatigue" test to find out.

"I'm soooooo tired!"

I hear this declaration every week in my office. Session after session, people complain about feeling chronically exhausted with barely enough energy to get through the day.

How bad is it? They don't want to venture out of their homes for weekly psychotherapy sessions.

"Do I have to come in today?" they whine. "Can't we just talk on the phone?"

What started this epidemic of fatigue?

The Pandemic Effect and "Lifestyle Fatigue"

Like most people, you probably spend too much time at home, scrolling through your cell phone, binge-watching shows, or mindlessly clicking on TikTok or YouTube videos.

I know. I've been there.

The pandemic played a big part in creating this new sedentary lifestyle. Being stuck indoors, couch-bound, isolated, inactive, with limited in-person social contact for months, you're certainly going to feel unsatisfied with life.

But what effects does this post-pandemic lifestyle have on your mental health?

Feelings of Depression

When you sense that you are slipping into depression, chances are you start to feel overwhelmed with insecurities and self-doubt. You may begin to ruminate, question your choices, scrutinize your history, and dissect your career and relationships. What's worse, you may start to lose your grip on reality; your mind may begin to play tricks on you. You may ask yourself, "Why do I suddenly feel depressed?"

Too often, the answer is hiding in plain sight.

"Lifestyle Fatigue"

Rather than comb through your history, book an appointment with a psychiatrist, or blame yourself for how you're feeling, consider this essential question:

Is your depression a product of your lifestyle?

When you consider the most common triggers for depression—such as social isolation, a sedentary existence, or a lack of creative stimulation—it's clear that such repetitive habits are a breeding ground for depression.

Depression Versus "Lifestyle Fatigue"

High-functioning depression (also known as dysthymia) can be hard to spot. Unlike major depressive episodes, high-functioning depression is low-level, chronic, and doesn't have a clear trigger.

"Lifestyle fatigue," however, does have obvious triggers and is more likely the result of feeling stuck in a rut rather than a predisposition for depression. ("Lifestyle fatigue" is a term I use and not an official diagnosis.)

"Lifestyle Fatigue" Checklist

Read through the list below and note which questions you answer "Yes" to:

1. *Does every day feel the same?*

2. *Is your work dull and unrewarding?*

3. *Do you dread leaving your house?*

4. *Are you avoiding friends and social interaction?*

5. *Do you spend more time with screens than people?*

6. *Have you lost your creative drive?*

7. *Has your sex drive gone missing?*

8. *Do you tend to ruminate or obsess about your failures?*

9. *Are you overeating or undereating?*

10. *Do activities that used to give you pleasure now feel like a waste of time?*

If you answered yes to five or more of these, you may suffer from "lifestyle fatigue" (although "lifestyle fatigue" does not preclude the possibility of depression.)

How to Break Free of "Lifestyle Fatigue"

"Lifestyle fatigue" lives and breathes in sameness and repetition; breaking free starts with one powerful word: *change.*

Any change in your daily routine, such as waking up earlier, going to bed earlier, contacting an old friend, or going to a concert or the theater, will do. Look for new activities that disrupt monotony or predictability.

It doesn't matter how big or small. Change is a powerful antidote. For example, a patient in psychotherapy with me says that she started to break free of "lifestyle fatigue" just by reorganizing her kitchen; another patient felt better after enrolling in a dance class, and another patient booked a trip to a tropical island with friends.

Such choices bring fresh energy and vitality and remind us that life is what we make of it. Even tiny changes can refresh your spirit and give you the boost you need to reboot your lifestyle.

The Key to Understanding High-Functioning Depression

The 3 most common causes of dysthymia and 3 reliable solutions.

The image most people attach to the word "depression" is of a solitary, lonely figure, despairing and downcast, silhouetted by a bleak landscape. We may wonder, *"What happened to that poor soul?"*

Yet this image isn't always accurate. On the surface, some depressed people appear to lead bustling, fulfilling lives; check out their social media, and you'll see their smiling faces and beautiful homes. They're functioning so well that even the thought that they could be depressed seems outrageous.

High-functioning depression, also referred to as dysthymia, can be hard to spot. It doesn't look like stereotypical depression. Unlike major depressive episodes, which are intense, debilitating, and time-limited, high-functioning depression is low-level, chronic, and doesn't have a clear trigger.

Its very existence can feel maddening.

Sadness vs. Depression

Sadness is a pure feeling that frequently springs from a clear precipitating event. We grieve a loss, miss a friend, or feel rejected by others. We cry or mourn because sadness feels appropriate; we allow it to flow through us.

In this way, sadness can feel relieving, even enjoyed. Some of the most beautiful poems, songs, and literature could be considered odes to sorrow. They offer relief because they validate our sadness; no longer are we alone.

Depression offers no such relief. Unlike sadness, depression is often a defense against unwanted feelings. The root of the word is *depress*—to push down, deny, or suppress. Unwanted feelings are frequently the cause of many depressive symptoms.

High-Functioning Depression

Though not a clinical term of diagnosis, high-functioning depression isn't prompted by a tragic event or change of fortune. Often you feel clueless about its source or cause.

If you struggle with high-functioning depression, you may still go to work, see friends, and attend events. But the heaviness rarely leaves you; you carry a feeling of exhaustion wherever you go. You feel weighed down by burdens. You think you have nothing to look forward to when you think of the future.

High-functioning depression is always there, a dark cloud on a clear blue sky. The substance of the cloud is a darkness that even you don't understand.

Causes of High-Functioning Depression

The three most common causes are high functioning depression are:

1. **Trauma.** Unfortunately, many childhood traumas are left unprocessed. People with high-functioning depression rarely have had time to consider their past. They press forward, aggressively avoiding memories or incidents that may draw attention to unhealed emotional scars.

2. **Inter-generational Depression.** Sometimes, depression is a part of the DNA of a family. When researching families' social/emotional history, one often discovers generations of depression—often, relatives who either self-medicated with substances or endured unstable moods their entire lives.

3. **Unresolved Frustration.** Frequently, people with high-functioning depression lead frustrating lives. They avoid dealing directly with emotional problems and prefer to remain task-focused. They store frustration, grudges, and disappointments that linger and zap their energy.

3 Ways to Resolve High-Functioning Depression

4. **Self-care.** People with high-functioning depression often live in a state of self-neglect. Even if they remain in good physical shape, they may neglect their emotional lives. Group therapy effectively breaks their emotional isolation, as group members learn to put their needs into words and heal emotional wounds.

5. **Creative Expression.** Art, music, and dance are some of the most potent tools for dismantling high-functioning

depression. Choose an activity that delivers pure joy: something you love. Chances are that you'll unleash energy and passion trapped by mundane, repetitive routines.

6. **Medication.** If you've exhausted natural cures such as changes in diet, exercise, routines, career, etc., and high-functioning depression still plagues you, it may be time to consider medication. As a therapist, medication is my last consideration, but often, it can open a door that had seemed shut forever.

The Destructive Voice of Self-Shame and How to Break Free

Five ways to disrupt your self-shaming cycle.

Living with self-shame is like having a 24-hour critical inside your head, constantly judging, labeling, and humiliating you.

That toxic self-shaming voice seeks to limit you, hold you back, and defer growth. Left unchecked, it eats away at your self-worth, undermines your confidence, and can morph into crippling anxiety that destroys any chance of lasting happiness.

Where does self-shaming come from? How did it gain so much power over you?

Derek's Battle With Self-Shame

Derek, a young man in one of my weekly therapy groups, talked about his crippling social fears. Tears trickled down his cheeks as he admitted, "I feel so much shame all the time."

"About what?" a group member asked.

"My weight, my voice, the way I walk, how people look at me." He paused and wiped his face with the sleeve of his shirt. "I guess I feel shame about being me."

Derek had been bullied at school, neglected by his family, and mocked by kids in his neighborhood. Over the years, he internalized those negative external voices. In other words, the hostile voices in his environment became his dominant internal voice. He learned to mistreat and judge himself the way he had been mistreated and judged by others.

To help Derek break free from the shackles of self-shame, let's investigate the personal historical roots of self-shaming.

The Roots of Self-Shame

Self-shaming is a learned behavior that originates from three possible sources:

1. **Family**

   Parents or siblings that engage in "teasing" leave emotional scars. Over-critical, punishing, abusive parents or siblings are perhaps the most common triggers of self-shaming behaviors.

2. **Peers**

   Children and teenagers can be particularly vicious in scapegoating the vulnerable by mocking and humiliating anyone they perceive as different or threatening.

3. **Society**

   Every culture perpetuates its prejudices and targets people who appear "different" from the dominant culture. External qualities such as skin color, weight, ethnicity, and sexual orientation are among the most targeted populations. Sadly, oppressed people too frequently internalize the oppressor.

Evicting the Self-Shaming Voice

Once you identify the roots of your self-shaming voice, you'll need a plan to evict it. It will be a mighty battle, but the rewards of eliminating your self-shaming voice will dramatically improve every aspect of your life.

1. Capture Painful Memories in a Journal

Childhood memories contain vital information about the roots of your self-shame. Categorize the times you were shamed by others and make a note of the particular words they used. Write those negative words and phrases down and see how they resonate with your self-shaming voice.

2. Break the Silence

Silence breeds shame. It's crucial that you find a friend, a therapist, a support group — anyone you can talk to about the role shame plays in your life. Gathering such supportive people around you is essential to winning this battle

3. Increase Self-Care

Exercise, creative outlets, meditation, and daily walks; such activities bring fresh energy into your day. If you have trouble motivating yourself, enlist the help of a friend. Think of this battle as an emotional marathon; you'll need to raise the bar on your self-care to win.

4. Set Positive Affirmations

Make a list of your positive qualities. What makes you unique? What talents do you have? What are you grateful for? One patient I work with found that covering her apartment with Post-it notes with inspirational quotes and positive self-affirmations was an excellent way to keep her focused.

5. Talk Back to Your Self-Shaming Voice

Start to talk back to your shaming voice and expose it for the fraud it is. Some people find it helpful to give the voice a name to separate from it. Remember, your self-shaming voice is not your authentic voice. It is not a part of your core identity. The weaker your self-shaming voice becomes, the stronger your true voice will grow. If your friends are critical and weigh you down, it's time to confront them or reconsider the value of those friendships.

Derek's New Life

After several months in group therapy, Derek's mood dramatically improved. He developed healthier friendships and experienced less anxiety in public. Recently, when someone noticed the changes and asked what shifted in him, he said simply, "I decided to be the awesome person I am."

Launch Your Battle to Break Free of Self-Shame

Breaking free of self-shame takes time and practice. There will be days when you feel liberated and days when you feel trapped. Keep applying the five steps, keep pressing forward, and focus on replacing self-shame with self-praise and compassion.

As Nelson Mandela wrote: " ... playing small does not serve the world. There is nothing enlightened about shrinking ... As we let our own light shine, we unconsciously give other people permission to do the same. As we are liberated from our fear, our presence automatically liberates others."

Why Do the Blues Feel So Good?

Soul singer Bobby Harden explains why singing the blues is good for you.

Broke, broken-hearted, or betrayed? Don't fret, there's a blues song for every hardship in life. But did you know that *singing the blues is actually good for you?*

Earlier this year I caught legendary soul singer Bobby Harden in his recent show at BB King's in New York City. What a night! A master entertainer, Bobby brought blues classics and his own original songs to life. But if you really listen to the lyrics, many of the songs are filled with anguish and hurt—songs that celebrate broken hearts and shattered dreams—yet Bobby had the audience jumping to their feet and begging for more.

Have a look at these excerpts of some of the lyrics of Bobby's latest CD, RIVER OF SOUL, and you'll find confessions of falsehoods, lost love, and lonely souls yearning for forgiveness:

> *"Some nights I want to cry...no one really cares...*

feeling all alone and sorry for myself... From "Try Again"

"You did have the right to walk out the door...

I did you wrong, and now you're gone.' From "Where is the Love?"

"She's outta my life...I'm not ready for the next love yet.

I have to ease the pain in my heart." From "Not Ready"

Bobby Explains Our Love of the Blues

I sat down with Bobby and asked him three simple questions:

1. *Why do the blues feel so good?*

When people listen to the blues, they relate whatever sadness or troubles they're going through in life. The original blues artists grew up in a chapter of history filled with so much pain and had to persevere through so many disadvantages in life. Men in particular, couldn't express their pain to their partners. Maybe it was pride or they just weren't taught to express feelings.

Many blues singers back in the day did so much road work that made it too easy to be unfaithful. All of the breakups and unfaithfulness gave them plenty of material for songs. I'm sure it was a way to turn a negative into a positive.

2. *What do we learn from the blues?*

Blues songs teach us three things:

1. They remind you that you're not the first to struggle with situations such as relationships or money problems.

2. They give you perspective. You start to think maybe your problems aren't as bad as you think they are.

3. You find humor in your situation and laugh about it. Maybe you could even write a great song yourself about the problems.

3. *Are the Blues making a comeback?*

The blues today has a much larger audience, young and old, black and white, and it's growing. Thanks to younger blues artists like Robert Cray and Keb Mo, and lots of fantastic young up-and-coming blues guitar players, the fan base seems to be growing to all races and ages.

The music festivals, especially in Europe, have blues artists, soul, R&B, Jazz, and Rock groups performing in the same festivals, which give people of all ages an opportunity to hear some great blues and all the other styles of music. Again, thanks to great, talented rock artists and groups that helped expose blues to a larger audience, Bird and Electric Flag, Rolling Stones, U2, Eric Clapton, and The Blues Brothers Band all helped to expose Muddy Water, BB King, Albert King, Albert Collins and others.

Even today, as I tour with the Original Blues Brothers Band, we see young kids, teenagers, moms, dads, grandmas, and grandpas dancing and enjoying our shows at every festival. They all love the blues and soul music.

Discovering You're Not Alone

The old adage *"A shared sorrow is half a sorrow"* may also explain why singing the blues is so good for us. In song after song, we discover we're not alone in our suffering. Everyone makes mistakes, fails, or faces obstacles in life. But with brilliant soul singers like Bobby, we learn to celebrate our sorrow, pick ourselves up, and, in Bobby's words, "Try again and again."

---

9 Ways to Cure Your Own Depression
It's easier than you think.

Defining Depression

Many folks confuse sadness with depression. Sadness is a natural state, a necessary part of living. Friendships end. Death steals loved ones. Life provides us with plenty of reasons to feel sad. Feeling sad is appropriate at such times — and indispensable. The need to mourn to feel sadness is an essential part of what it means to be human. Honoring sadness provides crucial space for self-reflection and greater empathy and compassion. It also may compel us to recognize brutal truths or inspire us to make better choices.

Depression, however, offers no solace. It brutally assaults us and promotes hopelessness. This is because depression is not a pure feeling but an effort to ward off a complex mix of unwanted ones. Anger, frustration, irritation, and grief are feelings we tend to find intolerable; we don't want to feel them. When we're depressed, we engage in a psychic battle to blot out these unwanted feelings. Common psychic defenses against painful feelings include denial (ignoring feelings), projection (transferring feelings onto others), rationalization (downplaying feelings), or binge eating (attempting to fill the emptiness we feel inside).

Unfortunately, as long as the true causes of our depression remain unaddressed, it will return again and again.

Hunt Down the Cause of Your Depression

Rather than viewing depression as a monster to flee from, look it in the eye; investigate the feelings you are "depressing" and avoiding. For example, you may say, "I feel depressed today." The questions that follow should be: *Why today? What am I ignoring? What issue am I not addressing?*

Here's a list of the most common situations that often trigger depression:

- **An Unresolved Conflict.** Is there a problem in one of your relationships? Is there something at work that is unsettling you? Unaddressed conflicts cause chronic psychological stress and are fundamental to many forms of depression.

- **A Repetition Compulsion.** Look for a common theme in your depression, one that repeats itself. This is most often a repetition of early experiences in your life. The most common themes I hear in my office include: *I'm always the outsider; I can't trust anyone,* and *Nobody understands me.* Without insight, we get trapped in a repetitive cycle and repeat the same problem repeatedly. Find out what that unresolved part of your history is that you keep replaying.

- **Self-Neglect.** Burnout and depression go hand in hand. When you neglect yourself, everyone suffers. You're no fun to be around; you don't enjoy work, play, or drag others down. Reward yourself, treat yourself, and give yourself the attention and TLC you crave. You'll be surprised how much better you'll feel.

- **Self-Slander.** Low self-esteem and self-slander are the major driving forces of all forms of depression. These negative internal voices shape your self-image and how you see yourself and others. You'll start to see others as better and more appealing than you, even when it's not even true. Such toxic affirmations drain your energy and leave you forever dissatisfied. After all, if you constantly tell yourself you're powerless or unattractive, you will eventually become both.

Battling Depression

To loosen the grip of depression, you'll need to take action—lots of it. Confronting depression is like going into battle. Here's a list of areas in your life that may need attention:

Body

- **Exercise.** A 30- to 40-minute cardio workout thrice a week can reduce depression symptoms. Walking or running is also a great way to clear your head.
- **Sleep.** Too little or too much sleep can trigger depression symptoms; shoot for 7 to 8 hours per night. Try your best to be consistent.
- **Diet.** Research has shown a correlation between high-sugar/high-fat diets and depression. Avoid foods that make you feel sluggish, as this might bring negativity.

Mind

- **Creativity.** Stimulate your imagination with new experiences; enjoy poetry, art, theater, and music, or try to reconnect with talents you've neglected.
- **Psychotherapy.** Invest in understanding yourself and breaking self-defeating patterns.
- **Education.** Challenge yourself by acquiring new skills; take classes or attend lectures.

SHORTCUTS TO A HAPPIER LIFE

Spirit

- **Meditation.** Learn to calm your thoughts and relax your mind through chanting, meditation, yoga, or other disciplines.

- **Altruistic Acts.** Helping others will get you out of your head and inspire you; look for opportunities to volunteer in your community.

- **Faith.** Consider spiritual matters; explore different philosophies and beliefs.

When depression appears in your life, think of it as a cry for help from your subconscious. Listen to it; find out what it's trying to tell you. If you've been depressed for a long time, antidepressants can give you the energy to make new choices. However, though medication may make you feel better, the cure for depression is still in your hands. Only when you confront and understand the actual cause of your depression, and then take action to address it, will you finally be liberated from it, no matter what the temperature outside.

CHAPTER 5:
GRIEF

How to Heal Your Broken Heart
Is it possible to speed healing?

Sooner or later, we all face dark times—times when we feel alone, isolated, and lost. Times when we want to hide because our hearts feel so broken.

No matter how we try to avoid it, we all suffer heartbreak. As long as your heart beats, it is only a matter of time before it is wounded.

You may barely notice tiny hurts, such as critical comments, a negative street encounter, or a bad day at work or school. Then there are the bigger hurts, such as being rejected by a lover, betrayed by a friend, or suffering financial hardship. Even if you manage to avoid such hurts, the heartbreak of illness or death eventually comes along and shatters your sense of security.

Since heartbreak seems inevitable, is it possible to speed healing?

The Broken Heart
I can recall several times in my life when I felt overwhelmed by emotional pain. I remember seeing a member of my family struggle with a life-threatening illness. I watched helplessly as she wasted away, unresponsive to every intervention. I searched for answers, prayed, and consulted professionals. Nothing worked.

Heartbreak reminds us that there are limits; not all life's dilemmas can be solved. Even when the body heals, emotional scars can endure. With each heartbreak, we emerge deeply changed.

When all the interventions failed to save my family member, hopelessness took hold and tortured me with unanswerable questions: *"Why did this happen? How could someone so young suffer so profoundly?"* Many nights, I went up to my roof and cried. I looked up at the stars and argued with the heavens about the unfairness of life. In time, I surrendered to my grief.

Mending Your Broken Heart

After long periods of mourning, if you grieve fully and surrender to your sadness, there comes a wish to recover; times you tell yourself, *"I have to move on."*

I've provided individual and group psychotherapy for hundreds of heartbroken people—individuals who lost spouses to cancer, children to accidents, or suffered profound betrayals or emotional hardships. While some remain mired in resentment and isolation, others seem to recover sooner. Here are there qualities I've noticed have helped them to heal their broken hearts:

1. **Healthy Relationships.**

   The adage, "Happiness shared is doubled, pain shared is halved," holds. I have noticed in my work that heartbroken people who surround themselves with good friends and a supportive community emerge from emotional pain enriched with a greater capacity for empathy and compassion for others in distress. As Buddhist peace advocate Daisaku Ikeda wrote: "There are countless people in the world whose hearts have been wounded in some way. At such times, what gives someone the strength to go on living? It seems to me that it is human bonds...There is no happiness as long as we are wrapped up in ourselves."

2. **Creative Outlets.**

   Creativity is a soothing balm for the wounded heart. Creative outlets such as music, dance, or poetry tap directly into our subconscious and provide emotional relief when words fail us. Find a way to be creative; write, draw, take photos–anything that focuses your attention outward and provides a distraction from the torment you feel inside. Or use that torment in a creative process. If you can't think of anything, take a class or course in something new and stimulate your creative juices.

3. Altruism.

I remember a friend finally receiving a kidney transplant after 10 long years of dialysis. The operation was a great success. Having faced death and won, he wondered what he would focus on next. A nurse offered him sage advice. She told him, "Use your pain to inspire others." It was a moment of such clarity that it took his breath away. Since then, he has written about his experience, spoken to dozens of patients, and, to this day, is a source of inspiration for many more. In my experience, people who engage in charitable activities, helping others by donating their time and energy, heal their broken hearts quicker and awaken a more profound sense of mission in life.

---

5 Ways to Deal with Despair That Won't Go Away
There is no quick fix for life's unavoidable suffering.

Simple tasks feel daunting when you're agonizing under the weight of despair; getting out of bed, showering, or leaving the house requires herculean effort. To live with despair means waking up every morning with a heaviness pressing down on your chest and a feeling of exhaustion no matter how many hours you slept.

Perhaps problems you face seem insurmountable, such as financial ruin, chronic illness, or grieving the loss of a loved one. Such daunting circumstances can make despair a way of life. It's understandable that many people, desperate to escape the intolerable hopelessness generated by despair, turn to drugs or alcohol for relief. Sadly, when they sober up, they discover that the problems that they ran from have grown even worse.

What do you do when despair doesn't go away?

Battling Despair

Recently a beloved family member was diagnosed with an incurable illness. The shock of it knocked me down. It was inconceivable. No matter how I tried, I couldn't believe it. How could someone I love so dearly receive such a damning diagnosis?

I withdrew from the world and stopped talking to friends and family. I even turned my back on my fellow Buddhists, who called relentlessly, trying to encourage me. I felt like part of my heart had cracked and fallen off, leaving me with a raw, exposed wound that would never heal.

"Why is this happening?" I wondered. "I'm a good person. Aren't I supposed to be spared from such misery?"

Over time, as I started to connect with others who faced similar hardships, I was forced to recognize a stark reality: Every life is eventually touched by tragedy. Life's most painful tragedies strike with cruel randomness.

After a long period of recalibration, I stopped asking "Why me?" and started asking "Why not me?" Did I really think that I would be absolved from universal hardships? Was it narcissism that led me to believe my family would be spared while other families would not? How callous of me to think other families should suffer while mine would be an exception.

Over time, a benefit of despair began to materialize: deeper empathy and understanding for the suffering of others. I left behind the delusion that we are all safe from harm; we are all equally vulnerable. In fact, in acknowledging that vulnerability, we unearth the deepest parts of our humanity.

Living with Despair

I wish I could say I resolved the despair that I felt. But the truth is, I've had to learn to live with it. When I was a younger, less experienced therapist, I thought there was a solution to every dilemma. I now realize how naive I was. No happy ending lasts forever.

Deep despair has a sinister, punishing quality. To regain your footing is to go to battle with your most brutal demons. Though you may not be able to resolve the problems that you face, here are some tools to weaken despair's grip on your heart.

5 Ways to Cope with Despair

These tips won't resolve despair, but they can take the edge off and open up a space for healing.

1. **Take your despair for a walk.**

    Once a day, try your best to get out of the house for some fresh air. A brisk walk raises your metabolism, boosts endorphins, and gives you much-needed headspace. Shaking off tension and gaining some vitamin D can also offer some relief.

2. **Give your sorrow words.**

    When I can't find the words for sadness, I always turn to poets and writers who are masters at capturing elusive feelings. Finding the words for your despair offers comfort and solace. As Shakespeare wrote in *Macbeth*: "Give sorrow words; the grief that does not speak knits up the o-er wrought heart and bids it break."

3. **Honor your despair.**

    Please don't deny it. Don't push it away. When you acknowledge your despair, you take away some of its power over you.

    For example, a friend recently said to me, "Today is a dark day. I think I need to be alone." I understood what he meant and was glad he shared his true feelings rather than "perform" feeling better. When he honored his despair, I could too.

4. **Seek out fellowship.**

    Isolation fuels despair. Seek out the company of people who share your experience. Faith-based communities or support groups such as AA or Al-Anon are free and give you a chance to connect with others. As the Buddhist reformer Nichiren Daishonin wrote, "Even a feeble person will not stumble if those supporting him are strong, but a person of considerable strength, when alone, may fall on an uneven path."

5. Avoid toxic positivity.

A patient in her weekly session shared with me that a friend cheerfully told her, "Don't worry, everything will work itself out." These may seem like comforting words; they had the opposite effect.

"I know he meant well," she said, "but I felt the strong urge to punch him in the face."

Her chronic illness was not going to work itself out. Such phrases, like "Everything happens for a reason," are insensitive to those who are truly suffering. Life's most devastating problems may be helped by a positive attitude but can't be solved by one. Toxic positivity from others feels insulting when you're faced with insurmountable grief.

In the end, you can learn to fly on wounded wings. Despair may knock the wind out of you, but when embraced and managed effectively, it can also lift you to even greater heights.

Finding Purpose in Your Pain

5 positive ways to turn pain into growth.

There is no shortage of tragedies in life. Yet 2020 proved to be a landmark year for pain and heartbreak.

It's difficult to imagine any time in recent history when so many hardships confronted us and altered how we live. Wearing masks in public and educating our children on-line have nearly become routine. But there are 2020 images that will forever remain distressing: spiking COVID death rates, explosive social unrest, disgraceful civil rights violations, and endless political scandals.

The Role of Pain

When confronted with something painful, it's natural to look away, particularly when you feel overwhelmed. Sometimes, during times of crisis, you need to deny pain and engage in compartmentalization. Other times it's essential to confront your pain and own it.

Denial can be adaptive, even helpful, but when you engage in unhealthy levels of it, pain denied can cause long-term health problems such as

- anxiety or panic attacks
- depression
- sleep disorders
- substance abuse
- social isolation
- hopelessness
- pessimism
- physical ailments.

Searching For Meaning In Your Pain

Pain has its place in life. When it is honored and processed in healthy ways, the positive aspects of pain begin to emerge. For example:

Pain can:

1. *Cause you to reflect and make new life choices.*
2. *Deepen your compassion and empathy for others.*
3. *Awaken gratitude and appreciation for what you have.*
4. *Move you to take action and confront injustice.*
5. *Inspire you to seek out healthier habits and relationships.*

Pain Can Awaken A Profound Sense Of Meaning And Purpose.

Finding purpose in your pain is an essential part of healing. You may never understand "why" such pain accrued; indeed, the randomness of life can be maddening. But deciding how you choose to live with your painful experience is essential.

When it comes to healing, altruism is one of the most effective tools you can apply. To illustrate, here are some powerful examples from people I work with:

- *A middle-aged man who is a stage 4 cancer survivor volunteers weekly at a cancer treatment center. He speaks to patients and their families, shares his experience, and supports them throughout their treatment. "Speaking to patients and encouraging them is the highlight of my week,' he says, "Nothing means more to me."*
- *A young woman who battled addiction in high school volunteers to support teenagers in recovery. Instantly, she becomes a role model for the girls in the program and an outspoken advocate for sobriety. "I don't want other girls to go through the hell I went through," she says. "I feel so happy when I visit them. Instead of regretting what I went through, I'm using it to make a difference."*

There will always be unavoidable sufferings in life: a relationship's demise, the death of a loved one, the betrayal of a close friend. Such pains demand attention. How you manage your pain can inspire you to a new way of being -- and encourage others as well.

---

5 Reasons Why People May Feel Nothing

Dissociative states can be terrifying and protective.

Think of the times you felt flooded with feelings—intense emotions such as joy, sadness, love, or fear. Such feelings can be electrifying. As they flow through you, they pack a powerful punch. They can deepen your empathy, keep you emotionally attuned to yourself and others, and guide you through good times and bad.

But what happens when you look inward and find nothing? What happens when you don't know what you're feeling?

What do you do then?

When Feelings Are Blocked Off

Many of us experience moments when we suddenly feel numb or apathetic:

"I went blank."

"I couldn't feel anything."

"I felt dead inside."

This is especially troubling when you find yourself in situations that normally produce strong emotional responses, such as holiday celebrations, weddings, or memorials. When you can't identify your feelings, it's not unusual to experience shame or even question your humanity: "What's wrong with me?" you may wonder. "Why can't I feel anything? Am I a psychopath?"

When the Body Switches to Survival Mode

When you can't feel your emotions, you're likely to be in a dissociative state. This frequently occurs when people are overwhelmed, and the body switches to survival mode, resulting in numbness or blankness. "Not feeling" is also a protective psychic defense during a time of crisis.

Here are five common causes of dissociation:

1. **Trauma.** Trauma comes in many forms. It can be a life-altering event, like the death of a loved one. Or an accident, injury, or illness. Traumatic events can be far more subtle for children, such as being bullied at school or facing classroom humiliation. During such events, feelings go numb, and the trauma is stored away in the body until the time is right to process it.

2. **Clinical depression.** The longer you feel depressed, the more trouble you have identifying your feelings. A heaviness takes over, emotions are dulled, and you experience life through a haze of indifference.

3. **Crippling anxiety.** When anxiety becomes a dominant force in your life, it tends to rob you of other emotions by keeping you in a state of constant fear and tension.

4. **Drug and alcohol abuse.** A friend once told me he lost ten years of memories due to drug and alcohol abuse. Blackout episodes and memory loss can rob you of feelings causing you to treat loved ones with cold indifference.

5. **Tragedy.** Unlike trauma, tragedy is driven primarily by loss. The bigger the loss, the more difficulty you may have

knowing your feelings. For instance, many people are upset when they can't cry at a funeral. They stare off into the distance or sleepwalk through the services. At such times of profound grief, dissociative states are common.

Recovering Lost Feelings

Frequently in therapy, people recover lost feelings. When you feel safe and out of danger, your defenses come down, and buried feelings emerge. This process can't be rushed; lost feelings only reemerge when you're ready. To force someone to feel something before they are ready can result in considerable harm. Always remember, everyone heals at a different pace.

As you begin to regain feelings and express them, a sense of relief takes hold, as if a weight has lifted off your shoulders. Even if the reactivated feelings are painful, you find yourself rejoicing; you're finally free of the burden of carrying them.

How to Reactivate Feelings

If you find yourself in a dissociative state, try the following steps:

1. **Take a deep breath.** People in dissociative states tend to hold their breath, sending their bodies into a panic. Remind yourself to breathe; help yourself to some nice gulps. Deep breathing brings fresh oxygen to your blood and raises your metabolism so you can focus and make better decisions.

2. **Step away.** When possible, give yourself a time-out. Step away and clear your head before you become impulsive or reactive. Think about your options, and then make a mindful choice.

3. **Move your body.** The body tends to freeze up during dissociation. Shake off tension through exercise. Be creative: Use music or dance to get yourself moving.

4. **Stimulate your other senses.** I worked with a young woman who told me that she would pause when she felt a dissociative episode coming on and take a shower. For her, a shower was a chance to reboot her feelings and reflect.

Other people find eating, journaling, drawing, or listening to music effectively disrupts dissociation.

5. **Talk to someone.** Pick up the phone, call a friend, and dialogue with someone. Healthy relationships are always stabilizing and the best way to find your way back to yourself.

Death Shock: How to Recover When a Loved One Dies Suddenly

5 stages of grief and 5 ways to recover.

It changes you forever. The news arrives, and time stops.

There are few things in life as devastating as the sudden death of a loved one. As your world descends into chaos and you're flooded with despair, you feel like you're trapped in a nightmare and can't wake up:

"How could this happen? It can't be true!"

A sudden death shatters our sense of security

We prefer to believe that our loved ones are safe from harm. We assume that accidents and illnesses will bypass them. So when tragedy strikes suddenly, we go into shock. Our entire being vibrates with a single word: *Why?*

A sudden death shakes you to the core. You can't turn away from it or reason with it. You know that life will never be the same.

Processing death: The five stages of grief

Kubler Ross identified five stages of grief to provide a framework for the processing of death. Ross spent much of her life working with terminally ill patients. While these stages are not universal, nor do they occur in lockstep, they can be useful in thinking about grief.

1. **Denial:** You experience shock and disbelief, frequently accompanied by numbness, detachment, or disassociation. You may focus on facts or keep busy, anything to delay

experiencing the pain and despair the loss of your loved one has caused you.

2. **Anger:** Rage emerges in you. You may point your anger at doctors, friends, spouses, siblings, society, or even yourself. But when anger is fixated on blame, it offers little comfort. As blame subsides, the pain returns. Anger also triggers a crisis of faith and rage at a God that would permit such a horrible thing to happen. You may even feel angry at the deceased for abandoning you.

3. **Bargaining:** In an attempt to ease the pain of your loss, you try to bargain with it. You may make sudden changes or promises, such as, "I'm going to be a better person." or "I'll honor his or her memory by changing my ways." But such grief-driven promises are hard to keep. Bargaining helps to soften your anger and is your first attempt to come to grips with the loss.

4. **Depression:** After passing through denial, anger, and bargaining, the painful reality of the situation sinks in. Depression pushes down on you until you collapse under its weight. Everything feels pointless. Exhaustion plagues you. You may fall back on self-destructive habits such as over-eating, sleeping, or isolating. Such patterns existed in your life before the loss and frequently increase during the depression stage.

5. **Acceptance.** You begin to accept your new reality. You recognize that, although everything has changed, you must go on living. You start to find moments of inner peace. Perhaps you take comfort in memories rather than feel depressed or hurt by them. You may dream about your loved one or talk to him or her in your mind. You start to seek new relationships.

The road to recovery from loss

The stages of grief can last months or years. Everyone passes through them differently. To help yourself recover, consider the following suggestions:

1. **Seek support:** A community of friends and family can be a great comfort after a loss. Accept whatever relief they can offer, and don't be afraid to ask for more.

2. **Reach out:** Isolation after a loss is common, but too much of it breeds depression. Reach out to others, enroll in a bereavement group, or find a religious community or meditative practice that offers peace.

3. **Maintain self-care:** Keep active and explore new habits such as exercise, journaling, or yoga. Find a way to step outside your grief by being more creative, such as taking a class, going to inspiring concerts, or visiting galleries.

4. **Find Meaning:** There is a beautiful new book written by David Kessler, "Finding Meaning: The Sixth Stage of Grief," In it, he discusses how the loss of his 21-year-old son due to an overdose gave way to depths of grief that he's never known. Books like this can be a great comfort in helping you to realize that you're not alone. They also offer you some tools to help you recover.

5. **Start Fresh:** At some point, you'll have a choice to make: *Do you let grief shrink your life and hold you hostage, or do you try to move forward?* I had a friend whose son was killed instantly when a car hit him while he was skateboarding. It was so shocking that even now, when I think about it, twenty years later, sadness washes over me. My friend emerged from his grief process as a changed person. He published a beautiful letter in a local newspaper to his son, celebrating and thanking him for their time together. In the letter, he shared that his son was an organ donor and wrote, *"His eyes returned sight to someone who couldn't see. His lungs breathe now in another body."* It was a beautiful tribute.

   When I asked him how he found the strength to go on, he said, "I decided the best way to honor my son was to live a happy life. I'm sure that's what he would want."

No one fully recovers from the sudden death of a loved one. We all are changed by such losses. But don't give up the battle to go on. A grief that is honored and processed fully frequently gives birth to a greater appreciation and commitment to living.

The Joy of Sadness

Studies find that sadness is actually good for you.

Recently, a woman visited my psychotherapy office for a consultation and expressed concern that she had been feeling sad since her mother passed away.

> "When did she die?" I asked.
>
> "About three months ago," she said, "From cancer. "
>
> "Isn't it appropriate to feel sad?"
>
> She sighed impatiently. "I don't have time for this. Can you prescribe antidepressants?"

Sadly, sadness isn't valued these days very much. Pushed aside by the dazzling smiles and gleeful selfies that bombard us on social media, the message is clear: Happiness is for winners, and sadness is for losers.

Studies on the Positive Effects of Sadness

According to 10 studies on sadness reported by Research Digest, more value is gained from honoring sadness than disowning it. The studies found that people who experience sadness benefit in many ways.

- Sadness enhances empathy.
- Sadness triggers self-reflection.
- A good cry discharges toxins, relieves tension, and lowers stress.
- Sadness induces greater patience.
- Sadness awakens gratitude by reminding us of the fragility of life.

Many types of theater, art, and music celebrate sadness. They touch us deeply because they permit us to mourn, grieve, and feel heartbroken, hurt, or disappointed. Such experiences deepen our humanity and often fuel our hunger for positive change. They cause us to assess our lives and relationships and consider new choices.

Alternatively, suppressed or denied sadness frequently erupts in a flurry of psychosomatic symptoms such as muscle tension, headaches, or backaches. It can also disrupt sleep, cause erratic moods, and weaken concentration.

Learning to Honor Sadness

Psychotherapy aims not to eliminate uncomfortable feelings but to expand our capacity to feel. We seek to honor all our emotions without placing a value judgment on them or labeling them as positive or negative. The more we embrace and welcome all our feelings equally, the more attuned we are to others and the world around us.

Jackson, a young man in weekly group therapy, suffered from many nervous tics. He always seemed filled with worry or on the verge of tears. Yet each time he felt the urge to cry, he released a whirlwind of self-criticism and apology.

> "Sorry! I'm too sensitive; I'm just being dramatic."

Week after week, the group watched as he disowned his sadness. Finally, one of his fellow group members protested heatedly,

> "I can't stand how cruel you are to yourself," she said. "You're allowed to cry, Jackson."
>
> Jackson was shocked, "Why are you so angry with me?"
>
> She explained, "You're abusing someone I care about."

It was the first time someone embraced Jackson's sensitivity and welcomed his tears. Throughout childhood, his sadness was met with impatience and intolerance; his siblings mocked him, and his parents responded with contempt. When he cried, his father barked, "Go to your room, and don't come out until you've fixed your face!"

The negative voices of his family became the inner critic that prevented him from honoring his sadness. He no longer needed his parents or siblings to shame him. He did that himself.

Over time with the support of weekly group therapy, Jackson discovered it was okay to cry. It wasn't shameful or unmanly. It made him more attractive and excited and expanded his emotional intelligence. His nervous tics faded when sadness became a good part of his experience. He no longer shied away from conflict or avoided expressing uncomfortable feelings. In honoring his sadness, Jackson discovered a wellspring of strength.

How to Recover When Life Crushes You

Life provides suffering, healing requires help.

Whether you saw it coming or not, the feeling is the same: You're devastated. You gasp at your vulnerability and wonder, *"Why did this happen?"*

Life has many hardships: heartbreak, illness, injury, death, and abandonment. Though we may share similar experiences, every hurt is personal. No matter how often well-meaning people say, *"We understand,"* they don't. You may even resent them for trying.

As a psychotherapist, I've sat with many wounded people. I witness their pain and do my best to make space for it. Even when they cry out, *"Why did this happen?"* I try not to engage in reactive comforting. When someone is deeply hurt, advice or quick answers always feel false, even insulting.

Suffering as a Teacher

After nearly 25 years of practicing psychotherapy, I've learned that when you're viciously knocked down by life, don't get right back up. Like tripping and falling, you have the impulse to rise and start moving again. But ignoring a severe injury will make it worse. Pain demands attention and must be acknowledged and embraced before you can move on.

Amanda's Story

When I met Amanda, she had just suffered one of the worst wounds: the death of her young child. In individual sessions, she sat in silence for weeks, detached and stoic. *"Tears won't bring my daughter back,"* she said flatly as she continued working at a finance job that she resented and avoided her grief.

When I asked her to attend one of my adult groups, she scoffed, *"Pointless."* But, with a bit of prodding, she agreed. *"I'll do it for you,"* she sighed, *"But it's a waste of time."*

When asked why she was in therapy during her first group session, she exhaled and replied, *"My daughter...she...my daughter...."*

Suddenly Amanda couldn't speak. She couldn't find words. She struggled to swallow her grief and choke down her tears.

"It was a mistake to come here. Sorry."

When she stood up and gathered her belongings to leave, an intuitive woman reached out and said warmly,

"I lost a child, too."

Suddenly, Amanda fell back into her seat and let her tears flow. She cried long and hard, gasping for air as the group made room for her pain. In the weeks that followed, she looked forward to group sessions. With the group's help, she slowly realized that the best way to honor her daughter was to find a new way to embrace life.

What to Do After You've Been Emotionally Hurt

I count myself among the heartbroken. I have nursed the dying, lost loved ones, and suffered heartbreak. I have cried alone on the street, in my office, sometimes with friends and family, and sometimes with patients. I tried to dodge heartache, but, like everyone, it eventually found me. It's one of life's cruel certainties.

How to Support Your Healing Process

1. Honor Your Pain.

Avoidance of pain increases it. To heal, you must pass through the doorway of grief. Emotional wounds are beyond "sadness"; they're felt in the depths of your being. Honor your pain; don't run from it. Unplug, put time aside to reflect, and permit yourself to grieve. If well-meaning people push you to *"Get over it,"* ignore them. Time and patience are crucial to recovery. Surround yourself with friends who understand that.

2. Reach Out.

Being alone is part of healing, but extended periods of isolation are unhealthy. Deep pain always brings out personal demons, such as blaming yourself, embracing victimhood, or bitterness. Such choices breed entrapment, not freedom. Reach out to friends, find support groups or twelve-step programs, and seek comfort in prayer, meditation, or philosophy—whatever brings you peace of mind. Instead of longing for a miracle, create one.

3. Take a Break.

Taking a break from your pain and engaging in healthy compartmentalization is essential. Everyone finds relief in different ways. Some find creative activities such as writing, reading, music, art, or movies. Others find it in movement such as dance, hiking, long walks, etc. Choose a task that allows you to escape by stepping into another reality, even if only briefly. Don't fret: Your pain will await you when you return, but you'll be better fortified, rested, and ready to face it.

4. Learn from It.

I've heard that the road to wisdom is paved with suffering. Reflecting, exploring, and pondering, without self-attack or blame, opens you up to greater understanding and compassion for yourself and others. An attitude of learning will help you unearth value in the experience. You may also discover a curious new freedom: Recovering from emotional trauma or heartbreak makes you stronger, wiser, and more resilient.

5. Move On.

Some people allow suffering to define, shape, and ultimately rob them of living. Many years ago, I was invited to a wedding between two widows in their 90s. Every person who attended was deeply moved, not by the service, but by the couple's spirit to keep living. After you give yourself time to grieve, mourn, and reach out to others for support and make space for your recovery, you have to decide: Will you allow emotional pain to hold you back, or will you choose to use it to propel you in a new direction?

Years after finishing her group therapy, Amanda phoned to update me on her life. She left her bank job and acquired a degree in early childhood education. She was working at the elementary school that her daughter was to attend before she died. When I asked Amanda how she felt, she replied, "*I still miss her. But I have so many children to care for now. I like to imagine that my daughter, wherever she is, is very proud of her mom.*"

CHAPTER 6:
GROUP THERAPY

Group Therapy in Your Living Room

Online therapy groups open a world of possibilities.

For 25 years, I've led therapy groups in my office. Week after week, members gathered in circles and shared their heartbreaks, breakthroughs, irritations, frustrations, and victories. They fell in love with each other (or in hate with each other) and experienced so many feelings in between.

Over time, the intimate relationships they formed in group therapy transformed and healed them. After sessions, they often exited the office, laughing and chatting as they made their way to the elevator. It's always a good sign when group members leave the group with more energy than they brought to the session.

The pandemic changed all that.

Online Therapy Groups? Really?

I prepared to shut down my group therapy practice when the quarantine hit.. After all, how could I allow 12 people in my office to sit in a circle and breathe all over each other? I thought my group practice was kaput, over and out, done.

Then a patient said to me, "My single mom's group holds weekly online sessions. You should look into Zoom."

To which I replied, "What's a 'zoom?'"

A New Online Community

After a tutorial, I gathered my group members' email addresses and scheduled my groups on Zoom. (I finally figured out what a "zoom" was). From the beginning, I felt trepidatious.

Will this work?

Will people feel safe?

Won't this be a lousy substitute for sessions in the flesh?

I didn't have high hopes. I decided not to charge for the first Zoom sessions because I was confident that online therapy groups would be a snoozefest. In other words, a complete failure.

I was wrong.

From the first session, I could see that group members starved for contact. They were thrilled to see each other. What's more, every group had at least one member who had the coronavirus and several members who lost loved ones. I sensed that they craved the love and support their weekly therapy group provided. Due to the quarantine, we couldn't meet in person, but to my surprise group sessions online were a damn good substitute.

3 Significant Benefits of Online Groups

Here are the top three benefits to online therapy groups I've noticed so far:

1. Members can participate in group sessions from different locations.

Often, members have to miss a session because of a schedule conflict, illness, childcare, etc. In the past, they would have to miss the session or even drop out of group. Now, they call in from home, the office, or other locations.

2. **Members who are sick or quarantined can continue to attend group sessions.**

   A member hospitalized with the coronavirus signed into her online group from her hospital bed. Her group members cheered when they saw her. She smiled, started to cry, and gushed, "Seeing you guys is the highlight of my week!" In the past, she could never have continued her group under such conditions.

3. **Members in crisis can continue to attend group sessions.**

   I have several group members who are facing crises, such as caring for a sick parent or child. They are unable to travel. Yet, they can still get the weekly support and encouragement from their group. In the past, those members would have had to suspend sessions or leave their group temporarily. Now, there's no reason for such interruptions.

Social Anxiety? 3 Reasons to Try Group Therapy

Studies show that group therapy is effective in reducing social anxiety.

Does this sound like you? Social gatherings fill you with dread. Panic starts even before you leave. You cringe at the thought of your own awkwardness, imagining all that could go wrong.

As you get closer to the event, your heart races, and your palms sweat. You start to consider excuses for canceling.

According to the Anxiety and Depression Association of America, anxiety disorders are the most common mental illnesses diagnosed in the United States, affecting over 40 million adults or 18% of the population.

Without treatment, anxiety disorders tend to get worse, shrinking your life and forcing you to withdraw from the world. The more you retreat into isolation, the worse your symptoms become. Soon, everyday events like ordering food in a restaurant or buying stamps at the post office induce panic. Unfortunately, some folks even turn to drugs or alcohol in an attempt to manage their anxiety.

While individual therapy can offer relief, studies published by Reuters concluded that group therapy is particularly effective for individuals suffering from social anxiety and suggest that group therapy should be one of the first choices of treatment.

What makes groups so effective? Folks with social anxiety are far more comfortable in the private one-on-one exchanges, the kind that individual therapy provides. In one-on-one exchanges, they don't experience the anxiety that they do socially. Typically, they report details from high anxiety experiences that happened outside of the therapy office, but the therapist may struggle to understand if the reports are distorted or inaccurate. For example:

- *"Was everyone really looking at them?"*
- *"Was someone really critical of them?"*
- *"Are they triggering negative responses in others?"*

In group therapy, however, therapists witness social anxiety in action and can identify its causes and triggers. For example, the anxiety may be the result of communication misinterpretations, negative projections, gender issues, or unresolved trauma. Armed with this insight, group therapists can intervene the moment anxiety appears and help the socially anxious person gain the skills to manage feelings, reduce distortions, and make healthier choices.

Here are three ways group therapy helps reduce social anxiety:

1. Group Therapy Disrupts Social Isolation

Group therapy ends social isolation by providing new, supportive relationships. Additionally, in group you'll discover that you are not alone; other people share your fears and concerns. As a result, you develop deeper compassion and empathy for your own and other people's struggles. The group experience nurtures kinship and fosters social healing.

2. Group Therapy Builds Social Skills

Group provides you with a place to practice essential social skills, such as self-expression, boundary setting, conflict management, and progressive emotional communication. And here's the best part: When your anxiety flares up, the group leader is there to help you manage it and build greater tolerance.

3. Group Therapy Recreates Social Settings

Social anxiety requires social treatment. Group therapy helps you better manage your fears by providing a safe, supportive social environment to process and understand the causes of your anxiety.

Marsha the Martian

Marsha battled social anxiety most of her life. Like many folks who struggle with anxiety, she has a history of social trauma. She remembers how she panicked in elementary school when the teacher called on her. *"My face would turn bright red and blotchy. The kids said I was Mars, the red planet. They started calling Marsha the Martian."*

Throughout high school and college, she avoided speaking in public, skipped parties, and dodged social gatherings. *"I spent most of my time in my dorm room or the library. I missed out on a lot."*

When I suggested Marsha try one of my weekly therapy groups, like most people with social anxiety, she responded negatively. *"Groups are firing squads to me. Why would I do that to myself?"*

Eventually, she agreed to join a group. *"I was desperate. I have an aunt who doesn't leave her house. I feared that could happen to me eventually."*

The moment she entered group she noticed a difference. *"People were thoughtful and mindful. They really listened. It wasn't like any group of people that I had experienced."*

Gradually, Marsha started to open up to the group, and express her fears and concerns. Rather than the impatience or criticism she expected, the group responded with warmth and affection.

"My friends started to notice a change in me. I was more expressive and more outspoken. I wasn't afraid to disagree or address conflict. Group gave me the skills I needed. At work events, I even became an expert mingler."

5 Reasons Group Therapy Is The Best Choice for Struggling Teens

Research shows a 73% improvement in teens in group therapy vs. other therapies

Individual therapy is a wonderful tool for helping teenagers overcome their fears, improve their moods, and explore their feelings. But why do so many teens with social problems fail to benefit from individual therapy?

The answer is simple: Kids' anxieties or difficulties socially—in classrooms, study groups, lunch rooms, or recess—will not emerge in individual sessions. Socially anxious kids frequently relate well, demonstrate intelligence, or have a sense of humor in individual sessions. That's because they aren't being challenged; they don't experience the same anxieties they encounter in social settings with peers.

A meta-analysis of 56 studies over 20 years, reported in the *Journal of Clinical Child Psychology*, reports that group therapy was proven more effective with children and teenagers than other forms of therapy. It says that the average child or adolescent treated by group treatment was better off than 73 percent of those not.

Group therapy provides therapists with the rare opportunity to see teenagers' social problems in action. Shyness, bullying, inattentiveness, fearfulness, social anxieties—all these tendencies emerge in group. A skilled group therapist catches these reactions in the moment and helps teens overcome bad habits and make new choices.

Who benefits most from group therapy? Kids who suffer from the following issues:

- Social Isolation
- Acute Shyness
- Bullying Issues
- Peer Rejection
- Anger Management Problems

- Identity Conflicts

The Benefits of Group Therapy

Group therapy is like a fitness center for social skills. Teens emerge from a positive group experience with new interpersonal tools and abilities. They speak up in class, resist negative peer pressure, and stand up for themselves. Group work also helps teens increase their capacity for self-expression and emotional assertiveness. As their social insecurities dissolve, they feel comfortable talking to peers or adults.

What are the benefits of group therapy? Here's a five-point checklist:

1. Social Confidence

Group sessions allow kids to incorporate new ways of relating and developing better social behaviors. As they build confidence and develop a knack for speaking in groups, they become more comfortable asserting themselves in social situations in their daily life.

2. Better Communication Skills

Many teenagers have difficulty communicating their emotions and tend to bottle up their feelings. Unrelieved emotional stress often triggers irritable behaviors such as moodiness, irritability, and defiance. In group therapy, kids rarely explore their feelings and fears with other teenagers. As they develop better communication skills, they experience a surge in maturity.

3. Positive Peer Influences

Peer pressure wields epic positive and negative influences on young people's lives. When kids are in the company of peers struggling to improve themselves and develop healthier ways of relating, they don't feel so alone. Each week, group members cheer and celebrate each other's victories. This positive environment gives kids the confidence they need to overcome self-doubt and take more social initiative.

4. Improved Relationships

Isolated teens are more likely to suffer from anxiety and depression; these teens withdraw from peers to quell fears and insecurities. Group sessions offer kids a chance to develop better-quality peer relationships. Kids trapped in poor relationships at school can start again and become part of a peer community off of school grounds that appreciates and values them.

5. Reduced Stress

Teens often feel humiliated by social and academic pressures. Group work relieves kids from stress by allowing them to unburden themselves with peers who understand them. They learn to keep difficulties in perspective and develop a healthy sense of humor.

A New Beginning

Not all kids are equipped with good social skills. The sooner they become skilled at managing themselves in groups, the better. Group therapy offers teens a rare chance to develop social confidence and self-assurance. And that's the best gift any teenager could ask for.

---

5 Ways Group Therapy Empowers You in Relationships

Tired of feeling like an outsider? Group therapy can help.

You can relax and listen without distraction when your favorite love song is played on a well-tuned instrument. But when the device is out of tune, even a master musician can't make it sound right.

Emotional attunement operates similarly in relationships. You're drawn to that person when someone listens to you thoughtfully and responds authentically. There's no static communication; there's no approval-seeking or narcissistic ranting. You feel understood and content.

Where can you learn to be so comfortable and at ease in relationships?

How Group Therapy Helps

Individual therapy is an excellent tool for strengthening your identity. A skilled individual therapist can help you better understand your history, feelings and impulses, and choices: it can help heal trauma, awaken passions, ease anxiety, etc.

As individual therapy focuses on improving your relationship with yourself, group therapy focuses on improving your relationships with others, specifically, how you communicate and behave in relationships. For example:

- *Do you get anxious or fearful in intimate exchanges?*
- *Do you become controlling, irritated, or combative?*
- *Do you feel let down or unfulfilled?*

Social difficulties require social treatment. Group provides a place to practice new ways of being with others. As your attunement improves, you'll learn to establish healthier, more satisfying relationships. Additionally, you'll begin to undo your bad habits that most often trigger social difficulties.

In group therapy, as you strengthen your attunement with others, you'll:

1. Communicate with greater clarity.
2. Stress less about conflicts.
3. Share your genuine thoughts and feelings.
4. Listen with greater empathy and consideration.
5. Develop your authentic voice.

The Tuned-Out Person

Have you ever worked for a boss who was constantly distracted, preoccupied, or unavailable? You get the feeling he's not listening – and you're right. You want to do your job well, but if he's so out of tune with you, you're never quite sure what he wants or if he's pleased with your work. One moment, he's supportive; the next, he's irritated. Sometimes he piles on demands; other times, he abandons you.

He's out of tune with you – and it's maddening. Feeling recognized, understood, and valued by others is an essential human need.

Eventually, you might muster up the courage to find a more positive place to work. But what if you couldn't quit that job because that distracted person is your parent, sibling, or spouse?

With attunement, relationships are manageable and satisfying. Without the tools to nurture attunement, you're left with an emptiness that no amount of therapy, self-help seminars, or life coaching will fill.

Practicing Attunement in Life

Knowing when you're in tune – and when you're not – is fundamental to improving your relationships. If therapy groups aren't available in your area, here are some basic suggestions to tune up your way of being with others:

Stop Multitasking

It's impossible to listen to someone when your attention is truly divided. Multitasking may feel good to you, but it's disrespectful. No one likes to compete for attention. Multitask when you're alone, but when communicating with others, for goodness' sake, stop and listen.

Put Down the Screen

Like it or not, we're all a part of "Generation Screen." How many times a day do we stop and stare at a glowing monitor? Cell phones, i-Pads, computers, the TV – you name it. While technology has dramatically improved our ability to share information, it's not a substitute for human contact. Many folks use technology as a defense against intimacy or to avoid complicated feelings. For mature, satisfying emotional communication, put down the screen and look into another person's eyes.

Focus on Listening

Today's world is built for distraction. Is it any wonder that ADD is among the top diagnoses? Ironically, the less time you spend with others, your insecurities and obsessions mushroom. Listening to someone else and being attuned ultimately strengthens and grounds you.

Stay Engaged

A distracted "uh-huh" is the empty calories of communication. If you feel someone is not listening, confront them. If you catch yourself not listening, stop and ask questions. If you say, "I'm sorry, what did you say?" more than two or three times a week, you tend toward disassociation; the distance you put between you and another person may feel comforting, but ultimately makes you less interesting, less attractive, and undermines your friendships.

Practice Mindfulness

A lack of attunement with others frequently stems from a lack of attunement with oneself. Attunement begins with getting in touch with your inner world. Mindfulness practice helps keep you balanced and grounded in the moment. It also empowers you to take responsibility for your moods, making you less likely to blame others or say destructive things to loved ones.

Toward a New Way of Being

Attunement is the beating heart of any relationship; it will never disappoint you. Group therapy offers the tools to strengthen attunement, live more fully in the moment, and build more satisfying relationships.

---

3 Ways Group Therapy is Better Than Individual Therapy

A backstage pass to group process.

Unlike individual therapy, group therapy focuses exclusively on relationships. In individual sessions, therapists receive patients' reports on events. These reports may be exaggerated, distorted, or just plain inaccurate. However, in group, therapists witness live enactments of your relationship difficulties. They observe when your anxiety suddenly spikes, notice your body language changes and see what intimate exchanges trigger in you.

In other words, whatever goes wrong in the space between you and another person is displayed in actual—time group therapy. And your therapist is there to help.

What Happens in Life, Happens in Group

The transformative power of group lies in its focus on the here and now. Rather than investigate your history, group therapy directs you to tune into your thoughts and feelings in the moment, particularly the feelings you experience toward your fellow group members.

Of course, this isn't easy. In fact, nearly all patients protest when I recommend group:

> *"How could I have feelings toward total strangers?*
>
> *"Why would I express personal feelings in front of others?"*
>
> *"I go blank when talking in group situations. I don't feel anything."*

Whether you realize it or not, you constantly have feelings toward others. Chances are that others are picking up on them, too.

For instance, when you step into an elevator with someone, you experience a wave of feelings toward that person.

> *Do you feel safe with that person?*
>
> *Are you attracted to that person?*
>
> *Do you smile? Avoid eye contact? Feel annoyed?*

You can stumble upon your projections as you tune into these feelings and investigate them further.

> *Does this person remind you of an old friend?*
>
> *A menacing high school teacher?*
>
> *Your first love?*

Tuning into your feelings is the first step toward living more fully in the moment; it transports you to the here and now and immediately strengthens your attunement to others.

The Group Contract

After identifying your feelings toward someone in group, more work must be done. Sharing your thoughts and feelings with group members is the best way to practice honest and meaningful exchanges. This will make your group experience so exhilarating; it empowers you to sustain intimate relationships in a safe environment. Gradually, you begin to apply the people skills you develop in group in the outside world.

To enrich your way of communicating and connecting with others in group, you'll be encouraged to:

- Voice your thoughts and feelings toward fellow group members.
- Share any associations, memories, or dreams brought to light by relationships in the group.
- Respond candidly to group members' responses to you.
- Express frustrating feelings maturely, refraining from verbal attacks.
- Strive to take emotional risks; step outside your comfort zone.

The therapist establishes a secure and structured environment for group members to feel they're in safe hands. Toward this end, group members are directed to:

- Refrain from outside social contact with group members.
- Respect confidentiality.
- Arrive at sessions on time.
- Pay for sessions on time.
- Attend sessions with minimal absences.

To ensure maximum emotional freedom with your group therapist, you're also encouraged to:

- Express feelings toward the therapist (i.e., frustration, anger, affection).
- Voice fears and concerns about the group to the therapist.
- Reach out for help or direction from the therapist as needed.

Group in Action

Steven, a prosperous real estate agent with rock-star looks, had a long history of failed romantic relationships. This had me particularly perplexed. In individual sessions, he was charming, thoughtful, and had a good sense of humor and high emotional intelligence. So why did women flee from him?

After several weeks, I asked Steven to join one of my groups. He balked, "What? Share my personal feelings with a bunch of strangers? No, thank you." I explained I couldn't help him form better relationships until I could study how he relates to others. "Forget it," he guffawed, "Group's not for me."

I responded, "You hired me to help you solve your relationship problems. I can't do that under these conditions. You're wasting your money."

Reluctantly, he agreed.

Within 15 minutes of his entry into the group, I was stunned by what I witnessed. Steven related to the men in the group in a relaxed and easygoing manner. But with the women, he was wooden, insincere, and arrogant. He adopted a false persona that proved disastrous in masking his insecurities with women.

Naturally, the women's reaction in group mirrored the women's response in his life. At first contact, they liked Steven, but the more he spoke, the more they lost his patience. Poor Steven felt hurt and abandoned by the women, just as he had felt all his life.

Then one day, Steven came to group with sad news; his mother had been hospitalized after a heart attack.

As Steven relayed his story, at times with tears in his eyes, the group members were moved. They understood his fears and shared their experiences with him. Steven listened and responded naturally and unaffectedly; gone were the superficial voice and arrogant manner.

As the group praised him for his openness, Steven discovered his authentic self was much more appealing than the counterfeit one. One woman confessed, "I like this Steven so much more. I would date this Steven in a heartbeat."

The more positive reinforcement he received, the more he began to share his feelings frankly and openly. As Steven began to form intimate relationships in the group, his anxieties dissipated, and he achieved a new level of comfort with others. Soon after, Steven reported a greater sense of social confidence in the world.

3 Ways Group Is Better Than Individual Therapy

1. Group focuses exclusively on relationships.
2. Group therapists get a live demonstration of social problems.
3. Group members have a place to learn and practice more effective communication methods.

Learning to Embrace Intimacy

Living fully in the here and now puts you at the intersection between your past and future—the best entry point for positive growth and change. In group, you'll learn to embrace intimacy, honor your feelings, and communicate with others with more excellent skill and authenticity.

Most importantly, group therapy helps you break free of unhealthy relationship patterns and social anxieties. As my mentor, Dr. Louis Ormont, the father of American group psychotherapy, often said, "If you can do it in group, you can do it in life." What could be more rewarding than that?

CHAPTER 7:
HAPPINESS

5 Steps to Finding Purpose and Feeling Happier

A commitment to personal growth is essential for starting the day with energy.

What gets you out of bed in the morning? What do you look forward to? How do you greet the day?

Many people fall into habits or mind-numbing routines without considering that their daily activities propel their lives in specific directions. From a short-term perspective, having a bad day may seem like no big deal. But over time, if bad days outnumber good ones, any happiness you feel will be fleeting, a short burst rebooting to a baseline of dread the next morning.

Finding direction and purpose

Purpose, mission, and *direction* are words loaded with meaning. Some people find fulfillment in work; others find it in family or relationships. Some may have talents that fuel passions or hobbies that have nothing to do with work or family. What do they all have in common? They engage in activities that revitalize and energize them, filling them with excitement, spike their creativity, or inspire them.

Finding joy in your work may seem ideal, but it's not the only way to achieve direction and purpose. Consider these examples from patients I have worked with.

- A lawyer who plays piano with his jazz band on weekends confesses, "Every gig is a jolt of adrenaline. I think of new chord progressions while standing on the subway platform. Sometimes I invite clients to come to hear my band. It's been good for business."

- A teacher feeling burnout who returned to school to get a degree in social work and transitioned to being a guidance counselor. "It's such a wonderful feeling; after all these years teaching, suddenly I feel born again," she says. "I love my new job."

- A psychotherapist who wrote a play about the challenges of being a therapist. After leaving his office, he dashes off to rehearsals, exhilarated as he works with the actors and the director. "Even when I was exhausted, seeing my play produced and performed was a thrill that I will never forget."

What do they all have in common? They committed to a path of ongoing personal growth. Rather than fall victim to burnout or routine, they found something new to inspire and awaken them. Not only did they feel happier, but they also started each day with more energy and drive. They didn't wait for the right time; they created it.

Getting started

Here are some prompts to get you started. Think of the following questions and activities as jumping-off points for mindful consideration.

1. Name three activities that you love and that rejuvenate, inspire, and energize you.

2. Are these activities related to specific jobs, or could they be hobbies?

3. What opportunities do you have to pursue these activities? For example, can you take a class or volunteer? Do you know someone in the field?

4. Talk to friends and brainstorm together. Sharing your feelings with others is always more effective than ruminating or obsessing alone. Talking to a therapist about lifestyle changes is also a great start.

5. Find a mentor. Having a mentor in your field of interest is the express lane to achieving your dreams.

Expanding your life

Life is full of built-in struggles. But having purpose and drive are chosen battles that give meaning to it all. They make common suffering less burdensome and give your day much-needed fun.

I return to the poem "George Gray" by Edgar Lee Masters again and again and often share it with patients. For me, this section speaks directly to the heart of the matter:

> To put meaning in one's life may end in madness,
>
> But life without meaning is the torture
>
> Of restlessness and vague desire —
>
> It is a boat longing for the sea and yet afraid.

Having a purpose encourages you to take risks and step out of the shadows. It also insulates you against fear, petty concerns, and insecurities while fueling you with vitality and energy.

5 Essential Steps to Be Happier and Achieve Your Dreams

Transform your frustration into fuel.

Do you want to live a happier life? And find the energy to achieve your dreams? Most people do. But with all the advice available, choosing the right path is challenging.

For more than 25 years, I've provided psychotherapy to people seeking a better life. They yearned for new careers, improved home lives, better relationships, or more creative activities. Over time, I've noticed that the folks who achieved their ambitions had one important quality in common.

Confronting frustration is the fuel that drives maturity. When you engage and resolve frustration, you trigger a leap in maturity, a surge of confidence, and a healthy burst of self-esteem.

The first step in this process is vital.

1. Confronting Frustration

At the root of frustration is discomfort. Chances are that you're dissatisfied; perhaps you feel stuck at work or in an unhappy relationship. The longer you experience dissatisfaction, the more tense and stressed out you become.

As internal pressure builds, many folks turn to substances to numb themselves, such as drugs or alcohol. Others may choose denial or compartmentalization. Such choices only temporarily diminish frustration; they don't resolve it. You may experience momentary relief but eventually, the frustration returns, and you feel stuck again.

Resolving frustration requires examining your choices when faced with frustration, which brings us to the second step:

2. Setting a Determination

After you identify the source of your frustration, it's time to consider your options:

- How can you confront the situation?
- What steps can you take to address it?
- Who are the players involved?

Engaging with frustration is never easy, which is why setting a personal determination is crucial. Determination awakens courage.

If your determination is, "I want a new job," some questions you may explore include:

- "Do I quit?"
- "Do I set up a meeting with my boss?"
- "Do I start interviewing for new positions elsewhere?"

- "Do I confront my co-workers about their behavior?"
- "Do I ask for a promotion or raise?"

Gather support, consider options, and come up with plans. It may be helpful to rehearse what you want to say, make lists, or journal about your concerns.

As Buddhist peace advocate Daisaku Ikeda writes:

> When your determination changes, everything will begin to move in the direction you desire. The moment you resolve to be victorious, every nerve and fiber in your being will immediately orient itself toward your success. On the other hand, if you think, "This is never going to work out," then at that instant, every cell in your being will be deflated and give up the fight.

Once you make your determination and confront your frustration, you will experience the next step:

3. The Test Period

Confronting frustration is always scary. Anxiety can spike. You may feel unsure, experience doubt, or question your judgment.

It also invites pushback. People may be critical of you, discourage you, deny your requests, or undermine your plans. Obstacles frequently appear during the test period. For example, an object moving forward through space meets resistance; it is the same when you take chances and push yourself out of your comfort zone, which brings us to the most dramatic step:

4. The Tipping Point

Everything hangs in the balance. The outcome is unknown; your determination comes under fire:

- Do you back down?
- Or do you press forward despite resistance?

The tipping point is exciting/terrifying because everything is on the line, and the outcome hinges on your choices. If you quit, abandon your determination, lose your patience, or do something destructive, you return to step one: frustration. This doesn't mean you failed; instead, it's time to return to the drawing board and start again.

Frustration isn't the enemy; it's how you choose to act in the face of frustration that determines whether you experience growth, decline, or stagnation.

5. The Breakthrough

You hung in there, didn't quit, persevered, and broke through. As a result, you experience a surge of confidence, maturity, and self-esteem.

Each time you make it through the five steps and experience a breakthrough, you should feel inspired and enlivened. It also triggers greater ambition and a healthy hunger for more personal growth.

---

3 Keys to Sustainable Happiness and Joy

Stop putting off your happiness until you achieve all your goals.

Most people come to therapy because they're disappointed in life. Things didn't turn out as planned; hopes were dashed, relationships ended, careers stagnated.

Is it possible to be happy when life doesn't work out as you planned?

How do you define happiness?

While most folks would agree that happiness is a worthy goal, few agree on how to achieve it, and even fewer know how to make happiness sustainable. The world is full of people who attached their happiness to wealth, romance, or materialism, only to discover that joy was fleeting; old anxieties and depressions returned, and they woke up one morning to find that dreadful weight of despair pressing down on them again.

When happiness slips away, we tend to repeat the same patterns: We chase it with even greater vigor. Sadly, happiness that depends solely on people, places, or things is fragile. Like a phantom, it can disappear suddenly and without notice.

Cultivating Sustainable Happiness

You can't wait to be happy sometime in the future; cultivating happiness based on your environment, relationships, belongings, appearance, weight, career success, or bank account won't do. Delaying happiness until you achieve any or all of these goals is a gamble that's likely to lead to – you guessed it – unhappiness.

3 Keys to Sustainable Happiness and Joy

Here are three things you can do today to build a foundation for sustainable happiness and joy in your life:

1. Gratitude.

There can be no lasting joy without appreciating what you have now. Gratitude doesn't develop naturally; it must be cultivated. Take a moment of quiet reflection – *now*. Enjoy what you have – *now*. Express gratitude for what you have – *now*. Chances are you already feel lighter, and your mood has improved. But here's the key: It takes more than just a moment, it takes a daily practice of gratitude. Before you can harvest sustainable happiness, you have to labor in the fields of appreciation. Appreciation and gratitude are the gateways to sustainable happiness.

2. Altruism.

A self-centered life, driven by ego, is a lifestyle that may be destined to end in burnout and loneliness. Studies have shown that people who regularly engage in altruistic activities consistently score higher on happiness measures than people who solely focus on themselves. The happiness experienced by bringing joy to others is more sustainable than happiness entirely based on satisfying our own needs.

3. A Spiritual Practice.

I've worked with hundreds of people in therapy. I've witnessed many of them overcome staggering hardships. But many of those who are able to cultivate sustainable joy in life had a daily spiritual practice that gave them strength and courage in the face of suffering. A spiritual practice strengthened their emotional core and empowered them to find joy even in times of adversity.

As Buddhist peace activist Daisaku Ikeda writes:

> "It is not others nor our fate nor the times we live in that make us unhappy; it is our own weakness. Inner weakness is the ultimate cause of unhappiness. It is what makes us fall into apathy and self-destructive patterns of behavior...and fills us with self-loathing. That is why to lead a happy life, the most important thing of all is to forge and develop our inner strength." (World Tribune, 2/21/22, p8)

Here's the best part: Sustainable happiness won't cost you a dime. It is available to everyone. Yes, it takes time and discipline. But how can you hope to master anything – even happiness — without practice?

Why You Don't Believe in Happiness Anymore

Five conditions that cause people to abandon happiness.

You start with big dreams, full of youthful enthusiasm. Over time, challenged by obstacles and hardships, your commitment to those dreams is tested. But you're still young, so you push on and persevere.

Then you get hit with big disappointments and let downs in your career, love life, or friendships. You feel unsupported and alone. "Why is this happening?" you wonder, "I'm a good person. I didn't do anything to deserve this."

Then you face a health crisis, lose a loved one, suffer injuries, or financial hardships. Unforeseen stressors continue to pop up and dash your plans.

You start to lose hope.

Losing the confidence that you'll ever be happy

When you're struggling, it's natural to want to give up. You may look around and feel that everyone has an easier life than you. You forget that no one is exempt from suffering, and some of the most outstanding individuals in history faced overwhelming personal hardships.

But no matter. The longer you stay in a place of hopelessness, the harder it is to believe that you'll ever be happy again. You may justify your unhappiness by proclaiming your powerlessness. You even start to question the concept of happiness.

"Happiness is an illusion sold by the media to make money," you decide. "Happy relationships? Happy families? Happy friendships? Bah! That's not real life."

Five conditions that cause people to abandon happiness

1. Heartbreak

Deep wounds to the soul come in many forms, but for me, the word "heartbreak" captures the catastrophic pain of unforeseen loss. No matter what form heartbreak takes when your heart is broken, gravity shifts, your body and mind feel sluggish, color is drained from the world, and every day is a battle with yourself.

2. Social isolation

You withdraw from the world. Stop seeing friends or family and embrace loneliness. The more you live in isolation, the more your thoughts and feelings become deluded. You distort the simplest of interactions and grow paranoid and suspicious of others. No one is who they seem to be.

3. Pessimism and bitterness

Complaining becomes your baseline functioning. You see fault in every-one. You watch people and judge them; no one escapes your criticism. "Phonies!" you think. "I'm better off alone." You convince yourself that the world has gone to hell. Even death seems like a welcome relief.

4. Creative stagnation

You have no curiosity. You stop exploring new experiences and become a slave to bad habits. There is no balance in your life. You eat too much or too little; you sleep too much or too little; time feels like it moves too slowly or too fast. Your reschedule has no consistency, and you feel permanently out of sorts. You don't like leaving the house, so you don't take walks or attend classes, lectures, or workshops. You stop going to performances. Creativity is gone from your life. Eventually, you grow disinterested in everyone and everything.

5. Living in the past

When you lose hope, you will start to live in the past. You revisit memories and embrace nostalgia, confident that the best times of your life are long gone. You stop living in the moment and lose your sense of wonder. There's nothing left to look forward to. "Weekends? Weekdays? Holidays?" you counsel yourself, "What does it matter? Nothing changes."

Steps to take to increase your chances of being happy again

Recently, a patient asked me, "When will my life get better?" I answered, "When you decide it will."

Needless to say, she was displeased. She met all five of the criteria for abandoning happiness. But I could sense she was holding tight to a childlike wish to be saved. As if someone would swoop down and save her from herself by blessing her with happiness.

My best advice: In adulthood, no one is responsible for your happiness but you. The wish to be saved by someone else will drive you to make reckless choices or ultimately reinforce the five conditions for abandoning happiness.

Breaking the cycle of unhappiness starts by taking a hard look at the choices you make that breed unhappiness. Until those conditions are addressed, happiness will remain elusive. To move in a new direction is going to require new choices.

---

3 Self-Defeating Habits that Destroy Happiness
The top three energy-draining, ambition-killing traits to lose.

Everyone struggles with negative internal voices; those nagging, critical, confidence-destroying voices that pop up when you're feeling anxious or want to try something new:

> *"You can't do that."*
>
> *"People will laugh at you"*
>
> *"You're not good enough."*

With the help of the right therapist, you can go to battle with self-defeating voices, unearth their origins, and evict them from your psyche. Even if they appear now and then (*who doesn't suffer bouts of self-doubt or insecurity?*), individual or group therapy can help you learn to manage self-defeating voices and keep them from undermining you.

But what about self-defeating habits? Those ingrained patterns that feel as comfortable as your favorite cozy blanket. What do you do about those?

Self-Defeating Habits

Self-defeating habits generally fly just under the radar of your consciousness. You're aware of them, but not enough to challenge them. They've become so ingrained and habitual that you're quick to normalize them.

> *"I know I should exercise more, but ..."*
>
> *"I don't make good decisions when I drink too much, but ..."*
>
> *"It should probably get out more, but ..."*

After every "but" is a reason not to justify poor choices and maintain your self-defeating patterns. To break free of them, let's take a closer look at the top three energy-draining, ambition-killing, and happiness-derailing traits that I've seen in my psychotherapy practice in the last 25 years.

Top Three Self-Defeating Habits

1. Complaining.

Complaint is the enemy of happiness. Whatever satisfaction it delivers can be considered empty calories at best. There's nothing wrong with feeling disgruntled, especially when it inspires us to grow and self-challenge, a dynamic Buddhists call "Turning poison into medicine."

However, chronic complaints without action forge patterns of negative thinking, pessimism, and hopelessness. It reinforces a sense of powerlessness in the face of frustration, saps your energy, and becomes a chronic source of discouragement for you and others around you. The result is an apathetic attitude that sucks the joy out of life.

2. Self-neglect.

No matter how you justify it, self-neglect leads to illnesses of the body, mind, and spirit. You can't sustainably enjoy life or develop resilience if you're sleep-deprived, don't exercise, ignore healthy eating habits, or rely on substances. The mind craves stimulation, the body craves movement, and the spirit craves balance—people who choose to ignore all three and engage in self-neglect craft a lifestyle that is destined to result in depression or social anxiety.

3. Procrastination.

Too often, we know what we should do, yet put off taking action. Procrastination leads to missed opportunities and regret. It feeds isolation, distrust, and emotional fragility. When we procrastinate, we deny ourselves a better way of being.

Challenging Self-Defeating Habits

Here are three simple ways you can start to undo self-defeating habits today:

1. **Write them down:** List the habits you'd like to change and put them down on paper so you can begin to be more conscious of them.

2. **Make an action plan:** what steps can you take today to address those habits.

3. **Seek out support:** therapy, support groups, career coaching, continuing education classes, spiritual practices; there are endless ways available to inspire yourself to action. Defeating self-defeating habits with support is always more successful than challenging them alone.

_____

6 Habits That Undermine Happiness and Sabotage Growth

Avoid these nasty happiness-destroying activities.

Everyone wants to be happy, right?

Yet many of us engage in activities that derail our happiness and point us toward misery.

Why would we willingly engage in happiness-destroying activities?

External obstacles to happiness

External obstacles to happiness are easy to spot, such as financial hardship, a failed relationship, a sudden accident, or illness. Such unsettling events jolt us into action: We apply for new jobs, start dating again, follow a doctor's guidance, and hopefully regain health. Like a movie hero, we see external obstacles are a call to action. They challenge and push us to make bold choices. It's the stuff of great drama.

Internal obstacles to happiness

Internal obstacles to happiness are harder to spot and less noticeable. Often there's no sudden change, no one to blame, and no transparent barrier in front of us. Internal obstacles ultimately lead to unresolved conflicts with ourselves, opposing impulses that create emotional tension and frequently lead us toward self-destruction.

Frequently, we engage in behaviors that we know are bad for us, yet we can't stop ourselves. The wish for instant gratification or relief from emotional tension tends to drive such impulsiveness and self-sabotaging life choices.

When we don't have mastery over our negative habits, lasting sustainable happiness will always remain elusive.

6 Happiness-Destroying Habits

1. Grudges.

Walking around wishing ill will on others is a terrible way to go through life. Worse, the grudges you nurse weigh you down and can trigger depression, increase anxiety, and zap your creative energy.

2. Compare and despair.

Comparing yourself to others and coming up short warps your world outlook. Some pitfalls of comparison and despair include lower self-esteem, a weaker core identity, and growth sabotage.

3. Creative Stagnation.

Curiosity will keep you young. Taking classes, exploiting new activities, and taking in art, theater, or dance stimulates your yearning to expand your life. Creative stagnation can breed despair and hopelessness.

4. Self-neglect.

Shakespeare wrote, "Self-love...is not so vile a sin as self-neglecting." Poor diet and exercise, lack of mindfulness, media binging, creative dullness, and intellectual decline are some outcomes of self-neglect. When you neglect yourself, all other aspects of your life decline.

5. Social isolation.

Few people thrive in isolation. A recent U.S. Surgeon General's report declared loneliness to be a national health epidemic in the United States; another report from the BBC shows increases in heart disease, stroke, and dementia among men who struggle with loneliness. Why are people so lonely? Buddhist peace advocate Daisaku Ikeda suggests that the depersonalization of society has resulted in more isolation and a loss of community.

6. Addiction.

Nothing can derail happiness faster than addiction. It destroys families and relationships, snuffs out creativity, and robs life of lasting joy. Whatever the substance, it's undoubtedly going to end badly.

"Warrior Approach" for Sustainable Happiness

Is your happiness fleeting? Does it flare up and then slip away?

Like most people, you want to be happy. Yet, you probably discovered that sustainable happiness is a real challenge. Sooner or later, old anxieties and insecurities flare up, and you find yourself back on that "mood roller-coaster"—happy one minute, despairing the next.

Is there a way to make happiness less erratic and more sustainable? Is there a form of happiness that endures even in the face of suffering?

Fragile Forms of Happiness

A problematic approach is viewing happiness as a destination, a phantom city on the horizon that promises to meet all your needs—a new job, a new relationship, or more money, all with the assurance of long-term happiness. But when you acquire them, you soon discover that the good times don't last forever.

That's the problem with happiness based on phantom cities: When they vanish, you find yourself right back where you started—searching for happiness again. This makes certain forms of happiness—for example, happiness based on sensory and material goods—the most fragile; when they disappear, so does your pleasure.

The Happiness Club

Another precarious view of happiness is thinking of happiness as an exclusive club. Whether you're a member or not, you're either born to be happy or locked outside the gates.

In the age of social media and wealth worshiping, the happiness club mentality misleads you into believing that some people are always happy. Scroll through all those shiny, cheerful images on social media, and you start to feel that other people's lives are endless parties. They get sunshine and rainbows while you're stuck in traffic or overpaying for bad coffee.

Unhealthy Habits That Derail Sustainable Happiness

Establishing sustainable happiness requires self-mastery—the ability to take a hard look at yourself and target self-inflicted forms of suffering that breed unhappiness.

First, target unhealthy habits that make sustainable happiness unattainable. The top three are these:

1. **Lifestyle problems:** Dependence on substances, fame, or superficial romance are among the most common self-inflicted forms of suffering that promote unhappiness.

2. **Discipline problems:** Lack of motivation leads to undisciplined finances; poor eating, sleeping, or exercise habits; too few tension outlets; and too few creative activities.

3. **Attitude problems:** A chronically negative outlook triggers complaining, blaming, and feeling like a victim. Life is a bore—and so are you.

Acknowledging Life's Universal Sufferings

Life serves all kinds of suffering: Illness, loss, financial crisis, etc. No one is exempt, no matter your bank account, the car you drive, or where you live. The idea that you should be personally immune to suffering succeeds in one way: It worsens suffering.

If you recognize that universal sufferings are inevitable, you cultivate enduring resilience; painful experiences, such as grief, illness, aging, or injury, when seen as a natural part of life, may strengthen and fortify you rather than doom you to unhappiness. They can even induce greater compassion and empathy, and awaken a sense of mission.

5 Keys to Sustainable Happiness

If you're serious about your happiness, then consider cultivating the following warrior traits:

1. **Gratitude:** Take time to appreciate the good things in your life; start a gratitude journal, call a friend, and express your love, or list the things you're grateful for.

2. **Acts of service:** Get out of your head; stop isolating. Help someone in need, volunteer in a neighborhood community program or animal shelter—people who perform acts of kindness score higher on happiness scales than those who are self-obsessed.

3. **Self-care:** Self-neglect is often the beating heart of unhappiness. Find ways to care for yourself. Join a support group, find a gym buddy, improve your diet, take a class, etc.

4. **Healthy relationships:** Healthy relationships are the cornerstone of happiness. If you surround yourself with unhealthy people, sustainable happiness will remain unachievable. Friendships should lift you up, not hold you down. Lose the friends that make you feel bad about yourself, then go out and find better ones.

5. **Community:** Isolation fosters loneliness and despair. Find a community that shares a common interest with you. Join a club, attend meet-ups, go to a lecture, or start a spiritual practice. Being part of something bigger than yourself can trigger a healthy dose of hope—and a better shot at sustainable happiness.

CHAPTER 8:
LIFESTYLE

3 Signs You're Eccentric, and 3 Reasons That's a Good Thing

Who wants to be conventional?

Recently, I ran into an old friend on the street near my group psychotherapy office in Manhattan. She looked me over, raised her eyebrows, and declared: "My goodness, Sean. Look at you! You've become so eccentric!"

Insecurity washed over me. *Was that a compliment? An insult? What exactly does "eccentric" mean?*

My quest for clarity led me down a twisted lane of confounding and sometimes disparaging definitions. According to the Oxford Dictionary, an eccentric is a "person of unconventional and slightly strange views or behavior." Unconventional, OK. But strange views or behavior? That didn't sound good. So I looked up the definition of "strange" and found it far more comforting: "Departing from what is ordinary, usual, or to be expected." Departing from the ordinary— I'm cool with that. And here's why.

Who wants to be conventional?

You will stand out and be noticed if you're authentic because you're less likely to conform to social norms and expectations. You're also free from the fears and anxieties that accompany worrying about others' perceptions of you.

While some people seem born with eccentric vibes, others grow into it with age. As my mentor Louis Ormont, the "father of American group therapy," once said, "Aging well means becoming more yourself and less concerned about the opinions of others."

In other words, aging brings greater emotional and psychological freedom. You're less likely to judge others and more likely to approach life with the openness, curiosity, and energy of youth.

3 signs you're eccentric

Whether you know you're eccentric or you're considering it while reading this post, here are some signs that you're on the path to eccentricity:

1. **You're not interested in following the crowd.** The latest fashions, music trends, or entertainment norms don't interest you. You follow your passions, indifferent to peer pressure.

2. **You're not afraid to stand out.** Being yourself is fun because you don't care what others think. You walk through the world unfettered and independent.

3. **You attract haters.** Sad but true. Some people disdain eccentrics. Deep down, they may feel threatened by someone who challenges their views and shrugs off social norms. Rather than search their hearts for the true cause of their hate, they'd rather target and blame you.

Eccentric and loving it

As your true self grows stronger and you follow your own unique path in life, consider these three significant benefits of being eccentric:

1. **Less social anxiety.** The less you're concerned with social norms, the less anxious you feel about being judged or rejected.

2. **Higher comfort levels.** You're at ease in your skin, not worried about other's perceptions or criticisms.

3. **An original thinker.** History is full of eccentric people who were outstanding leaders, inventors, and artists. In fact, It's nearly a requirement.

So, the next time someone calls you eccentric, be sure to thank them.

---

3 Signs You Need a Lifestyle Change

When exhaustion is a way of life.

If you're reading this post, chances are you feel dissatisfied with life. You may feel unhappy with your relationships, stuck in your career, or sick and tired of battling anxiety or depression.

Yet, despite many efforts to improve your life, every day still feels uninspired. What do you do then?

Common triggers for a lifestyle change

Most often, three stressful external events trigger lifestyle changes:

- **Trauma:** a health crisis, an accident, a brush with death.
- **Loss:** death of a loved one or the tragic end of a relationship.
- **Hardship:** a layoff, unemployment, mounting debt.

These events send shockwaves throughout your life, make you question your choices, and consider new options. They most commonly provoke an existential crisis that forces you to examine and evaluate all aspects of your life.

Signs a lifestyle change is needed

Frequently, the signs of the need for a lifestyle change are right in front of you.

1. Life lacks joy or wonder.

Days are depressingly predictable. You feel stuck in the same dull patterns; there is a "Groundhog Day" element; each moment feels the same, and you have nothing to look forward to.

2. Chronic stress.

Even simple chores are burdens. Tasks like cleaning your house, shopping, or visiting relatives can feel like a slow march to the gallows.

3. Habitual disappointment.

Everything, and everyone, eventually let you down. You feel disappointed even when you do your best to be outgoing and upbeat.

The power of choice

You read the criteria above and thought: "Yep, that's me." It's time to analyze what changes need to occur. And here's the good news: You don't have to wait for a stressful event to trigger a lifestyle change: you always have the power to make new choices.

But before you run out and quit your job, keep this in mind: Reckless change without mindful planning is always a gamble. Once you've identified that change is needed, don't take action right away—schedule time with a therapist, coach, or counselor to explore new choices and bounce ideas around. Talk to your close friends. Start journaling about your options.

Investing time into exploring possibilities will never let you down. The more mindful you are in this process, the more apparent the need for change. Setting personal goals like honoring your authentic voice, following your passions, traveling, and attending classes or lectures will also clarify the new lifestyle you want.

Remember, a new job or zip code change doesn't guarantee happiness. As Buddhists say, "You can't outrun your karma." Without working on yourself, you could change your environment only to discover you suffer from the same problems.

A simple question to start your journey

Before you decide to make a lifestyle change, here's one final suggestion: Imagine yourself far into the future and finish this sentence:

"Thank goodness 20 years ago I decided to _____."

Answering this question could awaken a hidden wish for a whole new way of living.

---

3 Signs That You're a Prisoner of Your Expectations

Overblown expectations can suck the joy out of living.

It's natural to have high expectations. But what happens when your expectations are overblown?

Over-hyped expectations can have a devastating impact on your life in three key areas:

1. Self-Esteem: You set the bar too high for yourself.

- *"I'm going to lose 10 pounds in three days."*
- *"I'm going to increase my income in the first quarter by 300 percent."*
- *"I'm going to wake up at dawn every day and write a best-selling novel in a month."*

Writing a novel, losing weight, and increasing your income are great goals. But when you marry them to unrealistic expectations, you're setting the stage for self-defeat. Consequently, your self-esteem takes a big hit as you give yourself too little credit for your efforts and fault yourself for missing impractical deadlines.

2. Relationships: You frequently feel hurt and disappointed by others.

- *"My romantic partner should know my needs without me asking."*
- *"I want all my friends to check in with me regularly and see how I'm doing."*
- *"My coworkers need to recognize how valuable I am to them."*

Turgid expectations strain relationships. Constantly putting pressure on friends, coworkers, or romantic partners to meet your demands is a real buzzkill. They start to feel bullied and burdened by you. The more emotionally demanding you are, the more people will avoid you.

3. Outlook: You develop a pretentious and arrogant outlook on life.

- *"Why does incompetence always surround me?"*
- *"I know I'm right no matter what anyone says."*
- *"No one knows better than me."*

Bitter, critical, and harsh, you expect the world to meet your extreme expectations. Rather than faulting yourself for expecting too much, you find fault in everything. In the end, no one escapes your condemnation.

How to Break the High Expectations Habit

High expectation habits cause you to focus on the future constantly. As a result, you enjoy the present moment less and have little appreciation for your past. Consider these three steps to regain some balance in your life.

1. Set ambitious and realistic expectations.

It's great to have big dreams, but don't expect them to materialize overnight. Better to make small, steady steps daily than to push for instant gratification. As Buddhist philosopher Daisaku Ikeda suggested: "True victories are the victories we achieve each day."

2. Foster gratitude.

You may not have written your novel in a month, but you probably finished a chapter or two. Recognize and applaud your efforts, even when they fall short of your expectations.

3. Be flexible.

If you miss a deadline, don't use that as an excuse to devalue yourself. Life is full of unexpected events that derail our plans. Be flexible. Take time to rest and reset your goals. Flexible expectations lower stress levels and breed greater mindfulness.

3 Traits That Breed Hopelessness and 5 Ways to Create Hope

How to create hope when you have none.

You have trouble getting out of bed. You think to yourself, "Why should I?" There's nothing to look forward to. Today will be the same as yesterday. Yesterday was the same as the day before, the day before, and the day before that, etc.

"Is it possible to die of sameness?" you wonder.

You check your phone—more bad news. The virus, the economy, the environment, politics, the world is coming apart. Why are you the only one who seems to notice? You scroll through social media and discover that your friends are living on another planet. They're riding bikes, picnicking, traveling—and you haven't been out of your pajamas for a week.

How do you go on living when you feel so hopeless?

The Science of Hopelessness

When you lose hope in one area of your life, it slowly bleeds into others and colors everything you see. Viewing the world through the lens of hopelessness results in blocking out hopeful events and only seeing the hopeless ones, a process psychologists call "confirmation bias." In other words, you seek out situations that reinforce your outlook while ignoring those that challenge it.

3 Traits That Destroy Hope

Before we consider how to generate hope, let's look at the most common traits that foster hopelessness:

1. Extreme thinking.

Always/never, good/bad, right/wrong, hero/villain. You divide the world into extreme fractions and ruminate on the negatives. You are quick to label others who are different from you or disagree with you, a choice that drains you of humanity. Sadly, in the world of relationships, labels block out hope by suggesting that people are one-dimensional and incapable of change—including you. Such extreme thinking ultimately leads to narcissism: You're a cult of one.

2. Resignation.

Convinced that nothing will ever change, you sink deeper into cynicism. Rather than take action, you blame, complain and resign to your hopeless outlook; you even take pride in it on some level. Such cynicism robs you of energy and prevents you from listening and learning from others or exploring new experiences.

3. Isolation.

The more you isolate, the more deluded your thoughts may become. When you shut out the world and live in seclusion, anxiety increases whenever you leave your home. Distrust spikes. Depression takes root. And the more entrenched you become, the more hopeless you feel.

Creating Hope

Psychologists have long held that hopelessness is a learned state from early childhood that we carry into adulthood. It's like a baby elephant tied to a post: He learns to stop struggling; he can't break free. By the time he is full-grown, though he could easily break the rope, he doesn't even try. Experience has taught him not to.

In the same way, adults frequently remain emotionally tethered to childhood traumas when they are trapped or powerless. Naturally, new choices, new behaviors, and healthier habits could help them break free. By carrying the hopelessness that we felt as children into our adult lives, we make an error in time that keeps us stuck and mired in our emotional past.

One of the key ways of creating hope is to disrupt patterns that promote hopelessness and challenge the behaviors that feed it. Here are five ways you can start to break free:

1. Engagement.

The opposite of isolation is engagement. Casting off passivity and neg-ative thinking requires that you engage more in the world around you.

Even if you don't want to, pushing yourself is essential. If hopelessness is a virus, engagement is the antibiotic you need.

2. Acts of Service.

Altruism is one of the least recognized and most powerful weapons against hopelessness. As the Buddhist saying goes, "When you light a lantern for another, it will also brighten your own way." Stop fixating on your problems and making them worse. Devote some time to helping others less fortunate than you and learn to value yourself more. When you give others hope, you receive it as well.

3. Humor.

Laughter is good medicine for the spirit. A hearty laugh also releases endorphins and adrenaline, raises metabolism, and reduces stress hormones. There are even studies that suggest that laughter strengthens the immune system.

4. A Mindfulness Practice.

A lack of mindfulness is frequently at the core of a hopeless outlook. Mindfulness practices such as meditation, yoga, or prayer pause our tortured thoughts and inspire us to live more fully in the moment. Self-reflect also disrupts emotional reactivity that so often breeds negative thinking.

5. Determination.

The most important and challenging tool for undoing your hopeless outlook is determination. No matter how much therapy, medication, counseling, or life coaching you engage in, at a certain point, you have to *decide the person that you want to be and redirect your thoughts and actions in that direction*. Short-circuit your complaint-and-blame process by giving yourself an order and following it. For example, "I'm going out today. I'm calling an old friend. I'm going to look into volunteering in my neighborhood."

In his inspiring collection of essays "Hope is a Decision," the Buddhist peace activist Daisaku Ikeda writes:

"When we change our inner determination, everything begins to move in a new direction. The moment we make a powerful resolve, every nerve and fiber in our being will immediately orient itself toward the fulfillment of this goal or desire. On the other hand, if we think, 'This is never going to work out,' then every cell in our body will be deflated and give up the fight. Hope, in this sense, is a decision."

How to Design a New Lifestyle in 3 Easy Steps

Rebooting your lifestyle is easier than you think.

You sometimes feel stuck in your tedious lifestyle—the same old mind numbing routines, blurring each day into the next. You greet every sunrise disinterested, unable to muster excitement or motivation.

Whether it's lifestyle fatigue or high-functioning depression, dullness feels similar. You've got a bad case of the "blahs" and are clueless about how to cure them.

Time for a lifestyle reboot

Chances are your lifestyle evolved without planning or thought. As a child, you rarely had to worry about your choices; they were usually made for you. What's more, the newness of life sparkled with excitement. Each day was a daring adventure filled with unknowns.

Even as a young adult, you had reasons to feel enthusiastic. Perhaps you started a new job or school, moved to a new neighborhood, or were in the honeymoon thrill of a new relationship. In any case, you hadn't established consistency or fallen into repetitive patterns. You didn't have to work to keep your lifestyle engaging. "Newness" kept everything fresh.

Boredom as a trigger

Familiarity is comforting but also breeds stagnation. With repetition, even the most exciting job can become a snooze fest.

SHORTCUTS TO A HAPPIER LIFE

Consider boredom to be a trigger for self-reflection. If you're feeling bored, chances are that you're taking a passive approach to frustration. Rather than push yourself to explore creative solutions to your boredom, you passively scroll or consume media. You train your brain to detach from frustration by disassociating rather than challenging it.

Unresolved frustration eventually transforms into repression that saps your energy and drains vitality from your life. Hopelessness about your future also sucks the joy of living in the moment.

Rebooting your lifestyle

The road to rebooting your lifestyle doesn't start with quitting your job, moving to a new neighborhood, or terminating your relationships. Such changes are often cosmetic because they frequently fail to resolve underlying emotional issues.

A change in environment may feel refreshing, but you take the same emotional script. In the end, your lackluster lifestyle follows you wherever you go: different environments, the same outcome,

Your new lifestyle

You entirely depended on your parents in your childhood to set your lifestyle. In adulthood, it's all up to you. Waiting and hoping won't do. You can't be passive when refreshing your lifestyle; you will have to get out of your own way.

To get you started, here are three simple steps you can take today:

- **Disrupt your routine:** Change is essential for growth, no matter how small. A simple change in daily patterns is a wake-up call to your senses. Take a different route to work, listen to other music, and challenge yourself to do something new every day or at least once weekly. These little changes will stimulate new responses in you and get things moving in the right direction.

- **Explore new passions:** Childhood is full of wonder; adulthood, not so much. That means the burden is on you to find new passions and interests. Take a dance class, start a new exercise routine, or join a writers' group. Whatever you do, choose something unique. Keep exploring, meeting new people, or traveling; stretch yourself, and you'll rarely feel bored with your lifestyle.

- **Develop a mindfulness practice:** The primary function of a mindfulness practice is to shine a light on parts of yourself that are poisoning your outlook. For example, if you are always complaining, everything you do will feel pointless. Dedicating time to reflect on the unconscious choices that shape your perspective empowers you to make new choices. There are all kinds of mindfulness practices. Take your time and find one that fits you.

CHAPTER 9:
PARENTING

7 Challenges Kids Face That Have Nothing to Do with Parenting

Is parenting really the omnipotent determinator of children's behavior?

Many mental health professionals quickly blame parents whenever young people exhibit behavioral problems. Of course, no one can deny parents' profound effect on children, but is parenting all that influential?

If parenting were genuinely all-powerful, children raised by the same parents would be carbon copies: same temperaments, personalities, and interests. But as we know, siblings with the same parents have vastly different characters.

Does parenting drive positive outcomes in children?

Over the past 25 years of working with parents and children, I've witnessed many children who received shoddy and incompetent parenting grow up to be outstanding adults. And children who had exceptional parents fare startlingly poorly in life.

The seeming randomness of some of the outcomes is always jarring to me. I often wonder, "How on Earth did that happen? For example:

- *How did a heroin addict grow up to be a pediatric nurse and outstanding mother?*

- *How did an award-winning star student end up pursuing a life of crime?"*

Why are parents so often blamed?

The rush to blame parents is often driven by the delusion that parents have total control over their children's behavior. Consequently, we turn a blind eye to the large part of child-rearing that is unpredictable. *Blaming every parent for their child's behaviors is like assuming every car accident is the driver's fault.*

For parents to admit they don't have control over their children's futures is unnerving. For example, we feel shaken when bad things happen to good people. Since the randomness of life can be so frightening, many of us pretend we have total command over our future. Naturally, we don't—especially when it comes to our children's future as well.

Nature and nurture

Nature and nurture play a dual hand in child development. To be clear:

- **Nature:** the wired-in qualities not determined by parenting, such as temperament and personality.
- **Nurture:** the family culture that parents create and how it impacts their child's way of being in relationships.

When nature overpowers nurture

Nature often overpowers nurture, leaving parents shocked by their child's behavior. These wired-in difficulties frequently fly under the radar of parenting and can be challenging to spot.

Wired-in challenges that have nothing to do with parenting

Let's examine the profound influence of nature more closely. Remember that these powerful wired-in tendencies shape behaviors despite parents' best efforts.

1. **Learning struggles. N**

   ot all children have the same learning styles. Neurodivergent children can have difficulties with focus and attention, auditory or visionary limitations, or slower processing skills. These differences can make learning painful and keep children in constant tension, fatigue, or irritability, leaving bewildered parents struggling to comfort or soothe them.

2. **Developmental issues.**

   Developmental milestones, such as walking and talking, are sometimes delayed or severely impaired. For example, problems with motor skills, communication or sensory issues resulting from cerebral palsy, autism spectrum disorder, or pervasive developmental delays require specialized schooling and other interventions to assist children and parents.

3. **Addiction.**

   Family histories of drug and alcohol abuse can reach back generations. Because addiction is unpredictable and sometimes skips a generation, it is not uncommon for parents who don't abuse substances to have a child who does. Such parents are shocked by their children's addictive tendencies and often blame themselves for a condition that is clearly in the family's DNA.

4. **Adoption issues.**

   Many adopted children struggle mightily during adolescence when identity issues and powerful biological family tendencies emerge. Many adoptive parents of easygoing or agreeable children are bullied or in constant conflict with their kids during their teen years. They witness radical, inexplicable transformations in their children and levels of defiance that baffle them entirely. Sadly, they may blame themselves or feel reproached by others for their children's demeanor.

5. **Temperament.**

   Some babies sleep through the night, while others don't. Some children eat everything on their plates, while others drive their parents crazy with pickiness. Temperament emerges very early in children and frequently feels incongruent with the parenting that they received.

I recall working with two very calm parents who had a child who "never stopped moving even in the womb." The mother said, "He skipped learning to walk and started running and climbing immediately." His temperament was wired in from the start and had little to do with the parenting he received.

6. Societal issues.

Racial tensions exist in every culture. When a child experiences oppression or discrimination because of their ethnicity, it can significantly affect how they view themselves. *Children who experience racism have suffered higher levels of depression and anxiety due to societal issues— not parenting.*

7. Medical challenges.

Every parent prays for a healthy baby. Sometimes medical issues emerge that create hardships, such as mobility limitations, diseases, or a compromised immunity system. For children facing medical conditions, life appears full of unfair restrictions. The intensity of their frustration and despair naturally affect their behavior. As a result, parents are likely to experience higher levels of tension and anxiety.

A new outlook on behavior problems

It's time to acknowledge that parenting has limitations and stop blaming parents for all children's problem behaviors. To judge good parents harshly is cruel and unnecessary. A deeper, more compassionate understanding of the complexity of childhood conditions is needed to avoid making struggling parents feel even worse about themselves or their kids.

---

3 Essentials for Healthy Family Communication

How to reboot your family's communication style.

So many parents feel trapped in negative patterns relating to their kids. They cycle through the same arguments week after week, leaving everyone feeling exhausted and battle-weary.

When faced with challenging or problematic behaviors in children, all parents are bound to make mistakes. The five most common are:

1. Blaming each other for their children's behavior.
2. Shaming, criticizing, and lecturing their children.
3. Relying too heavily on punishments.
4. Dictating rules without discussion.
5. Modeling impulsive or disrespectful behaviors.

Such choices escalate conflicts and leave families battered and disheartened. Even worse, as long as parents continue to make these five mistakes, their relationship with their kids will steadily deteriorate.

Rebooting Your Family Communication Style

The single most powerful skill for strengthening and improving family relationships is *healthy communication*. The quality of parents' communication ultimately determines the success of their parenting and the happiness of their children. The three essentials for healthy family communication:

Behavior. Modeling positive behavior is a vital part of successful parenting. For example, when parents disrespect one another or their children, they're training their children to disrespect them, their siblings, their peers, or teachers. Parents must model the positive behaviors that they want to see in their kids.

Language. Parents' choice of language has a powerful effect on children. It is never permissible for family members to abuse each other verbally. Avoid language that is degrading or demoralizing. Crude or hurtful language damages children's fragile egos and undermines their self-esteem.

Listening. Parents who are poor listeners are more likely to have defiant, depressed, or anxious children. Listening is curative; it is the basis for nearly all talk therapies. Children who feel their parents are engaged listeners develop a positive sense of self and trust their parents more.

Launching a New Culture of Communication

Setting out to change your family's culture of communication takes time and isn't easy but will bring you sustainable results. Here are four areas to focus on:

1. Parental Unity.

Improving communication between you and your partner is crucial. Discuss parenting decisions before including your kids. Work out your conflicts in private. Put your ego aside. Avoid making executive decisions, work as a team.

2. Meetings.

Too often, families discuss behaviors under stressful conditions. Hold family meetings at a time when everyone is well-rested and relaxed. Use such meetings to establish family rules and routines. Let everyone get an equal share of the talking time. Be sure to process conflicts, acknowledge progress, and set shared goals. Always start each meeting with a round of gratitude before you delve into more thorny situations.

3. Positive Reinforcement.

Parents tend to be too critical and ignore improvements in behavior. Praise your kids' positive choices. Pay particular attention to improvements in your communication style. Simple acknowledgments such as, "I like the way you said that" or "I appreciate that you told me that" reinforce gains.

4. Healthy Family Activities.

Put down your cell phone, unplug from technology, step away from academic concerns or housework. Every family needs healthy activities that they enjoy together. Consider the following five kinds of healthy family activities:

- **Physical** activities, such as bike riding or going to the gym.
- **Creative** activities include making art or going to a gallery or concert.
- **Intellectual** activities include attending a lecture, playing, or reading a novel together.

- **Spiritual** activities include attending religious gatherings or practicing meditation.
- **Altruistic** activities include volunteering with neighborhood organizations or participating in donation drives.

You'll have to confront your own emotional immaturity to break free of negative communication patterns. You'll need to be more patient, mindful and thoughtful. This will be challenging, but when you rise to the challenge, your children will follow.

How Parents Can Empower Their Daughters

3 keys to self-empowerment that every girl needs.

What can we do to help empower our daughters in today's world? How can we help them to develop self-worth?

I sat down with Yoon Im Kane, a Yale-trained psychotherapist and the founder & executive director at Mindful Psychotherapy Services, a private outpatient therapy center with offices based in Manhattan. Yoon is passionate about therapy and women's empowerment. Here's what she had to say:

We've trained girls to be nice and sweet. We rewarded girls who showed empathy and cooperation. Now, we have an issue on our hands. Young women are confused and conflicted about how to be there for others while caring for themselves. This is evident in the thoughts that arise from young women in my practice:

> Sometimes I don't speak up when I don't want to do something because I want people to like me.
>
> I don't want to be difficult and cause problems, so I act responsibly and cooperatively even when I don't feel like it.
>
> I get resentful when I sell myself out by caring for other people's needs instead of listening to mine.

From a young age, women receive messages about how to be friendly and compliant, accommodate others, and gain approval from the families and the communities they grow up in. Messages are often subtle and not conscious. They can sound like: *Be nice to your brother. Don't interrupt. Stop being so dramatic. Why are you being so difficult? Don't you care how I feel?*

These messages can hinder women's natural development of a sense of self-worth and entitlement. Healthy self-worth involves cultivating self-acceptance that validates a full range of desires and feelings. Healthy entitlement requires self-compassion, accepting negative feelings without self-criticism, and making mistakes without shame. Not developing self-worth and entitlement early on can lead to more significant problems as girls become women.

Life is full of ups and downs, and while we can't prevent the downs, how can we provide the proper nutrients to bolster girls' sense of self early on in a way that will insulate them later in life?

Empowerment is best modeled in the environment. Most learning comes from what's demonstrated moment-to-moment. Opportunities abound in daily interactions with your daughter. For example, sometimes your daughter doesn't feel like being nice to her brother, seems angry for no reason, or refuses to join a family gathering. You may tell her to behave and stop being difficult. Whether she refuses or complies, consider that she also hears a disempowering message that harmony and keeping the peace is more important than what she feels and wants. This doesn't mean you can't have expectations and set boundaries. Setting healthy limits will foster her sense of self-worth. When you try to understand the source of her feelings and help her put them into words, she will feel empowered to express herself.

For example, when you are annoyed at your teen's interactions with her brother, say something like, *"You seem angry at your brother; I get that."* This statement helps her feel understood and accepted. It's essential to support her in expressing her feelings constructively and negotiating conflict. Validating her feelings and helping her communicate them effectively is empowering.

Young women today are growing up in a culture in which people may be uncomfortable with women expressing feelings like anger. This sets up a dichotomy where the cost of feeling powerful and expressive is a loss of connection and belonging. Encouraging messages about "girl power" and women's rights are juxtaposed with our public debate over issues of gender and power in which women's voices are not always equally valued.

What can powers do to help empower their daughters? Here are three suggestions:

1. Foster Healthy Entitlement

Encourage your daughter to express her needs and provide opportunities for her to make real choices. Girls need to feel that their needs are worth as much as others, even if they don't get what they want. Help them tolerate disappointments. Healthy entitlement grows from balancing self-care with caring for others.

2. Teach Boundary Setting

Too often, girls are taught to take on the burden of other people's feelings. Help your daughter set healthy boundaries by saying no when uncomfortable. She can stay connected in relationships without complying with demands or becoming a caretaker. Relationships are more about give and take and negotiation rather than requirements.

3. Nurture Self-Worth

Adults who share their feelings and own up to their mistakes are great role models for their children. They are demonstrating the courage to be vulnerable. Validating your daughter's feelings has big rewards. Teenagers are going through a confusing phase of life - it makes a big difference to them that you recognize their struggle.

Teaching and modeling compassion and acceptance of vulnerable feelings are crucial. Supporting healthy communication and inviting girls to make healthy choices that foster new beliefs offers opportunities to test new ways of being. These experiences will encourage your daughter and give her the confidence to counter dysfunctional cultural norms.

The Blueprint for Raising Happy, Resilient Children
Are You Using Sue Atkin's Four C's?

Many years ago, the UK's favorite parenting expert, Sue Atkins, wondered Why some children become 'successful' in life and others don't. She concluded that the children who succeed have close relationships with others (particularly their immediate family), feel valued, and have control over their lives. I asked Sue to explain more. Here's what she had to say.

The children in trouble are missing four necessities to manage life's challenges.

- Feeling connected to others.
- Feeling capable of taking care of themselves.
- Feeling that they count.
- Feeling courageous.

These Four C's are vital for children to feel they can meet life's challenges.

What the Crucial' C's Give Children.

Feeling that we connect, are capable, that we count, and have courage will go a long way to encourage a positive attitude about life and give it purpose.

If we ensure that our children develop the Four C's, they will take life on and make it work for them. They will develop a 'Can Do Kid' mindset & they will have the ability to handle whatever life throws at them.

Kids who are brought up with the four Crucial C's become

- Responsible
- Self-reliant
- Happy

Feeling Connected.

Our ability to survive physically and psychologically depends on our ability to connect to others. We move from being babies, totally dependent on others, to interdependence with others. Compared to other animals who mature far sooner than human beings do, the process of moving toward total dependence takes much longer.

As children grow into toddlers, they experiment, make mistakes, and learn through trial and error, and the more capable they are allowed to feel, the more self-confident they become.

Teenagers who are secure in their belief about belonging to others feel connected, so they are able to cooperate because they don't feel afraid of rejection or isolation. They are more resilient to peer pressure and being drawn to gangs or the wrong crowd.

A child who doesn't feel connected feels insecure and isolated and will seek attention and believe that any attention is better than none.

Feeling Capable.

Toddlers begin life as babies learning to hold their heads up and walk. A toddler doesn't fall over the first time and decide that walking isn't for them!

Children develop their capabilities through being allowed to explore and make mistakes, and they must be given meaningful activities. We live in a busy world, and parents are often in such a hurry that they rob their children of the opportunity to 'struggle' putting on their shoes or doing up the zip on their coats.

It's often more manageable and quicker to do it for them, but this way of helping children may have severe consequences in the long term.

Children may interpret your failure to trust them to do these things as a sign that they can't do them. You rob your child of the experience of feeling competent and capable. The message they receive is: 'You don't think I can do things for myself.' Over time, they may learn to resent you and to feel inadequate.

An overprotected child may become overly dependent on others, may be afraid to be alone later in life, or become so confused that they 'boss' people around to get their needs met!

Teenagers are encouraged to feel capable, develop self-control, and become self-reliant. They will develop respectful relationships with others.

Teens discouraged from feeling competent become unsure of their capabilities and may resist your attempts to guide them.

Disempowered teens resist responsibility – needing to be nagged to get up, do their homework, or wash up. So, maybe allow them to face the consequences of their actions, such as getting detention for late arrival at school, to begin feeling responsible for themselves.

Feeling Significant – 'I Count'

We all like to feel that we matter and count - children are no different.

If parents respond to their child's needs and care for them, a child feels secure. They think that they can trust the world and can count on others. They learn that they are important and that they matter.

A baby whose needs are unmet may learn that they can't trust the world and that the world isn't a safe place, and they may not move beyond that self-centered experience.

Children who are encouraged learn that they count and that they matter. Children who are not made to feel significant look for a way to feel valued in more destructive ways.

Teenagers who feel valued become more involved in school or community activities. They are less likely to break the rules or avoid responsibility. Whereas a teen who doesn't feel that they count behaves in more destructive ways, thinking that what they do doesn't matter.

Feeling Courageous

It takes courage to ride the ups and downs of life, the good and bad experiences, and the frustrations and challenges. It's a precarious adventure, so developing courage in your children is essential.

Toddlers show courage in everything they do, from learning to walk to learning to talk. They show courage as they go from one mistake to another until they master many skills. That takes courage.

Think back on your life – it took courage to start school, to leave home, or to get married. 'Feeling the fear' and doing it anyway, as Susan Jeffers said. Children experience frustration and disappointment just like we do, and that courage stands them in good stead for their lives.

As Franklin D. Roosevelt said, 'Courage isn't the absence of fear but the ability to overcome it.'

Children without courage focus on what they can't do. They give up and avoid situations. They miss out on life through fear. A child with a 'Can Do' attitude shows courage & feels hopeful & optimistic. They embrace life and all its opportunities.

Becoming a teenager is a challenging time of confusion and uncertainty. It's a constant feeling of three steps forward and five steps back. Teens who don't have courage blend into the background, afraid to put their hand up in class or join sports clubs. They'll find it hard to resist the pressure to drink alcohol or take drugs as they won't be brave enough to say 'No.'

Children are encouraged to be courageous and trust themselves. Children who lack courage can't get over their fear. It controls them.

Is Parenting Burnout Destroying Your Marriage?
How self-neglect undermines partnerships and parenting

Why do so many couples unravel after becoming parents? Why do so many marriages self-destruct?

Of the kinds of parenting dilemmas I see in my office, parent burnout is among the most common and unrecognized. Remarkably, most parents don't even realize they're suffering from it. Ask these parents when was the last time they took a break from parenting, and they stare at you stupefied: *"You're allowed to take a break?"*

Alarming Statistics

According to the *Wall Street Journal* article, "Here Comes the Baby, There Goes the Marriage," approximately two-thirds of couples see the quality of their relationship plummet within three years of the birth of a child—with mothers' dissatisfaction leading the way, and more women filing for divorce than men. Within five years after the birth of a first child, over 40 percent of couples will go their separate ways. Some studies report marriages failing within 18 months after the first child is born.

Couples are painfully unprepared for the demands of parenting; in fact, parenthood may be a frequent cause of separations, divorces, and failed relationships.

Signs of Parent Burnout

If you're a burnt-out parent, you're exhausted; you've neglected yourself without mercy. Depleted emotionally, intellectually, and creatively, you stumble through your routines, doze off mid-sentence, or stare at a computer or television screen in a weary hypnotic trance. You may have forgotten that you have needs. Is it any wonder you suffer low energy, mood swings, and over-the-top reactions to frustration?

If you find yourself humorless, angry, or critical often—maybe it's not your child, partner, or friends; perhaps it's you.

The Roots of Self-Neglect

From the very beginning, parenting is rough on your body and mind. You sleep less and eat more. Healthy habits deteriorate. You stop exercising or socializing (especially with "non-parent" types). Gradually, your life drifts off course, and your relationship sours.

Moreover, children are gifted crisis creators, no matter their age. They get sick, have accidents, lose things, and continually rearrange your priorities. The more time you spend running after them and tending to their needs, the less time you spend tending to your own. Self-reflection is gone from your life. Soon, you live in a reactive state, forever responding to your kid's never-ending wants while ignoring your partner's needs. Is it any wonder that your relationship starts to unravel?

Personal Experience

The year after my first child's birth, I unwittingly gained 33 pounds. With new financial demands, I worked more hours than ever before. I ate poorly, slept poorly, suffered chronic back pain, and the little hair I had left on my head soon disappeared. Seriously, all of it—gone!

The worst part was the toll it took on my marriage. My wife and I spent less quality time together. And when we did, one of us usually fell asleep during a conversation. In the mornings, we'd bump up against each other near our coffee machine with this intimate exchange:

"Hey."

"Hey."

It took us years to overcome parent burnout—but it doesn't have to take you that long.

From Self-Neglect to Self-Care

Taking care of yourself is a vital part of being a good parent and a good partner. You don't need to spend a fortune on therapy to get your life back. Start your recovery by reviewing this burnout prevention checklist.

1. **Schedule a weekly date.** Being a parent is not an identity—it's part of who you are. As soon as possible, arrange for babysitters—relatives, neighbors, friends. You must put aside time for yourself and your partner. This is often surprisingly difficult, especially when you've fallen into the habit of self-neglect. Turn your attention to new topics and activities, not about parenting. A well-rounded parent is always better than a burnt-out parent.

2. **Keep exercising.** I say this all the time in parent workshops, and here I go again: *A cardio workout, 30 minutes 3 times a week or more, cuts anxiety and depression up to 70 percent in most people.* Walk, run, swim, bike, dance...whatever you fancy. You'll feel better, have more energy, and less appetite for comfort food. If you have trouble committing to a weekly workout, sign up for a class, or get a trainer or a gym buddy. Most parents report feeling better almost immediately.

3. **Reboot creativity.** Creativity is a wonderful tension outlet. It soothes angst, awakens your muse, and brings new dynamism into your life. Look for new creative outlets or resurrect inspired activities you enjoyed before becoming a parent. Children love to see their parents be creative. It's good modeling for your kid and good self-care for you.

4. **Personal adventures.** Parenting doesn't end personal growth. If you're stagnating in the same old routine, surfing the net or watching an entire season of a Netflix series in a few days, chances are you've stopped challenging yourself. Kids respect parents who have a sense of purpose or mission that is beyond parenting. Take a class, visit a museum, explore continuing education, attend a concert, join a writing group or book club, or learn another language. Look for activities that will stimulate you intellectually, emotionally, and creatively in new ways.

5. **Keep socializing.** Parenting can be very isolating. Spending every moment of your free time with your kids is unsuitable for you or them. Don't let your friendships fade away; pick up the phone and schedule a time to see each other. And, for goodness sake, give the parenting-themed conversations a rest. You'll be surprised how relieved you feel.

Revitalize Your Life & Revitalize Your Relationship

Children want parents that they can be proud of. It strengthens and fortifies them, builds their confidence, and strengthens their sense of self. When you neglect yourself or succumb to burnout, you deny your kid a crucial need for pride in their parents. To cure your burnout and get your relationship back on track, start by weeding out the toxic roots of self-neglect for you, your partner, and your child's well-being.

Top Ten Parenting Mistakes

Boo-boos, blunders, and screw-ups... and how to avoid them.

One moment, you're elated, and the next, you're discouraged or frustrated. One morning, you wake up feeling inexplicably euphoric, only to go to bed that evening feeling utterly heartbroken.

Children add rocket fuel to your emotional life; your feelings intensify when you become a parent. Managing these powerful emotions will ultimately define your relationship with your kid.

Next time you're at your wit's end, remember: Making mistakes is natural — correcting them is not. It takes courage to admit your faults, especially to your children. Starting over and creating a new, healthier relationship with them is a challenge. But that's the gift of parenting; children give you the chance to keep evolving and developing as an individual. *Growing with your kids won't just make you a better parent —it will make you a better human being.*

In my book, *When Kids Call the Shots: How to Seize Control From Your Darling Bully—and Enjoy Parenting Again,* I discuss the greatest hits of parenting blunders—the sanity lapses and slip-ups that I've culled from 25 years of working with families. Take your time, read through the list, and find your tendency. Develop a knack for knowing your weak spots, and keeping cool in heated moments will be much easier.

So let's count down parenting mistakes that every parent is bound to make:

10. Micromanaging

Micromanagers are dedicated and hardworking; they love their kids and want them to succeed. The problem is that they do too much for them. As a result, their kids remain dependent on their parents and have great difficulty standing on their own; they have trouble self-governing, they lack drive and motivation, and, despite their intelligence, they're emotionally immature. Instead of micromanaging, give your kid the tools to be self-reliant and independent. The more your kids can succeed without you lording over them, the more drive they'll have to grow independently.

9. Enabling

A parent's actions are usually well-intended, but enabling is one of the most disastrous parenting tendencies. When parents pander to their kids' every need, their kids fare poorly in relationships; they expect everyone else to cater to them. They shrink from challenges, avoid hard work, and maintain a sense of entitlement. Emotionally, they suffer from a bizarre mix of low self-esteem and arrogance. To sidestep the trap of enabling, strive to engender personal responsibility in your kids and encourage them to achieve independently. Stop enabling—and start empowering.

8. Bad Modeling

A parent's first job is to be a good role model. Yet, many parents' misbe-haviors serve as poor examples for their children. Parents who erupt in rages, blame others, tell untruths, or play the victim are subconsciously training their kids to do the same. Blaming your kids for the behaviors and bad habits you taught them is like blaming the mirror for your reflection. Behave the way you want your kids to behave. Be the person you want your kid to be. Above all, before you fault your kids for their conduct, consider amending your own.

7. Bullying

Bullying parents tend to be control freaks. Rather than understand their kids, they overwhelm them with orders, directives, threats of violence, or actual violence. They aim to shape and define their kids by intimidating them rather than letting them unearth their individuality. Sadly, children of bullying parents suffer low self-esteem and anxiety problems; they have difficulty trusting others and fear intimacy. Bullying parents may get their way, but their kids suffer mightily for it.

6. Inconsistency

Inconsistent parenting drives kids (and therapists) up the wall. Parents who change their minds often, don't take a stand, and have difficulty making decisions or providing strong leadership are likely to produce emotionally volatile children. These children emerge with unstable cores and weak identities. They have trouble defining themselves and often develop oppositional and defiant behaviors to camouflage their insecuri-ties. Providing a stable and consistent home may not always be possible, but providing consistent parenting is always within reach.

5. Criticism and Comparison

No one enjoys criticisms or comparisons. Yet many parents compulsively criticize and compare their children daily: *"Why can't you be more like _____?"* or *"Why are you so _____?"* This is a surefire way to damage your kids' self-esteem and fragile egos. Children who are criticized grow up to think of themselves as outsiders and underachievers. They don't celebrate their strengths because they were never taught to, a direct result of having internalized their parents' negative voices. It only takes a thoughtless moment to hurt your kids with criticism or comparisons — but it can take a lifetime for them to recover.

4. Poor Structure, Limits, and Boundaries

Providing balanced structure, limits, and boundaries is essential to good parenting. What exactly are structure, limits, and boundaries? Here's the breakdown:

- Structure means consistent schedules and routines.
- Limits mean curbing destructive or risky behaviors by engendering good judgment.
- Boundaries mean honoring and respecting the physical and emotional space between people.

Some parents are too strict with limits; some don't provide enough structure or boundaries. Strive to find the right balance for your children; they will be better prepared for relationships, jobs, and the world outside your door.

3. Neglect

Parents don't set out to neglect their kids, but many do. Adults get absorbed in their work, delegate parenting responsibilities to eldest children or grandparents, miss important events in their kids' lives, or, worst of all, become terrible listeners—all forms of emotional neglect that undermine a child's healthy sense of self. Emotionally neglected kids always suffer from mood and behavioral problems. The simple act of listening to your kid has a healing effect that remedies many parenting dilemmas. Children who feel understood by their parents don't act out for attention and are less likely to engage in destructive behavior. Spend quality time listening, understanding, and identifying with your kid. It doesn't cost you anything, and it will save you a fortune in therapy bills in the future.

2. Disregarding Learning Problems

Many academic and behavioral problems are the direct result of undiagnosed learning difficulties. Impatient parents who are too quick to label kids lazy, unmotivated, and apathetic about school often fail to consider what might trigger their kids' attitudes toward learning. Even brilliant kids struggle with processing speed, executive functioning, and sensory and memory deficiencies. These under-the-radar complications often emerge in middle school or high school. Such difficulties make learning a painful and exhausting experience. So save your money; psychotherapy isn't going to help resolve these problems. If your kid has even the slightest difficulty with learning, an educational evaluation is the first step to finding a solution.

1. Invalidating Feelings

When your children reveal their feelings and insecurities to you, for goodness sake, don't contradict them, correct them, offer unsolicited advice, or use it as an opportunity to lecture about your experiences. Remember, they are taking a risk in doing so; therefore, your sensitivity is imperative. Kids want to feel understood; they want to feel validated by their parents. Many symptoms of hyperactivity, defiance, and mood problems are generated in children of parents who invalidate their feelings.

Parenting: The Ultimate Learn-as-You-Go Experience

Parenting is a full-time job without any training or supervision. Everyone is sure to make mistakes, especially during those chaotic first years. But there is no need to fret; parenting is an evolutionary process. You grow into it day by day, year after year. Strive to learn from your mistakes and improve; your parental journey will be far less hindered by self-doubt and worries and more joyful for you and your kids.

The Best Technology-Screen Time Contract for Kids
Use this 10-point checklist to end tech battles in your home

Battles over screen time disrupt families every day. Eavesdrop on most households, and you're likely to hear:

"Put your phone down!"

"Turn the computer off!"

"Stop texting!"

Parents are frustrated and concerned for their kids—and they should be. Numerous studies have suggested that unlimited use of technology can harm a child's emotional intelligence, temperament, and social development. A national movement supported by top technology innovators strongly recommends that children do not have smartphones until age 14 (8th grade) and are not given a data plan until age 16.

Technology can be highly addictive, particularly for children and teens. In therapy sessions with me, many admit that they *want* to put their screen down, but *they just can't*, forcing parents to become dictators of screen time.

In my parenting workshops, parents always ask: I'm tired of policing my kids' screen time—what should I do?

How to Create a Family Culture for Screen Time

Kids crave structure, consistency, and leadership from parents. So, rather than go to war over screen time, I recommend establishing a family culture around technology by sitting down and creating a Family Screen Time Contract.

The contract below provides a basic framework, allowing for flexibility and customization based on your kids' ages and your family's use of technology. Set aside time to fill it in together, edit it, or use it as a jumping-off point for discussion. Each family is different, so that each contact will be too.

Remember, the contract is not a punishment but a way to set healthy screen time boundaries for everyone in your family, including parents. Screen time devices include smartphones, computers, laptops, televisions, and all game systems.

THE _____ FAMILY SCREEN TIME CONTRACT

1. School Nights & Weeknights

Our family shuts down all our devices at _____ o'clock. The devices remain off until the following day. Devices will be turned back on once everyone has finished breakfast and is dressed and ready to leave.

2. Weekends & Holidays

Our family limits screen time on weekends and holidays to _____ hours/minutes per day.

3. Travel Vacations

After arriving at our destination, everyone in our family limits screen time to _____ minutes in the morning and _____ minutes in the evening. We leave our devices in our hotels or vacation homes and don't take them on activities like hiking, going to the beach, cycling, etc. If needed, one device may be designated for directions, photos, or emergency calls.

4. Screen Time Blackouts

Our family does not use our devices when we have: (check all that apply)

____ Meals together

____ Family gatherings

____ Friends visiting

____ Playdates

____ Sleepovers

____ To walk or drive

Add your personal family guidelines here:

_____

5. Device Storage & Charging

Our family does not store or charge tech devices in our bedrooms or playrooms. Instead, we keep our devices in a communal space, which is _____.

6. Screen Time Privilege

Devices aren't available after school until homework and chores are completed. Chores may include:

___ Making beds

___ Tidying up rooms

___ Doing dishes

___ Taking care of pets

___ Helping prepare dinner

Add your additional family chores here:

_____

7. Alternatives to Screen Time

Our family recognizes that too much screen time is unhealthy. As a family, we each have weekly physical and creative activities such as (check at least three):

___ Exercise

___ Sports

___ Musical instruments

___ Art

___ Dance

___ Reading for pleasure

Add your special activities here:

_____

8. Web Use and Passwords

Family members under __ years old are not allowed to surf the web unsupervised to protect our children from inappropriate material and frightening images. Parents also keep records of all passwords, including social media passwords, and don't allow secret accounts.

9. Social Media Behavior

Our children agree never to use social media to be hurtful or mean to others.

10. When the Contract Is Broken

Our family recognizes that screen time is a privilege, not a right. Devices will be taken away if someone in our family repeatedly breaks the family contract. Parents will decide for how long.

DATE: _____

SIGNATURES:

_____

_____

_____

Healthy Structure Is the Key to Screen-Time Management

Parenting is full of challenges, but one thing is certain: Technology is here to stay. Structuring screen time helps to limit parent/child battles by setting clear guidelines for everyone. Remember, technology is a tool, not a way of life. Help your kids manage screen time better and enrich their lives with quality bonding time and greater self-mastery.

---

5 Things Parents Do to Enrage Teenagers
Plus three parenting tools that will never let you down.

Yes, teenagers are moody. But before you label your kid with anger issues, ask yourself this question: *Could I be the cause of my kid's angry outbursts?*

So often in my psychotherapy office, I witness well-intentioned, loving parents make spirit-crushing comments to their teenagers. I sit in shock while parents shame, criticize, or blame their kids, dumping frustrations on them and saying things they would never say to another adult.

So before you hire a therapist, ask yourself if you are guilty of the following crimes:

1. **Criticism.** No one thrives in a critical environment. Constantly criticizing your kids makes them feel like failures. Parents' words are powerful and impact a teenager's evolving identity. Teenagers may act tough, but they have a fragile sense of self underneath. Golden rule: Never say anything to your kid you wouldn't want someone to say to you.

2. **Unsolicited Advice.** Unsolicited advice nearly always backfires with teenagers. Especially when advice is given with a built-in directive, such as *"You need to do this..."* Teenagers spend most of their lives being ordered around by adults. Unsolicited advice is likely to increase defiance and undermine trust.

3. **Comparison.** Does anyone enjoy being negatively compared to others? If you start a sentence with, *"Why can't you be like..."* trust me, you've just hurt your kid. Such hurt is frequently at the root of teenagers' anger at their parents. Many teenagers feel they are under attack when their parents compare them to peers or siblings. It also undermines their peer/sibling relationships and increases emotional tension.

4. **Victimizing.** No one said parenting would be easy. Yet many parents make a hobby of complaining about their kids. They whine, lament, and martyr themselves to friends or relatives—at home and in public. Such negativity weakens a parent's leadership and breeds a toxic environment. It's also terrible role modeling. If you complain about your kid,

your kid will complain about you—and that's a dead-end for everyone.

5. **Self-Aggrandizing**. Does this sound familiar: *"When I was your age,...blah, blah, blah."* Boasting about yourself to your kid sends the vexing message: *"You should be like me."* Remember, teenagers are working on separation and individuation. They don't want to be like you; they want their unique identity. Moreover, self-aggrandizing transmits arrogance and insecurity—making you a bore to any teenager.

These three power parenting tools will never let you down:

1. **Listen More Than You Talk.** Listening is healing; it's the basis of all talk therapies. Teenagers who feel their parents listen and value their opinions are more cooperative and less defiant. Try this simple suggestion: Listen to your kid without judgment, self-references, or advice, and keep a close eye on your kid's responses. They will share more and feel more comfortable turning to you for support.

2. **Celebrate Who They Are, Not Who You Want Them to Be.** Kids crave attention. No matter how aloof they appear, they desperately want their parent's approval. Find a way to highlight your kid's strengths. And if they fail, don't engage in "I told you so." Teens feel bad enough when they fail; they don't need their parents' disapproval to add to their burdens. Do your best to praise your kid's efforts regardless of the outcome. It will lower their stress levels and increase their self-esteem.

3. **Model Mindful Behaviors: Be The Change You Want to See.** Lead by example. Kids internalize their parents' way of communicating and their habits. I've witnessed parents blame their kids for behaviors they themselves model. In other words, your kid is more likely to be impulsive if you're impatient. If you bully your kid, your kid will eventually become a bully. Don't blame the mirror for your reflection.

Clean up your act, and your kid will, too. In the end, mindful parents raise mindful kids.

The 8 Essentials for Preparing Your Kid for College

And three ways to help them thrive in freshman year.

For many years, I've sat with stunned parents who asked, *"What went wrong with my kid in college?"* Their son or daughter left home upbeat and full of hope, only to return from freshman year overwhelmed, anxious, or depressed. Yet they had excelled in high school.

What happened?

The leap to college is loaded with challenges for teenagers. Take a look at the many "firsts" teenagers confront freshman year:

- *First time...living on their own.*
- *First time...managing their own budget.*
- *First time...setting their own schedule.*
- *First time...structuring their studies alone.*
- *First time...living in a new city or town.*
- *First time...without parental supervision.*

Add academic pressures and social problems to those challenges, and it's not difficult to understand why some college freshmen crash and burn.

Preparing Your Teenager for College: An Eight-Point Checklist

The best way to help your kids prepare for college is to start preparing them before they leave home. Believe it or not, many teenagers arrive at college unprepared for independent living, needing to learn how to do simple tasks such as laundry, cooking, or managing their finances.

To help prepare your teenager, consider the following:

1. **Summer Camp**

   A few weeks at summer camp is an excellent way to help teens explore independence and sharpen their social skills.

2. **Summer Jobs**

   Teens love to make their own money. Summer jobs boost self-esteem and are a great way to inspire teenagers to set financial goals.

3. **Internships**

   Internships always inspire new levels of maturity in teenagers. Look for internships that appeal to your kid's interests, with an eye on their future career.

4. **Study Abroad**

   Living in a different country and speaking a foreign language is a challenge. But if your teenager can manage that, college will be a breeze.

5. **Bank Accounts**

   Rather than handing cash to your teenager, open a savings account and deposit allowance or paychecks into it. Teach basic accounting skills in high school, and your kids will be well-prepared to manage their money in college.

6. **College Prep Courses**

   What better way to prepare for college than sampling academics and social life?

7. **Household Chores**

   Pass on healthy habits to your kids by encouraging them to do their laundry, cook meals, and exercise regularly. Teenagers will take those healthy habits to college.

8. *Teen Therapy Groups*

If your kid is shy, withdrawn, or struggling socially in high school, college will quickly become unmanageable. Teen therapy groups are the best way to strengthen social skills and build confidence.

How College Support Groups Can Help Freshmen Year

For nearly twenty-five years, I've led college support groups for students in the New York City area. College students file into my office every week to share their struggles and fears.

As they develop positive relationships with their fellow students, sighs of relief abound. Finally, they feel understood. Finally, they have a community. Finally, they have a place to share their anxieties and get help from their peers.

Nearly all student health centers offer college support groups. However, some students resist contacting their college student health center for help and will prefer private college support groups off campus.

3 Ways College Support Groups Can Help

1. *College Support Groups Strengthen Social Skills*

Isolation is the enemy of positive adjustment. College support groups help students develop the confidence they need to feel more comfortable in social situations and be more assertive and expressive.

2. *College Support Groups Encourage Independence*

Sometimes, struggling students turn to their parents for support. Though parents can offer long-distance relief, when college students remain too emotionally dependent on their parents, they suffer gaps in their maturity. College support groups help students develop the confidence to stand on their own and become self-reliant.

3. *College Support Group Provide a Positive Peer Community*

Drug and alcohol abuse in college is well documented. To feel socially accepted, students sometimes engage in destructive behaviors. College support groups provide students a positive community to resist negative peer pressure.

How Technology Lowers Emotional Intelligence in Kids

Have we raised a generation that relates better to screens than human beings?

I define technology as any external mechanism that disrupts your kid's ability to be present with their thoughts and feelings and attuned to others. That includes any device that draws your kid's attention away from the moment—such as earbuds, smartphones, and laptops—and dulls their senses to the world and its people.

Out of Touch and Out of Sync

Recently, I watched a family in a restaurant eating dinner in stony silence as each member glared intently at smartphones. Most of the children in the restaurant were eyeballing some kind of screen. One teenager, chatting on her cell phone, shoved her way out of the restaurant, nearly knocking over an elderly couple.

Fundamental human interactions—thoughtfulness, kindness, courtesy—were completely absent among the youth. Worse, their parents supported their behavior by modeling insensitive, tech-dependent behaviors.

Plugged Into Technology and Unplugged From the World

The ability to dissociate from a stressful environment can be helpful. For example, listening to music can release stress by allowing you to take a break and escape a difficult moment. Some apps are designed to boost mindfulness and reduce anxiety through guided meditations or relaxation exercises.

The trouble begins when interacting with technology takes priority over engaging in meaningful communication. As tech dependence increases, kids move through the world in a narcissistic bubble, divorced from their thoughts and feelings and the thoughts and feelings of others. As conversation skills and positive interactions crumble, technology starts to warp kids' sense of humanity; they are less compassionate to others.

The Rise of Technology and the Fall of Emotional Intelligence

Daniel Goleman, in his book *Emotional Intelligence*, defines emotional intelligence as the ability to identify one's feelings and the feelings of others. He notes that people with high degrees of E.I. have healthier relationships, adapt better to environments, and are more skilled at working toward their goals.

Dr. Goleman identifies five essential qualities that foster emotional intelligence: *self-awareness, self-regulation, social skills, empathy, and motivation.*

What do these qualities all have in common? Pay a visit to your local kindergarten; chances are you'll find these qualities absent among most children, particularly during playtime. To develop these qualities, teachers and parents strive to foster mindfulness and thoughtful attentiveness to others. In this way, children develop emotional intelligence by becoming better attuned to the world around them and the people in it.

Let's see how tech dependence negatively impacts Dr. Coleman's essentials of emotional intelligence:

Technology Dependence:

1. Undermines Self-awareness

More time on technology means less time with your thoughts and feelings, the beating heart of mindfulness. As tech dependency increases, kids live in self-alienation, estranged from their emotional selves, turning off self-awareness and self-reflection. Instead of thoughtful choices, they grow more reactive and less reflective.

2. Weakens Self-regulation

Research has proven tech dependence increases impulsivity and lowers frustration tolerance. Without developing the ability to self-regulate, kids remain emotionally immature and mired in early childhood behaviors such as bullying, temper tantrums, and angry outbursts.

3. Diminishes Social Skills

Even when kids play games online with others, such faceless relationships rarely lead to genuine friendships. In this way, tech dependence tends to breed isolation and reclusiveness. The more tech dominates, the less community develops. This leaves kids with poor coping skills and limited tools for navigating relationships.

4. Undermines Empathy

When screen time replaces family or friend time, kids move through the world in trance-like states, self-absorbed and detached from others. Unempathic and unsympathetic, they lack attunement and rapport. The basic building blocks of healthy compassion remain underdeveloped.

5. Stunts Motivation

Motivation toward achieving personal goals, which requires drive, sustained attention, and high frustration tolerance, declines rapidly. Like any addict, kids neglect themselves and their future as they become more dependent. Watch what happens when tech-addicted kids are suddenly forced to interact with the world. They quickly grow discontented and irritable. That's because, unlike technology, they can't control the real world or its people. As a result, when faced with difficult life choices, tech-dependent kids are likely to suffer symptoms of anxiety or depression.

Guidelines for Parents

Everyone suffers when tech dependence goes unaddressed. After all, technology should enhance kids' lives, not control their lives. Strive to put structure and limits around tech use for all family members. Remember, technology should be a tool for kids -- not a way of life.

---

4 Reasons a Bad Marriage Is Worse for Children Than Divorce

When marriages turn toxic, divorce can actually help kids.

When I was a kid, divorced parents were given the evil eye. Heads shook, tongues clicked; divorcees were homewreckers, selfish and unloving; they destroyed children's lives. Some churches banned them from services—apparently, even God wasn't a fan. The message to married couples: Keep your marriage intact by any means necessary.

Times have changed; today, nearly half of all marriages in the U.S. end in divorce. Whether divorce hurts or helps children depends on how their parents handle it, but one thing is certain: Staying in a toxic marriage is sure to cause children more damage than good.

Kids forced to endure loveless marriages and to tolerate emotional tension day after day bear the full brunt of their parents' dysfunctional relationship. They intuitively feel their parents' unhappiness and sense their coldness and lack of intimacy. In many cases, children blame themselves, feeling their parents' combative relationship is somehow their fault. In such cases, staying together "for the kids" is a cruel joke.

Here are four ways kids suffer through a bleak marriage:

1. Chronic Tension

Our parents' relationship leaves an emotional imprint on us that never fades. A natural part of children's development is internalizing both their parents. When parents are consistently at odds, their kids internalize those conflicts. Rather than feeling soothed or comforted by both parents, they feel tense. Such ongoing tension can produce serious emotional, social, and physical ailments in children, such as depression, hopelessness, or chronic fatigue.

2. An Unstable Sense of Self

James Dean cried out to his bickering parents in Rebel Without a Cause, "Stop it! You're tearing me apart!" because the war between parents does take root inside children's minds. The strain eats away at their security and leaves them with little internal peace, putting them at odds with their own impulses. For example, they long to be loved but reject closeness; they yearn for friends but choose isolation; they will have great intellectual or creative abilities yet sabotage their own efforts. The external conflict between their parents eventually becomes an internal battle with themselves that complicates their lives and hinders their emotional development.

3. Fear of Intimacy

Children raised by battling parents have great difficulty getting close to others. Intimacy triggers the traumas they suffered when witnessing their parents' dysfunction, so they avoid closeness to steer clear of getting hurt. If they establish an intimate relationship, they remain cautious or guarded. When conflict arises, they're most likely to flee or reenact their parents' conflicts with their partner.

4. Mood Problems

Warring parents produce children who struggle with serious mood problems, such as dysthymia. These problems, if left untreated, may fuel personality disorders or substance abuse. At the root of these problems is a profound lack of hope. They learn at an early age to abandon optimism and expect the worst. Sadly, bad marriages cause kids to mature too quickly and lose out on their childhood.

Before You Consider Divorce

Ending a marriage is a brutal undertaking that should only be an option after all other efforts have been exhausted. Before you call your lawyer, here are a few suggestions:

Couples Counseling

Couples counseling works best when it teaches parents how to work through their conflicts without resorting to emotional warfare. It also gives ill-tempered parents a place to work through their differences rather than exposing their kids to them. The goal of couple's therapy is to enrich communication and enhance intimacy. But be warned: Couples therapy can be treacherous, and the wrong therapist can spell doom for your marriage. Gather trustworthy recommendations, take your time, and interview several professionals. Make sure you both agree on the therapist you choose; otherwise, the therapy will become just another bone of contention.

Individual Therapy

Nothing stirs up unresolved childhood issues like marriage. Too often, couples have unrealistic expectations of marriage and become disillusioned when they discover that good marriages take work. Before you blame all the problems in your marriage on your partner, get some help for yourself. A skilled therapist can help you identify problems from your past that are resurfacing in your relationship.

Support Groups

The best outcome of group work comes from sharing your feelings and discovering that you're not alone. Hearing about other couples' struggles and difficulties and how they work through them can bring much-needed inspiration and relief. It also provides a community of people who can inspire you with new choices in your marriage.

Zoe's Story

Zoe, a shaggy-haired thirteen-year-old with sad eyes, glares at me, arms folded and jaw set; a therapy hostage if I ever saw one. Parents exert executive power with therapy, so I don't expect Zoe to cooperate, especially during our first tumultuous session. To kids like Zoe, therapy is an insult.

Zoe, however, offers me a deal: *"I'll be in therapy with you only if you promise one thing. I want you to convince my parents to get divorced."* I was flabbergasted by her request, but it opened my eyes to something I had never considered—the positive side of divorce

Due to her parents ' combative relationship, Zoe suffered ongoing humiliation in public, in school, and in front of her friends. The verbal abuse she witnessed her mother suffer at the hands of her father never let up. As a result, Zoe struggled with ongoing headaches, depression, and weight problems.

After meeting with her parents and witnessing their sneering contempt for each other, I understood Zoe's request. If I could barely stand them for 30 minutes, what would it be like to live with them?

Within a year after her parent's divorce, Zoe's depression lifted: She went from failing school to being on the honor roll. She also had her first boyfriend and became socially outgoing. I was amazed at how much better life became for everyone.

———————

How Parents Can Make Their Kids Experts in Happiness

Is your kid's happiness short-lived or long-lasting?

Admit it, you love to see your kid happy; your home is filled with smiling photos grinning from your computer screen, bookshelves, and even your refrigerator door.

Everyone wants to raise a happy child. But when raising children, are all forms of happiness equal? What kind of happiness should you shoot for?

Starting with the Self

Before we begin, I will tell you something you may want to avoid hearing that I included in my book *When Kids Call the Shots*. Parents have fired me because of this personal viewpoint, so if you're fainthearted, skip this section and go on to the next. For those of you who have stuck with me this far, here it is:

No therapist is going to completely "cure" your child. No amount of medication, biofeedback, cognitive-behavior therapy, psychological testing, solution-focused, short-term therapy, or long-term psychoanalysis will genuinely help your kid in the end unless you take full responsibility for your own behavior, i.e., your moods, motives, relationships, your feelings about yourself, your partner, your job, and most importantly, your way of being in the home and the world.

A parent's first and most important job is demonstrating how to live a fulfilling and happy life for their children. It doesn't matter if a single parent, same-sex parents, or adoptive parents raise a child. I've seen trust fund kids raised in wealthy homes who have everything–yet they are depressed. I've also worked with children with very little material wealth yet experience far more joy in life. True and lasting happiness is not based on externals; it's generated from within.

Here's where you come in. Parents pass their children a blueprint for living; no life lesson lecture, order, or directive is more powerful than your own behavior. Your child absorbs your life state, your happiness or unhappiness, every day; it shapes their way of being. No one can match your influence, especially during those crucial early years.

Relative vs. Absolute Happiness

Now, to the question of the kind of happiness you want to foster in your home. I want to share a wonderful Buddhist concept of happiness with you. It divides happiness into two camps: relative and absolute.

Relative Happiness

Relative happiness is a kind of happiness that involves getting stuff or going places. It can be a high-octane experience that gets your heart pumping: an amusement park, a birthday party, a gift, eating your favorite food—all these special moments bursting with happiness.

If you're looking for instant gratification, relative happiness is for you. The difficulty with relative happiness is that it fades quickly. No matter how awesome it feels, it diminishes from the moment it ends. This is because relative happiness is a dependent form of happiness; it depends largely on things outside yourself. Take away those things and happiness goes with it.

Of course, we all want to have fun with our kids; relative happiness can supply plenty of that. The difficulty is that lasting happiness remains elusive when our children's lives become too focused on relative happiness. Any fulfillment they receive from relative happiness expires quickly and is replaced with a ferocious hunger for more. Over time, they grow unsatisfied and belligerent, even bullying. When this happens, parents find themselves trapped in an endless cycle of supply and demand, an exhausting undertaking that undermines everyone's happiness.

Absolute Happiness

Absolute happiness is the kind that isn't dependent on others, objects, or things. It doesn't fade with time. It isn't discarded after the batteries run out. It comes from a more profound sense of purpose, pride, identity, and satisfaction with oneself.

A high score on an exam, a home run in a decisive baseball game, a successful piano recital, a well-written essay, a painting, a report card full of A's. No one can take away the happiness that comes with these achievements; that's why it's absolute; it stays with us forever. We recall these prideful moments well beyond our childhood. They provide nourishment that lifts us when we are down and fortifies us when we feel deadlocked.

Children who experience this kind of happiness are much better equipped to handle life's challenges. They are less dependent and more self-motivated because their happiness isn't dependent on others; it springs from personal triumphs. Parents who cultivate absolute happiness in their children's lives pass along creativity, energy, and passion. Their children are rarely imprisoned behind computers or phone screens or sapped by the trappings of social media. They've learned to seek fulfillment that comes from more enriching activities.

A Balance Approach

Which kind of happiness is the best for your kid? The truth is, your kid needs both. Though short-lived, relative happiness is just too much fun to ignore! Birthday presents, water parks, family outings; some of our kid's best memories are tied to holidays and celebrations. You can't deny the long-term benefits that absolute happiness brings in developing your kid's unique talents and strengths.

A balanced approach to relative and absolute happiness is your best bet –– for you and your child. It's a universal truth that every parent wants a happy child, and every child wants a happy parent. Cultivating happiness in your family is more than just good parenting; it provides you and your kid with memories you will cherish for a lifetime.

---

5 Questions for Kids Fearful of Trying New Things
Bestselling author Paul Smith teaches parents how to encourage hesitant children.

Bestselling author Paul Smith knows a lot of ways of encouraging hesitant kids, 101 ways to be precise. In his book *PARENTING WITH A STORY*, Paul documents 101 inspiring lessons to help kids build the kind of character they and their parents can be proud of.

I asked Paul to share his thoughts on a common parenting struggle: what do you do when your kid resists trying something new? Here's what he had to say:

One of the most common fears young people face early in their lives is trying something new. The uncertainty and apprehension of failure can be crippling. And if it's not overcome as a child, it can haunt someone throughout life. One person who's earned some valuable wisdom while struggling to find courage is Kerri Whitfield.

When she was 12 years old, her family moved. Two years later, Kerri still felt a bit like the new kid in town. She'd made a few friends but still didn't know many other 12-year-olds. Watching one of her girlfriends play on a softball team that summer, Kerri sat in the bleachers and secretly wished she was on the field with her.

"It looks like fun to play," she thought.

And she'd make so many new friends that way, too. Eventually, her friend asked Kerri if she wanted to join the team. This was her big opportunity! What did Kerri do?

"I told her, 'No.'"

Three-plus decades later, Kerri explains that decision this way:

"I was so scared. I'd never played softball before. I'd never played any organized sport before! So I didn't know anything about the game. I didn't know the rules or how to play. All I could think about was how I would fail because I didn't know how. It never occurred to me they could teach me those things. So I just said no."

The remorse didn't take long to set in.

"I was so sad. I kept going to the games and watching them play. There were times I had to wipe away tears, hoping no one had seen me cry. I so wanted to be out on that field. It's a decision I still regret."

That event kicked off a lifetime of what Kerri now sees as missed opportunities. Her fear of failure kept her from succeeding at many new things. Sometimes, it kept her from trying in the first place, like the singing lessons she never took or the new job she never applied for. And sometimes, that fear made her quit soon after starting. She recalls a failed attempt at gymnastics.

"I hadn't been in the class for long, and we were learning how to do the splits. One of the coaches said that if we couldn't get all the way down, they would push us the rest of the way. I never went back. Somehow, my parents never challenged that decision. So that was the end of my gymnastics career."

One of her more memorable successes was in learning to waterski. A friend had invited her to ski. But when it was Kerri's turn, she was too afraid to get in the water. After a few minutes of grace and ineffective coaxing, her girlfriend's father pushed her off the boat. Kerri Whitfield learned to ski that day. And the next time, she jumped off the boat by herself.

It probably wasn't until she had children of her own that Kerri decided her insecurities would no longer impact her or her growing family. She shares these stories with her son and daughter to help them have the courage to try new things. Looking back, there are three lessons she thinks she learned.

* "First, I wished I'd shared my desires more openly with my parents. They could have encouraged me to play softball.

* "Second, I wish I'd understood then that I didn't have to be the best at everything on the first day. Everyone has to learn, even the experts. If I'd known that, I might have returned for the second day of gymnastics class.

* "Third, I learned that part of life is getting unexpectedly wet. Because sometimes good parenting means pushing your kid off the boat.

The best way to find wisdom in this or any story is to share it with your kids and then discuss it. Do so. Here are five questions to get you started.

1. *Can you recall two or three things you tried but gave up on soon after? What were they? Is it too late to try again?*

2. *Name something you'd like to do now but have been afraid to try. How can I help you with that?*

3. *How long do you think it takes for people to get good at something new, like learning to play the guitar, throw a baseball, or write poetry?*

4. *Can you think of something some people are naturally good at without learning and practicing?*

5. *Let's have this conversation again next month to see what's changed and what you're interested in then, okay?*

Paul Smith is a bestselling author of the book *PARENTING WITH A STORY*. He's a keynote speaker and trainer on leadership and storytelling techniques and the author of two other books: *LEAD WITH A STORY* and *SELL WITH A STORY*.

Happy Parents, Happy Kids
Peace activist Daisaku Ikeda's newly published parenting book

It's a universal truth that every parent loves to see their children happy. But when raising happy children, you'll soon find yourself sorting through mountains of complex and conflicting advice. This makes *HAPPY KIDS, HAPPY PARENTS* such a unique and timely parenting book. It takes child-rearing back to the basics with clear-headed and sensible guidance that will leave parents smiling in recognition and sighing in relief.

Starting with the Self

The beating heart of *HAPPY PARENTS, HAPPY KIDS* is this simple message: parents' most important job is demonstrating how to live a fulfilling and happy life for their children.

Daisaku Ikeda, a peace activist and Buddhist leader who has spent his lifetime promoting peace, culture, and education, believes that creating harmonious families is vital in creating a more peaceful and harmonious world. Sharing his wisdom and insights, Mr. Ikeda asks parents to reflect deeply on their behavior and become models for the behavior they want to see in their children.

Distilled from Mr. Ikeda's selected speeches, essays, and books, *HAPPY PARENTS, HAPPY KIDS* is organized into themes that every parent will recognize, such as *Disciplining With Love, Viewing TV and Video Games,* and *Overcoming Problems at School.* Each chapter is edited and organized into inspirational bites that parents can use for daily affirmations. Mr. Ikeda skillfully directs parents to polish their own behaviors and view their children with greater compassion and understanding.

Here's a sample of what you'll find:

Parents' Love & Sincerity

"You may sometimes make mistakes, become overwhelmed, or lose your temper. What is important, however, is to make a wholehearted effort. Children grow up watching their parents. It is not the parents' words that children hear. No matter what wonderful things parents may say, children will not listen if their words are not accompanied by action. Children's lives will be determined by how parents live. The parents' love and way of life will, like magma beneath the earth's crust, form the innermost core of children's hearts and become a source of energy to support the rest of their lives" (p.8)

Respecting Children's Personalities

Every child has a unique mission. There is a budding potential in everyone. I think the greatest nourishment for children's growth is our trust in them. Some children show their potential early on, while others start to develop later. Whichever the case, we must continue to give children steady encouragement and warm support, believing that their potential will definitely sprout and grow in time. The key is how much we can believe in children." (p.27)

When the Budget is Tight

"More children are being raised in a relatively comfortable environment, one in which people are willing to buy them almost anything they want. If children continue to be indulged in this way, however, they will grow to be people who avoid anything unpleasant and end up weak and defeated in life. In this way, a too-comfortable childhood can pave the way to unhappiness

later. Rousseau said, "Do you know the surest way of making your child miserable? Let him have everything that he wants." (p.48)

HAPPY PARENTS, HAPPY KIDS reminds readers that parents provide their children with a blueprint for living. In this way, no lecture, order, or directive is more powerful than parents' own behavior. Mr. Ikeda clarifies that children absorb their parents' life state every moment; no one can match a parent's influence. As the title suggests, when happiness thrives in parents' lives, it naturally thrives in their children's lives.

Boys Without Fathers: 3 Myths, 3 Miracles

"Who's missing" from a child's life isn't as important as "who's there."

Do a quick search for "boys raised without fathers," and you'll quickly find yourself buried under an avalanche of horrifying statistics. More likely to drop out of school, more likely to develop drug or alcohol problems, more likely to be incarcerated; the bad news goes on and on. One study went so far as to claim that fatherlessness permanently alters brain structure, causing higher levels of aggression and anger in children.

This is what makes the new documentary IN A PERFECT WORLD... such an important and timely film. Director Daphne McWilliams bravely explores the health and hardiness of men raised by single mothers.

Ms. McWilliams begins the film with her own pregnancy and fearlessly records her parenting struggles with his son from infancy through his teen years. We see Ms. McWilliams pregnant and dancing with her baby's father. By the time her son is a toddler, his father's smile is fading, and soon he is missing entirely. Ms. McWilliams suddenly finds herself unwittingly thrust into the world of single moms.

IN A PERFECT WORLD... also follows the lives of eight men from different socioeconomic backgrounds and cultures raised by single mothers and reveals how they triumphed over their father's abandonment and became outstanding fathers themselves. We see many of them in action, waking their kids in the morning, preparing meals, and dropping their sons and daughters off at school. They move through parenting tasks with a passion and commitment rarely seen in men.

The film's most remarkable and inspiring aspect is the hope it conveys. The men in the film speak of their deep love and respect for their mothers. In raw and unscripted interviews, each man opens his heart, sheds tears about his mother's struggle, and expresses how his mother remains a constant source of inspiration. The men also exhibit sensitivity and compassion for their absent fathers.

Ms. McWilliams and I recently screened the film for teenagers at Williamsburg Charter High School in Brooklyn. I was struck by how a room full of boisterous teens fell silent as they watched the film that mirrored many of their own experiences. The teenagers shared their disappointment and anger toward their fathers during a discussion group after the screening. Yet, they were quick to identify men in their lives who stepped in as father figures.

One young girl pointed to the school dean seated next to her, a tall, imposing man with a firm handshake and determined look, and announced:

"Mister Sanford is my true father. He's a better father than my father ever was."

When I asked why, her answer was straight to the point:

"He's always there for me, and he cares."

Soon Mr. Sanford and other adults in the room were choking back tears.

Outdated and Misleading Studies

Statistics are tricky. Cold, hard facts can leave us feeling hopeless or scapegoating others. When lives are reduced to numbers on a page, we risk losing touch with our humanity. Worse, simplistic statistics can feed unfound prejudice and fear. They rarely consider men like Mr. Sanford, who step up and change children's lives every day.

Before I get to the myths and miracles, I was able to speak to Daphne McWilliams about her experience as a parent and the director of IN A PERFECT WORLD.... Here's what she had to say:

Do you think there are any positive aspects of boys growing up without fathers?

I wouldn't label it with the word "positive" as in the positive aspects of boys growing up without fathers. That said, I know that a boy can be raised in a household without a father, and there doesn't have to be a negative outcome. It's in the child's best interest (boy or girl) that they can have a relationship with their father. Naturally, this would be case-by-case, but I think children should "know" both of their parents. One important message I would like to get out to all the single parents reading this article is that you must find nurturing things for you! I am still raising my son, but he sees my commitment to several activities that keep me calm and balanced.

With all the endless negative statistics about fatherless households, do you ever feel discouraged about your son's future?

Absolutely NOT! I have never let statistics dictate my life nor my son's future. Statistics have their place in our society, but at the same time, they are broad strokes and not based on an individual case.

What did you find inspirational about the interviews with men who grew up without fathers?

I was inspired by how genuine each of the men was. They may have been speaking directly to me, but somehow, they knew their voices would be heard beyond the lens and the editing room. Each of their stories was the very thing that pushed me to complete this film (which I did with my own savings and credit cards). It was a blessing to have been in the room with each of them; they spoke, and I listened.

3 Myths of Children Raised by Single Mothers

1. *Fatherless boys inevitably suffer delinquent tendencies.*

   The biggest problem with the fatherlessness label is that it is oversimplified. It doesn't reveal why some children in the studies are without a father.

   Was it caused by a divorce?

   Is the mother a widow?

Did a female couple raise the child?

These details completely transform study outcomes. For example, boys raised by a mother and stepfather (a two-parent home) have the highest negative outcomes, much more than those raised by a single mother. In fact, juvenile delinquency and substance abuse are highest among children raised by parents in hostile marriages (two-parent homes).

High conflict levels at home inherently cause the most significant damage to children's well-being. Consequently, an intensely negative parent relationship can do more damage than a missing parent.

2. Fatherless boys suffer from anger issues or depression.

Once again, the quality of the relationships in a child's life determines their mental well-being. Boys without fathers don't choose their biological father but can choose their father figure, role model, or mentor.

All the men in the film, including the director's son, adopted loving and supportive men to fill their father's role. Ms. McWilliams's brothers, interviewed at her son's soccer game, gladly stepped into the father role for their nephew.

3. Fatherless men don't know how to be good fathers.

As the fathers in IN A PERFECT WORLD ... demonstrate, being a parent offered them the opportunity to be the father that they never had. It motivated them to bond with their sons and daughters and heal their own painful childhoods.

Many men raised by single mothers I've worked with in therapy have demonstrated the same impressive tenacity and grit as the men in the film. By loving their children deeply, they also stop letting their past define them.

3 Miracles Of Children Raised by Single Mothers

1. Men raised without fathers are equally successful in life.

The history of the United States is filled with stories of single mothers raising successful men. It dates back to our first president, George

Washington, to President Obama. You can also find endless lists online of inventors and innovators, Olympic athletes, and musicians raised by single mothers.

2. *Men who grew up without fathers can be outstanding parents.*

The men featured IN A PERFECT WORLD... quietly grew into and embraced their role of dad. In fact, it is their history that fuels their deter- mination to honor and love their own sons and daughters even more.

3. *Men raised by women are often more sensitive and attuned emotionally.*

In my 22 years of leading therapy groups, I've discovered that men and teenage boys raised by single mothers are frequently more sensitive to the feelings and needs of others and more mindful in relationships with women.

Parenting Over Biology

Growing up in ideal circumstances doesn't guarantee happiness. IN A PERFECT WORLD... reveals that the "who's missing" isn't as important as "who's there." After all, everyone faces obstacles in life: health complications, sudden tragedies, and divorce. IN A PERFECT WORLD... drops the labels and proves that any child can succeed with the proper support, role models, and love.

---

3 Mistakes Parents Make by NOT Considering Boarding School

And affordable options to get your teen back on track.

There was a time when I thought sending your kid away to boarding school was just plain cruel—a failure of parenting or schooling. I thought therapy could fix everything.

Boy, was I wrong.

When a kid has too many negative influences in her life, particularly during her teen years, therapy loses its effectiveness. Even the most resilient teens waste away under the influence of toxic peers or lose themselves in an environment that encourages dangerous or destructive behaviors. You may have to take more drastic steps to reestablish sanity in your family and safety for your child.

In this excerpt from my book, WHEN KIDS CALL THE SHOTS (Amacom, 2015), I outline for parents when to consider boarding school. Most of the candidates for boarding school are teenagers, although it's not limited to them. The top three reasons parents choose boarding schools for their kids are substance abuse, delinquency, and school failure.

Substance Abuse

If your kid has tried marijuana or alcohol at parties, don't freak out. These days, it isn't easy to find a teenager who hasn't. But if your kid drinks alcohol regularly, has blackouts, or smokes marijuana daily—either alone in his room, during the school day, or with a particular group of peers (e.g., "the stoners")—there is cause for concern, particularly if your family has a history of substance abuse or if you find that your kid is using more severe drugs.

Substance abuse triggers severe mood swings, violent outbursts, and extreme defiance. If you see these side effects and feel like you're losing your child—it's time to take action. Preventing addiction isn't easy, but reversing it after becoming part of a kid's identity can take a lifetime.

Delinquent Behavior

Shoplifting, trespassing, and other delinquent behaviors typically fall under adolescent limit testing. But if you have these problems, in addition to more severe misconduct such as selling drugs, gang involvement, or police arrests due to misdemeanors or felonies, hoping for the best won't do. Getting your kid away from an environment that encourages such behavior—and fast would be best.

School Failure

Failing grades, school suspensions, truancy, or ongoing conflicts with teachers or peers signal that a new school may be necessary. Consider your child's more pressing needs first rather than just a quick change of schools. I've worked with parents whose kids were expelled from two or three-day schools before they felt boarding school was an option. As your kid gets older, the options for boarding school become more limited. If you suspect that the day school your child attends is a poor fit and things are going from bad to worse, don't waste time. Find a therapeutic boarding school to help undo your kid's destructive behaviors and meet his academic needs.

The Benefits of a Therapeutic Boarding School

All boarding schools manage kids twenty-four hours a day, not just the six or seven hours that regular day schools provide. Therapeutic boarding schools, however, provide intensive therapy, counseling, and empowerment programs designed to strengthen teens' core identities and undo destructive behaviors. Choose a school designed to address behavior problems; otherwise, your kid may be expelled, and you could find yourself right back where you started.

Here's how boarding school can help.

1. *Boarding School Removes Kids from Toxic Influences*

Once in boarding school, your kid no longer has access to drugs or alcohol or peers steering him down the wrong path. Boarding schools provide a complete break from a world that's out of control. Once negative influences are removed, skilled counselors or therapists can begin to address the underlying issues that are triggering self-destructive behaviors.

2. *Boarding School Introduces Healthy Structures*

Boarding schools provide highly structured daily schedules, such as set times for classes, study periods, homework, bedtime, morning routines, meals, exercise, and counseling. Though kids initially resist such structures, their behavior and moods drastically improve when implemented. Such positive frameworks nourish healthy emotional and psychological development.

For example, I worked with an obese teenager addicted to video games. His sleeping schedule was erratic; he was failing school, had few friends, and bullied his parents. To make matters worse, he had no vision for his future.

After all, the interventions failed, and his parents found an appropriate boarding school. During his first year at school, he lost thirty pounds, became a rugby player, and had his first girlfriend. He was finally on a regular eating, sleeping, and exercise schedule. During family weekends, his parents were thrilled by the changes in him. They had their child back! By the time he left the school, nearly all his bad habits had vanished. He was ready to move on to college and major in computer programming.

3. *Boarding School Replaces Negative Influences with Positive Ones*

I'm always awed by the positive impact role models can make in a troubled kid's life. I've seen drug dealers become ballet dancers or athletes once they were given access to positive role models and mentors. Teenagers crave adults that they can look up to. Counselors and older peers at boarding schools often fill this need and offer kids a chance to make better choices.

Alternatives to Boarding Schools

There's no denying it: Boarding schools cost an arm and a leg. Some parents spend their child's college savings on boarding schools, knowing there might be no college without it. Other parents attempt to get their health insurance to cover the costs. If you have no insurance or savings, many states have government-funded boarding schools that will require extensive applications to meet requirements. If boarding school isn't an option, I've seen parents take the following alternatives with some success.

Change of Environment

Removing your kid from a hostile environment can also be achieved by temporarily moving homes or sending her off to briefly live somewhere else with adult supervision—an aunt or uncle, a cousin, or a friend will do. This may seem ridiculous (I can feel my colleagues rolling their eyes!), but when negative influences are out of control, this can be a quick fix until professional help is secured.

Social Action Programs

Never underestimate the power of altruism in turning a troubled kid around. I've seen teens come back from building homes in hurricane-devastated parts of the country or return from Peace Corps–style programs profoundly changed. Coming face to face with the intense sufferings of others and offering them help may change a kid's outlook. Such programs also boost self-esteem, purpose, and personal value.

Wilderness Programs

Programs such as Outward Bound usually have rolling admissions. In other words, your kid can start right away. A combination of healthy outdoor exercise, group and individual counseling, and wilderness programs provide kids with much-needed time for self-reflection. Many counselors of wilderness programs are graduates of the programs, a testament to their excellent work.

Rebooting Your Kid's Childhood

What are the three mistakes parents make by not considering boarding school? Very simply, they wait until it's too late and their kid has aged out of boarding school, rationalize their kid's destructive behaviors to justify not taking action, or chalk up their kid's dangerous choices as "just a phase of adolescence."

I think of boarding school as a last resort, something you try when all else has failed. Yes, it's an unpopular decision, but the alternatives are far more painful when you see your kid heading toward self-destruction or a criminal record.

Over the years, teenagers who went off to boarding schools have come back to visit me in their twenties and thirties. No matter how difficult a decision it was at the time, they nearly all expressed appreciation for the intervention. As one told me, "My life was so out of control; I think deep down I was relieved when my parents stepped in. I don't know where I would be today if they hadn't."

----

3 Mistakes Parents Make With Technology

#1. Not Setting Limits

Everywhere you look, children are staring at cell phone screens, computer screens, tablets, iPads, etc. By the time you finish reading this article, someone will probably have invented a new glowing screen for kids to stare into.

The real question is this: has technology improved our kids' attunement and empathy with others, or is it adding to their self-absorption and isolation?

Tuned-in and out-of-touch

Never before in history have kids had instant access to so much information. With endless data at their fingertips, kids can breeze through entire libraries or view their homes from outer space. A tap or a click can deliver facts and statistics that would have taken hours to find in books.

While technology has expanded our knowledge of the world, advanced education, and provided medical breakthroughs, it is quickly becoming the number one source of conflict between parents and their children at home.

Technology and Temperament

Some kids don't fuss over technology. These kids lead full lives filled with hobbies and activities such as school clubs, social events, sports teams, band, or music practice. To them, technology is just another pastime.

For other kids, technology devours their lives. They can't put it down or turn it off. These kids tend to be more isolated and anxious, have poor people skills, have difficulty maintaining friendships, or have an unstable sense of self. For them, technology is just another way to avoid a frustrating world that they have difficulty handling. They can shut out contact and communication by placing a glowing screen in front of their face. Sadly, the more connected they feel to technology, the less connected they feel to the people around them.

For example, the best summer camps don't allow any technology. That's because they know that the more connected kids are to technology, the less connected they will be to each other.

If technology becomes your kid's primary activity, if your kid spends hours a day gaming or surfing the net instead of hanging out with friends or participating in school activities, be warned: you may have a budding tech addict in your home.

Tech Addiction

Many kids who visit my office spend unlimited hours each day tied to some form of technology, such as a cell phone, a tablet, or a portable gaming device. They can't travel without it or put it down without a fight. In this way, technology looks a lot like addiction.

Like any addiction, as dependency increases, personal functioning decreases. Kids become more impulsive, moody, and less empathic. As their hunger for more tech time grows, clashes with parents increase.

Tech-addicted kids are more likely to suffer:

- *Social isolation*
- *Poor social skills*
- *Unstable moods*
- *Impulse problems*
- *Sleep disorders*
- *Low self-esteem*

The biggest problem with technology is simple: it doesn't turn itself off. Setting limits on unhealthy behaviors is a crucial part of good parenting. Taking the "guardian of technology" role may make you unpopular with your kid, but it is critical to preventing tech addiction tendencies.

The three big mistakes parents make when it comes to technology are:

1. **Not Setting Limits on Technology**
2. **Not Having Enough Family Activities without Technology**
3. **Parents are also Tech Addicts**

Tech Rules

Here are some basic recommendations for parents who have a child obsessed with technology. Of course, every kid is different; what works for one child may be a disaster for another. Consider this list a jumping-off point for discussion. But be warned, the more dependent your kid becomes on technology, the more difficult it will be to wean them off it.

1. **Tech Blackouts**

   Set aside specific times at home when no one (parents included) uses technology. Cell phones, computers, iPads...everything is off. You must lead the way if you want your kid to be less tech-addicted. Tech-free time can be spent reading, talking, playing games, cooking, making art... anything creative or social will do.

2. **Tech Hours**

   Kids resist structure — but fall apart without it. Technology needs limits. For instance, I often recommend that families establish tech hours, time for homework, gaming, or Internet surfing. Scheduling tech time will help to limit battles by setting clear guidelines. For instance, when it comes to gaming, many parents may allow thirty minutes a day during the school week and two hours a day on the weekends.

3. **Tech Spaces**

   Keep all technology in a shared space like the living room — not in a child's bedroom when possible. Establish communal places for tech time; avoid allowing your kid to disappear behind a closed door for hours.

4. **Tech Limits**

   Plenty of online services can filter out inappropriate or violent material. These services can also limit Internet access by scheduling times that the Internet is available and times when it is not. One example of such a service is Net Nanny.

Stop Tech Addiction Before it Starts.

The bottom line is that parents must control technology or risk technology controlling their kids. Technology without supervision is not healthy for any young person. When staring into a glowing screen replaces meaningful communication in a child's life, they will suffer mightily with intimacy in the future.

Find the right balance for technology use in your home and eliminate tech addiction in your kid's future.

----

3 Signs Your Child has Learning Disabilities

... and what you can do about it.

Schoolwork can be difficult, but it shouldn't be torture -- for you or your kid. If your child is struggling academically, it's time to consider that your kid isn't just being difficult. There may be something more going on than meets the eye. After all, who wants to do poorly in school?

Nonverbal learning disability (NVLD) is under-the-radar perceptual difficulties that affect how children process information. NVLD often appears in middle or high school when work becomes more demanding. Longer essays, complicated math, and more intensive reading and writing assignments, and suddenly, your good-natured A student morphs into a moody and irritable procrastinator struggling to pass.

Parents who bring their children or teenagers to me for therapy always balk when I suggest a neuropsychological evaluation, a psychological assessment that identifies NVLD.

> *"My son was a perfect student in elementary school."*
>
> *"My daughter has never had difficulty in school before."*
>
> *"He's just being lazy. He doesn't apply himself."*

Commonly, children with NVLD compensate by being highly proficient in other areas. Sometimes, elementary school academics weren't challenging enough.

Here are three warning signs that your kid may be struggling with an NVLD:

1. Struggles are Centered Around Academics

If all your kid's struggles are centered around school work, then the solutions you need are academic, not therapeutic. Kids with NVLD usually have some social difficulties. But when it comes to schoolwork, everything falls apart. If you can't wait for school vacation so your kid is her old self, start thinking about an assessment for an NVLD.

2. Difficulty Concentrating and Completing Assignments

Does your kid need help with focusing in class? Has note-taking become unbearable or illegible? Are certain subjects more difficult than others, resulting in wildly uneven grades? Such academic imbalances are often a sign of undiagnosed NVLD.

3. Erratic Moods and Fatigue

After a day at school, is your kid irritable, sullen, anxious, or depressed? Kids with NVLD are in a constant state of tension that eats away at their mood and energy levels. Simple assignments are exhausting. Even if they can keep up with the schoolwork, their outlook is bleak. No matter how much they try, they're always behind. They give up without trying or telling their parents they don't care. Anytime a child says, "I don't care," always look for hurt feelings or fears of failure, which are familiar to kids with NVLD.

Primary Deficits in NVLD

Dr. Preetika Mukherjee, a Manhattan-based neuropsychologist who specializes in assessing children and teenagers with NVLD, explains the four primary deficits seen in individuals with NVLD:

1. Tactile Perception:

Tactile Perception (sometimes called touch perception) is the brain's ability to understand (perceive) what the hands are feeling. When you put your hand into your handbag and fish around to retrieve your keys, your touch perception helps you find your keys without using your eyes. If a child has poor touch perception, it feels like they are doing everything with rubber gloves on, as the brain is not processing the information sent by the child's hands properly. The child may be clumsy, constantly dropping small items or letting things slip out of their grasp. Or maybe the child squeezes the pencil tightly so they can "feel" it properly to control it.

2. Visual Perception

Visual Perception is the ability to see and interpret (analyze and give meaning to) the visual information surrounding us. Without accurate visual perceptual processing, a student would have difficulty learning to read, give or follow directions, copy from the whiteboard, visualize objects or past experiences, have good eye-hand coordination, integrate visual information with other senses to do things like ride a bike, play catch, shoot baskets when playing basketball, or hear a sound and visualize where it is coming from (like the siren on a police car).

3. Complex Motor Skills

Motor clumsiness is often the first concern parents observe with NVLD children. There may be more noticeable problems on the left side of the body. Children hesitate to explore their environment motorically. Instead, they explore the world verbally by asking questions. When children start learning to walk, they are unstable and often fall. They avoid jungle gyms and activities that require a lot of motor activity. Fine motor skills are also impacted. For example, the NVLD toddler resists eating with a spoon or fork due to their fingers' lack of dexterity. The NVLD teen may have trouble writing class notes. Look for difficulties tying shoelaces and unusual ways of holding scissors, pens, or pencils.

4. Dyscalculia

Math involves visual-spatial abilities. Conceptualizing math problems involves visualizing the operations. Addition, for example, is a mental operation of "seeing" sets of things being put together. Research has shown that NVLD individuals can understand the language and verbal reasoning aspects of a math problem but cannot "visualize" efficiently the relationships between the parts of the problem to perform the arithmetic operations.

Dr. Mukherjee notes that these primary deficits lead to secondary deficits, including difficulties with attention and social cue recognition, concept formation, organization, and planning. Academically, we will see difficulties in the following skills:

- Graphomotor Skills
- Computational Skills
- Quantitative Reasoning
- Reading Comprehension

- Written Organization

What to Do

Dr. Mukherjee suggests that if parents think their children suffer from an NVLD, they should talk to their teacher, reach out to a school guidance counselor, or arrange a private consultation with a neuropsychologist specializing in learning disabilities. Getting an accurate assessment of your kid's learning style is vital to avoiding the pitfalls of undiagnosed NVLD and keeping your kid's school and home life harmonious.

Questions for Preetika Mukherjee, Ph.D.? Visit: drpreetikamukherjee.com

---

3 Good Reasons Not to Give Kids Too Many Presents
... and four ways to keep them grounded on the holidays and all year long.

Too many gifts can turn little darlings into ungrateful bullies who are never satisfied—no matter how much they get from their parents. So before you go overboard and shower a child with gifts, consider these negative outcomes.

Too Many Gifts...

1. Increases destructive behavior.

Kids who engage in greedy gift-grabbing during holidays suffer negative social and emotional ramifications that extend well beyond their childhood. According to a study from the University of Missouri, such children are more prone to credit card debt, gambling, and compulsive shopping as adults. Sure, unwrapping a mountain of gifts produces a burst of happiness—but it has no staying power. Instead, it feeds an insatiable hunger for more.

2. Lowers self-esteem.

Lasting self-esteem is rooted in a strong sense of identity—not materialism. Excess does not equal increased self-worth. Studies have shown no correlation between material possessions and self-esteem or happiness. Children with fewer material possessions but positive relationships with parents and peers score higher on self-esteem assessment tests. They also have fewer behavior problems and demonstrate more resilience when facing obstacles than kids with overindulging parents.

3. Robs children of lasting happiness.

Researchers publishing in Harvard's *Journal of Happiness* found that people valued gifts they purchased for *others* more than gifts they bought for *themselves*. And when those "givers" completed a personal satisfaction scale, they consistently scored higher than those who purchased gifts for themselves. Helping your child develop generosity fosters a healthy sense of interconnectedness. It boosts personal happiness—kids who only value *receiving gifts* are more likely to grow to be egocentric and lack empathy.

3 Kinds of Holiday Bullies

I always ask parents who attend my parenting workshops which kids are more likely to have parents who overindulge them during the holidays. Believe it or not, it's the bullies. Kids who bully parents into overindulging them are more likely to get more gifts than kids who don't:

1. The Defiant Bully—demands gifts and feels entitled. (*"I deserve this, you owe me."*) Engages in blackmail and threats to wear away parents' resolve. Eventually, parents buy gifts to buy peace. But it's never enough. The more parents give, the less these kids will appreciate—and the more they will demand.

2. The Anxious Bully—equates gifts with love. Constantly feels deprived, compares and despairs with peers, worries about not having enough, and fears being left out or forgotten. Guilts and shames parents into buying more.

3. The Manipulative Bully exploits parents' insecurities by lying and manipulating them to get what they want. Knows precisely which buttons to push to make parents feel insecure. Does anything to achieve their gift goals. But be warned: Even after manipulative bullies get what they want, they start plotting for more.

What to Do

1. Set gift limits.

Meaningful gifts have more emotional value than a mountain of generic presents. Setting limits on gift-giving triggers more thoughtfulness and consideration in children. It also guarantees that everyone experiences an equal amount of giving and receiving. And remember, homemade gifts such as artwork or poetry can create memories that last longer than AA batteries.

2. Keep household schedules and limits intact.

Too often, parents allow sleeping schedules, chores, and other household structures to fall apart during holidays. Without structure, though, kids' behaviors will deteriorate. For example, if your child suddenly has unlimited access to sweets, stays up all night, and sleeps all day, you'll see more meltdowns, moodiness, and bullying. Losing structure during the holidays is the Number One cause of problematic behaviors.

3. Focus on esteem-building gifts.

Aim for gifts that enhance creativity, talents, or motor skills, such as musical instruments, paints, cameras, etc. Children love to discover new talents. It strengthens their self-esteem and confidence. They also learn they don't need excessive belongings to feel too good about themselves.

4. Teach the joy of giving.

Kids whose parents encourage them to give gifts to others experience a stronger sense of community and interconnectedness. Help your kids learn the value of giving by engaging them in altruistic activities such as volunteer work or helping those in need. After all, isn't that giving the *true* spirit of the holiday?

---

4 Ways Altruism Produces Happy and Empowered Children

What's missing from your kid's life could make all the difference.

During my 20 years as a psychotherapist working with young people and their parents, I've witnessed certain youth make sudden leaps in maturity that catapulted them far ahead of their peers. Their amplified sense of well-being astonished their parents and me. What was the magic ingredient that was added to their lives? It was the power of altruism. That's right, teaching kids the value of helping others was instrumental in improving their mood and behavior—and reducing bullying. It also roused in them a greater sense of personal worth, an essential condition for fostering feelings of happiness and empowerment.

Too often, there's a misconception that altruism involves some personal sacrifice. It's not uncommon to think of altruism as a charity that solely benefits others. Nothing could be farther from the truth. Researchers have found that when parents teach their children the value of helping others, their children benefit as much as those they helped, sometimes even more. Here's how:

1. Altruism Increases Personal Happiness

Too often, young people fall into the trap of focusing exclusively on their own needs. This narcissistic tendency is a breeding ground for depression or anxiety. Altruism breaks through the hard shell of self-absorption by nurturing compassion for others. Sonja Lyubormirsky, in her wonderful book *THE HOW OF A HAPPINESS* (1), cites a study in which women were trained in compassionate listening techniques. Afterward, for three years, they visited MS patients to talk and listen for 15 minutes at a time. The study found that the volunteers, who were MS patients themselves, experienced measurable increases in happiness in areas such as self-esteem, self-acceptance, and life satisfaction.

2. Altruism Fosters a Healthy Sense of Interconnectedness

Isolation is the enemy of happiness. Visit any high school lunchroom, and you'll see that teens yearn to be part of a community; until they do, they suffer much discomfort. Researchers at Harvard support this need to feel connected to others in the Journal of Happiness (2). The study found that people valued gifts they purchased for others more than gifts they bought for themselves. During the research, participants completed a personal satisfaction scale to measure their happiness level. The happiness that they experienced when giving gifts consistently scored higher.

Generosity gave birth to a healthy sense of interconnectedness, which boosted their happiness.

3. Altruism Strengthens Personal Identity

For years, I've witnessed many young people's identities fortified and strengthened when they helped others. Altruism triggers a surge in self-esteem, which promotes confidence and assurance. In a national study by the American Journal of Community Psychology (3), 56% of those surveyed indicated that altruism was an immutable part of their identity. In other words, altruism reinforced a positive view of themselves. A young woman in the study, who donated her time to visiting senior citizens in her community, stated: "If I give it to you... I'm not giving it to you because I know you need it. I'm giving it to you because ... I'm being just the person I am."

4. Altruism Inspires a Sense of Mission

So often, young people feel adrift. Unsure of their future, they struggle with internal feelings of emptiness and indifference. Altruism inspires them by directing their attention outward and allowing them to experience the value of helping others. I recently encountered a young man who said his life was transformed when he traveled to a nearby city to help with relief efforts after a devastating hurricane. An unhappy and aimless teenager, he experienced a dramatic shift in his perspective. In his words: "I thought I was helping rebuild the city, but I was really rebuilding myself." Today, he is employed as a program designer for not-for-profit organizations.

Surprisingly, altruism doesn't get much respect when it comes to child development. Yet, I've witnessed its transformative power again and again. Many children diagnosed as anxious or disruptive improve dramatically—socially, emotionally, and even academically—when their parents introduce them to altruistic activities such as volunteer work or supporting neighborhood projects. Kindness, compassion, gratitude, empathy, and many other positive qualities emerge when children learn that helping others is also a great way to help themselves.

CHAPTER 10:
PSYCHOTHERAPY

When Therapy Fails

What to do when therapy isn't helping you.

Are you frustrated with your weekly sessions and thinking of quitting therapy? Perhaps you have friends who gush about their therapist and brag about the progress that they are making. You wonder why you don't share their excitement.

What do you do when therapy isn't delivering results?

When therapy isn't working

Let's consider some possible reasons why therapy is failing you:

1. **A lousy therapist:** Just as there are bad plumbers or teachers, there are bad therapists. A burnt-out, inexperienced, or poorly trained therapist isn't likely to be very dynamic or helpful. If your therapist looks bored, disinterested, or isn't challenging you enough, confront them. If nothing changes, move on.

2. **A poor fit:** Therapy isn't one size fits all. If you don't feel safe, comfortable, or understood by your therapist, you're probably working with the wrong person.

3. **A severe mood disorder:** If you're suffering from extreme anxiety or overwhelming depression, talk therapy alone

may not be enough, particularly if you have a long family history of mood disorders. It may be time to consider adding medication to your treatment.

4. **Lack of motivation:** If you're attending sessions, but your heart isn't in it, you're not likely to see much progress. Waiting for your therapist to cure you without putting forth effort isn't going to produce sustainable results.

5. **Poor self-care habits:** If you're not exercising, your diet is dismal, you don't have creative outlets, you engage in unhealthy relationships, or you abuse drugs or alcohol, such choices can undermine the benefits of therapy.

What to do if therapy isn't helping

Before you fire your therapist or abandon treatment entirely, take a moment to identify what went wrong and consider the following options:

1. **Be choosey:** Too often, people go with the first therapist that they meet. They rush into therapy without considering the actual therapists that they are hiring. Take your time; interview at least three therapists before you decide. Bring a list of questions to your first session. Trust your intuition. If the therapist transmits confidence and inspiration, that's a great start.

2. **Try different kinds of therapy:** There are more therapy types today than ever, such as art or dance therapy. You may benefit from a more engaging and stimulating treatment than traditional talk therapy.

3. **Consider group therapy:** When it comes to social anxiety, chronic relationship problems, or self-isolating tendencies, you can't beat the power of group therapy. Joining a group of individuals committed to each other's growth is an incredibly healing experience. I've led groups for 25 years, and I'm still awed by the progress I've seen in group members.

4. **Educate yourself about different schools of therapy:** Certain forms of therapy target specific symptoms and

are most effective. For example, if you're struggling with symptoms of OCD or phobia, studies have shown that CBT or DBT therapies are your best choice.

5. **Explore other interventions:** If therapy isn't working, consider other interventions, such as working with a nutritionist or life coach or consulting a psychiatrist. Keep trying until you experience the personal breakthrough that you crave.

Is Therapy Ruining Your Relationships?

Change triggers conflict.

You started therapy, and you're feeling much better. You feel empowered and understood; your voice is stronger, and your confidence is growing. However, you discover that your friends are less than thrilled by the changes they see in you. They're perturbed by your fresh lease on life.

What's happening? Why are your friends suddenly rejecting the new you?

Not Everyone Will Like the New You

Remember, you went into therapy to improve your life. You may discover that some of your relationships are unhealthy in that process. Once you become aware of unhealthy dynamics, it becomes harder to tolerate them.

As your point of view changes, so does your outlook on your friends. You start to confront them about their unhealthy behavior or poor treatment of you. They shrug you off, grow defensive, or accuse you of being too sensitive. They may even try to discourage you from continuing in therapy. They don't like the changes in you because you're disrupting the status quo.

Changing Triggers Conflict

A big part of being in therapy is learning to refrain from unhealthy habits and toxic relationships. As you start to make healthier choices, friends who embrace unhealthy habits will feel threatened or rejected by you. After all, you changed, they didn't. The new you is a challenge to them.

The top five reasons your friends reject the new you:

1. **You're more assertive.**

   In the past, your friends cancel plans on you, didn't include you in gatherings, and rarely showed appreciation for your support. Up until now, you didn't even think you deserved better treatment. Now, their thoughtlessness is unacceptable, even offensive. When you confront them, they feel attacked rather than accepting responsibility for their actions. They reject your claims and cling to their old behaviors.

2. **You complain less.**

   Complainers love company. They enjoy dishing the dirt, talking behind others' backs, finding blame, or sulking about the unfairness of life. There was a time when you supported such habits. That time has passed. You don't enjoy complaining anymore. You find their bitter, self-serving rants exhausting. When you confront them, there is a backlash against you. Complainers hate positive, proactive people, and you're becoming one of them.

3. **You're not interested in drug/alcohol-fueled parties.**

   Friendships built around partying frequently fall apart when one friend stops relying on drugs and alcohol to have fun. Rather than support your healthy decision, they accuse you of being uptight, dull, or old. They mock your healthy lifestyle.

4. **You crave deeper connections.**

   Your authentic voice is growing, and you crave more intimacy. You're unsatisfied by shallow surface talk. You ask more profound questions and ponder weighty issues. You start to find conversations with your friends less satisfying. Your friends accuse you of becoming too serious.

5. **Your personal values change.**

   You've become interested in changing careers and doing more rewarding work. You want more than a paycheck; you want to feel your work is of value. You're less driven by materialism and more attracted to social issues. Your friends accuse you of growing snobbish and self-serving.

Friends Who Grow Together Stay Together

Therapy awakens a hunger for a better life and healthier relationships. Embracing that hunger may cause you to reevaluate your relationships. The reality is not all relationships pass the test of time. If your friends reject the positive changes in you, it's time to find new friends.

Want to Be a Therapist? 5 Signs You'd Be Great at It

These are personality traits every therapist needs.

For nearly 25 years, people in my office have shared their secrets, fears, and hopes. They've confessed wrongs, explored love and relationships, worked through childhood traumas, pondered dreams and nightmares; some lasted a few sessions, others stayed for years.

Occasionally, a person asks me, "How could you spend your life listening to people complain? I could never do it." They're correct—that statement alone proves that person would likely be a sub-par therapist.

If you're thinking of becoming a therapist, here are five essential personality traits that you'll need:

1. You're a people person.

You enjoy time with people, feel energized by emotional exchanges, and are interested in people's backgrounds. You relish a hearty laugh and a good cry. You delight in hearing stories and sharing a close bond with others. Even if you're shy, intimate talks invigorate you.

2. You're a good listener.

You're the designated "therapist" in your social group. Friends tell you their secrets and seek out your advice and counsel. No doubt it's because you're a good listener. This skill is the bedrock of therapy—not advice, analysis, or guidance. People trust and open up to good listeners. When people feel heard and understood, healing begins.

3. You think analytically.

You're fascinated with human behavior and question what makes people tick. You love a good mystery and enjoy piecing together clues about individuals. You take note of character traits and have an excellent memory for detail.

4. You're an altruist.

You enjoy helping people. That's right—you're a do-gooder. Helping people recharges you, gives your life meaning, and boosts your self-esteem. Social justice is also a keen interest. When you give to others, you give to yourself as well.

5. You may have struggled with anxiety or depression.

Many worry that their mental health challenges preclude them from becoming a therapist. But believe it or not, your struggles are welcome here. Many of the best therapists (but not all, of course) have battled mightily with their own emotional problems. Often, their therapy awakened a wish in them to be a therapist. Struggling with personal demons can empower you with greater empathy and the ability to identify with others in pain.

The Next Steps

If you have most or all of these qualities, you have the raw materials to become a great therapist. You can hone these talents into a profession you'll love with the proper training.

These days, there's a therapy for everything: drama therapy, dance therapy, art therapy, etc. First, figure out what kind of therapist you want to be. What area interests you? Next, consider the folks you want to work with: children, teenagers, or adults? Couples, families, or groups? Community building or traditional social work?

Your Guide to Mental Health Professionals

Social workers, psychiatrists, and psychologists are all therapists. So how do they differ? They have vastly different training and unique specialties. Here's a glance at their specifications:

- **Clinical social workers** have master's degrees in social work and are generally trained in empowerment and advocacy. Social workers take a practical approach to problem-solving through talk therapy, counseling, or group work.

- **Psychiatrists** have medical degrees and can prescribe medication. For example, if someone were considering antidepressants or medications for anxiety, they would likely visit a psychiatrist.

- **Psychologists** have doctoral degrees and engage in testing and evaluations, such as neuropsychological evaluations. For instance, working with children may help identify learning differences, such as dyslexia and attention deficit disorder. They also may engage in research.

There are other licensed or masters-level therapists, such as Marriage and Family Therapists, Licensed Professional Clinical Counselors, or Credentialed Alcoholism and Substance Abuse Counselors, a certification that doesn't require a college degree.

States often have different requirements and names for each profession. To find the right path, read up on the other helping professions in your area. Talk to someone in the field or attend a lecture or workshop. Alternatively, volunteer in an organization you like or sign up for a class. You'll know pretty quickly if this profession is for you.

A Life in Therapy

Loving your profession is a blessing. It adds years to your life and life to your years. Every day, I look forward to seeing my patients. I strive to understand them; I celebrate their progress; I feel upset when they suffer. In session after session, we examine their lives like puzzle pieces on a tabletop and fit them together so they can start to feel whole again.

Ultimately, the goal of therapy isn't about changing people. It's about helping people to reconnect with their true selves. It's about healing injuries and building trust. It's about crafting healthier relationships and living more fully in the present. These are the actual goals of therapy: helping people become healthier, stronger, and more empowered.

If this sounds like an exciting way to make a living—what are you waiting for?

When Therapists and Patients Fall in Love

Freud wrote "Analysis is, in essence, a cure through love." What did he mean?

After such cozy and intimate attention, many people wonder, "Are my therapist and I falling in love?"

Love in the Therapy Office

Hollywood filmmakers and writers of romantic novels seem to cherish scandalous stories in which therapists break professional boundaries and fall madly in love with their patients. Perhaps, since traditional therapists can seem somewhat scholarly and detached, it's fun to imagine them dropping their guard and acting with breathless, unrestrained passion.

All that makes for thrilling erotic fantasies; even Shakespeare enjoyed a good forbidden love story. However, in real life, therapists are forbidden from engaging in sexually inappropriate behaviors with their patients. I recently spoke with Lisa Grover, founder of Surviving Therapy Abuse and an outspoken advocate for people who have been abused by their therapist. On the website, Lisa bravely shares her experience of sexual abuse by her former therapist. Lisa is also a volunteer with TELL, an online support group. If you've had a similar experience, visit TELL's website, TherapyAbuse.org, for resources, help, and support.

Romantic Love vs. Loving Acceptance

When Freud wrote, "Psychoanalysis is, in essence, a cure through love," he didn't mean therapists should have affairs with their patients. However, many of his colleagues did, causing him to issue strict rules regarding professional boundaries. Due to its enormous healing powers, Freud implied that love is central to the therapist/patient alliance.

For example, many people report conflicts in their relationships with their parents. Often, these conflicts originate from a lack of loving acceptance from their parents or caretakers. These primitive, unsatisfying experiences leave people feeling incomplete. Such gaps in loving acceptance can remain with them throughout their lives, resulting in problematic relationships and difficulties with intimacy. For example:

- A woman who didn't feel loved by her parents may have trouble trusting or being intimate with others.
- A man who felt neglected by his father may have difficulty maintaining loving friendships with men.
- A youth who feels rejected by his family may also find romantic relationships unfulfilling.

People who grew up feeling unloved struggle mightily with giving or accepting love. They also find it difficult to love themselves.

In such cases, the love and understanding they receive from their therapist can fulfill those unmet needs. Such loving acceptance also translates into feeling understood, valued, and cared for, feelings they yearned for but were denied.

Therapists and Their Feelings

In addition to love, therapists are bombarded with all kinds of feelings, such as hate, yearning, rage, or despair. Learning to manage such dynamic and often erratic emotions is essential. But before therapists can help their patients, they have to help themselves.

Experienced therapists spend years in their own therapy, two or three times a week, in addition to group therapy, supervision, and post-master training programs. They are taught to scrutinize their personal history, analyze and dissect life events, and pour over the intricacies of their relationships. In the process, they become skilled at experiencing, investigating, analyzing their feelings, and enhancing their sensitivity. In my training seminars for therapists, I always ask therapists to reflect on their personal experiences of love and acceptance.

Ongoing personal analysis is essential for therapists. Being an effective therapist requires stepping into the patient role. An unceasing commitment to personal growth and self-understanding allows therapists to offer the authentic, curative, and nurturing relationships many people need to heal.

Beyond the Session

Like an attentive parent, therapists offer acceptance and understanding while modeling a respectful, loving rapport. Masterful therapists don't encourage dependency; they inspire people to seek more rewarding relationships outside of their sessions and achieve greater intimacy and emotional well-being in all areas of their lives.

---

5 Signs You Have the Wrong Therapist

Doubt the value of therapy? Maybe your therapist is the problem.

- They rushed into therapy without interviewing different therapists.
- They didn't get a referral from a reliable source, such as a friend or colleague.
- They hired the cheapest therapist (and got what they paid for).

The attunement between a therapist and a patient is vital to success, so taking your time to find the right person is crucial. You have many options if you can pay out of pocket; there's no need to rush. Take your time and interview at least three before choosing one.

If you're lucky enough to have good insurance, work through that long list of providers. Yes, it's frustrating, but it's well worth it. Be patient and find a therapist you can trust and open up to.

If you're broke and have no insurance benefits for therapy, search for local mental health clinics, hospitals, or training institutes. Whenever I provide clinical training seminars in such places, I'm always impressed by their quality of care. Even with a low fee, you still have the selection process on your side.

5 Signs Your Therapy Is Going Nowhere

If you're in therapy and discouraged with the results, here are some warning signs that you're probably working with the wrong therapist.

1. You don't look forward to your sessions.

Your session is a high point in your week when therapy is working best. You leave your therapist's office feeling invigorated by insights motivated for change. Naturally, sometimes sessions can be sluggish or dull. But if this is the majority of the time, there's a problem.

Therapy is a growth experience. Even when it is painful, it should be empowering. If you find yourself chronically bored, confront your therapist and tell him you want to get more out of your sessions. If nothing changes, pack up and spend your money elsewhere.

2. You don't feel challenged.

Many patients complain that their former therapists were too passive and never said anything. Naturally, every good therapist needs to be a good listener—but there's more to therapy than listening. A good therapist confronts challenges and inspires you to make new choices. Therapy should encourage you. If your therapist is too passive and unresponsive, move on. Therapy should never be a snoozefest. If you're bored, chances are your therapist is too.

3. You don't quarrel with your therapist.

A therapist who always agrees with you may feel good, but you won't see much progress. Bottom line: Therapists are not paid friends. You don't hire them to enable you or passively listen to you vent. For therapy to work well, you and your therapist should occasionally clash. The patient/therapist relationship works best when you express a full range of feelings toward your therapist: affection, irritation, admiration, and even hate. Such a dynamic, active relationship is the hallmark of sound therapy.

4. You don't see any growth in your life.

Why keep going to therapy if you don't see the payoff in your daily life? There has to be some kind of positive emotion, such as better relationships, more confidence, and less depression or anxiety. If you see no change or growth from therapy, something's seriously out of whack that your therapist needs to address.

5. Your therapist isn't a good role model.

Is your therapist expressive and engaging, or dull and passive? Therapists need to be good role models for their patients. Even if your therapist reveals nothing, you can sense if he practices what he preaches. A lot of therapists suffer from depression. If they can't cure themselves, how could they possibly cure you?

CHAPTER 11:
RELATIONSHIPS

What Is 'Toxic Caretaking'?

Passively or actively enabling a friend or loved one's destructive choices.

Caretakers are a thoughtful and generous lot, ready to lend a hand, especially for a friend in need.

- *Need a ride to the airport?*
- *Someone to watch your pet?*
- *Want to borrow a few bucks until payday?*

No worries! The caretaker will be there. Empathic, loyal, kind, dedicated; what's not to like? After all, who doesn't love to be cared for?

When Caretaking Turns Toxic

Recently, a young man who struggles with addiction confessed that his father was supplying him with drugs. This was particularly shocking because his father was paying for his therapy sessions and expressed concern about his drug dependency.

When confronted, the father became enraged and defended enabling his son's addiction:

"At least I know the drugs that I'm giving him are clean. Safer than the drugs he would buy on the street!"

In a way, he was right. The drugs may have been safer, but was supporting his son's addiction the best way to help him?

Sadly, as the young man's dependency increased, the father couldn't keep up with his son's demands for more drugs. After the young man survived a near-fatal overdose, his father came to his senses and enrolled him in rehab.

I genuinely believe the father thought that he was helping his son. But in the long run, like all toxic caretakers, he did more harm than good.

Signs of Toxic Caretaking

Unlike bad friends, toxic caretaking can be challenging to spot because the caretakers frequently appear loving and generous. Furthermore, toxic caretaking often yields short-term benefits.

What's behind the toxic caretaker's decisions? Most often, their decisions are driven by fear. Rather than face the fallout of confronting someone about their behavior, the toxic caretaker chooses to support it. They choose comfort over growth for themselves and the person they care for.

Toxic caretaking behaviors include:

- *Lying to protect a loved one or friend from negative consequences.*
- *Not confronting a loved one or friend about their negative behaviors.*
- *Passively or actively enabling a friend or loved one's destructive choices.*
- *Disregarding detrimental outcomes for fear of retaliation.*

Toward Healthy Caretaking

A healthy caretaker isn't afraid to confront a friend or loved one about their negative behaviors. It may be difficult, but ultimately, it's a growth choice for both individuals.

Healthy caretaking behaviors include:

- *Enabling and applauding a friend or loved one's positive choices.*

CHAPTER 11: RELATIONSHIPS

- *Supporting a friend or loved one's growth even during challenging times.*
- *Pointing out destructive behaviors.*
- *Expressing love and affection freely without ulterior motives.*

In the end, confronting a friend or loved one about their poor choices isn't rude or mean; it's an act of love.

---

3 Ways That Grudge-Dumping Destroys Relationships

... and 5 better ways to manage frustration.

Frustration is unavoidable in any relationship, particularly with close friends or romantic partners. The space between people will always be fertile ground for miscommunication and misunderstanding. It would be unthinkable for even the healthiest intimate relationship not to experience intense frustration or hurtful moments.

But before you read any further, take a moment and answer this question:

When you feel wronged by someone, do you store up frustration or process it with the person and resolve it?

Take your time. The answer to this question ultimately determines whether you can sustain healthy intimacy.

Common Responses to Frustration

Since frustration is a natural part of any relationship, let's consider three typical responses to it:

1. **Ghosting.** Ghosting is one of the most common responses when things go wrong. If a relationship becomes frustrating or anxiety-producing, the ghoster will flee without explanation. Ghosters claim they didn't want to hurt the person. Ironically, ghosting is one of the most hurtful things you can do to someone you have been intimate

with. Ultimately, the ghoster protects themselves, not the person they ghosted.

2. **Blame-Shifting.** Blame-shifters find a reason to end a relationship without a confrontation. They may blame society, their family, or their childhood. They may even blame themselves (*"It's not you, it's me"*). Their goal is to let a person down gently; ultimately, blame-shifting is most often permission to be cruel without consequence.

3. **Grudge-Collecting.** On the surface, grudge collectors appear to be people-pleasers: quick to smile, always willing to accommodate, and the last to provoke a confrontation. But beware: Behind their tense grin may be a loaded gun, and each bullet a stored-away grudge aimed directly at you. Whether they ghost you or shift blame, the outcome is the same: The relationship will end badly.

The Grudge Dump

Unrelieved frustration can morph into epic grudges and resentments, which, when stored away, gather in strength and toxicity. As pressure builds, even the most simple misunderstandings can trigger explosive responses:

- *You were late...again.*
- *You didn't return my texts...again.*
- *You were insensitive...again.*

Grudge-dumpers are usually at the end of their rope; their patience has run out. Because the unrelieved pressure is so significant, they feel justified in dumping their grudges in the form of temper tantrums, explosive arguments, or words designed to produce maximum hurt.

Most shockingly, grudge-dumpers feel *justified* in inflicting harm. While grudge-dumping offers some relief to themselves, the discharge is so toxic that it frequently damages relationships beyond repair.

5 Ways to Better Manage Frustration in Relationships

1. **Speak up early.** Don't store frustration. Address it early, and it can strengthen intimacy rather than destroy it.

2. **Write a letter.** Letter writing allows you to sort out your feelings and be mindful of how you express yourself. If you're worried about your tone, you may want to have a friend read it before the letter is delivered.

3. **Find a mediator.** A mediator, professional, or good friend who can mediate a conflict could bring greater clarity and direction. Most importantly, they can guide you toward mutually acceptable resolutions.

4. **Join a group.** Group therapy is the best treatment for strengthening communication skills, boundary setting, and establishing healthy intimacy.

5. **Accept responsibility.** If you wronged someone, don't be stubborn; apologize and set the tone for a healthy reconciliation. Take the initiative. Mistakes are natural; processing them thoughtfully together will ultimately bring you closer.

When Sexual Attraction and Hate Collide

5 reasons why you may experience sexual attraction and hate simultaneously.

First impressions are powerful. The moment you come into contact with someone, you may have any number of responses: You may instantly like or dislike them, feel annoyed by them, or feel drawn to them. This list is seemingly endless.

To complicate matters, sometimes powerful emotions collide. You may find yourself hating someone while feeling attracted to them simultaneously; such cognitive dissonance can pack quite a punch.

How do you know which feeling to trust when hate and attraction collide?

The origin of hate in attraction

If you hate someone you're attracted to, the conflict will likely spring from your history, particularly past intimate relationships with family, friends, colleagues, or lovers.

When someone hurts you, that hurt lives inside you. The more painful the experience, the more likely you will transfer those feelings onto others. This psychological defense is known as "transference" — transferring a feeling you have for one person onto another.

The less you know about someone, the more vulnerable you are to transference reactions, which have the potential to distort reality and color your view of relationships.

For instance, I worked with a patient whose girlfriend in high school hurt him deeply. Unsurprisingly, as an adult, he tended to distance himself from women he found attractive and developed a resistance to intimacy. He carried that bitter experience from his childhood into his adult relationships and transferred the feeling of hurt onto women that he found attractive. Avoiding relationships kept him from being hurt again but left him lonely.

Another patient confessed that she viewed all men as potential abusers. Her history of trauma started with her abusive father and led to relationships with abusive men; who could blame her, considering men with distrust?

Why you may hate someone you find attractive

If you feel attraction and hate simultaneously, chances are there's an underlying discomfort you're not acknowledging. Rather than exploring the source of your discomfort, you may blame the other person for it, hate them, or avoid them entirely. Here are some possible reasons why you may hate people you feel attracted to:

1. **You fear rejection.** You're afraid that the other person will reject you, so you reject them first, a preemptive strike to avoid the anticipated hurt of being turned down.

2. **You distrust your attraction because of past trauma.** Trauma has a powerful effect on how we experience others. Trusting an unknown person is a real challenge for

someone who has experienced a hurtful relationship or childhood trauma.

3. **You don't want to suffer again.** If your last intimate relationship ended badly, you're likely to feel skeptical of new people that you find attractive. You may keep your distance or even treat them coldly. We tend to protect areas of our body that have been wounded. It is the same with feelings of vulnerability.

4. **You feel insecure about your appearance.** Sometimes, when people feel an attraction to someone, they have the impulse to run and hide. They may feel shy, overwhelmed, or angry at the person for "making them" uncomfortable. At the core of the conflict are social insecurity and low self-esteem.

5. **You think attractive people are arrogant and feel superior.** I've worked with several fashion models who reported that they frequently experience hostility from strangers. Such reactions may spring from people feeling competitive with them or jealous of the attention that they are receiving.

Breaking Free of Transference

It's natural to have transference reactions to others based on your history, but you don't have to be stranded there. Cycling through the same adverse transference reactions doesn't promote growth or leave you feeling good about yourself.

The key to breaking free of transference lies in examining and understanding your emotional responses to others. By understanding the origins of reactions, you can make empowered choices and break free of negative relationship patterns.

While individual therapy can help you to unravel your transference reactions and understand your history, group therapy is far more effective at helping you to navigate intimate relationships, set healthy boundaries, and remain true to your authentic self.

---

3 Ways 'Ghosting' Undermines Your Emotional Health

How ghosting sabotages intimacy and forfeits growth.

Unfortunately, "ghosting" continues gaining popularity, particularly on social media platforms and dating apps. You know the routine: you participate in a virtual conversation, it seems to be going well, and suddenly—poof!—the other person goes silent, disappearing into cyberspace and leaving you wondering: *"What happened?"*

Ghosting can happen in established relationships as well. For example, a young woman in one of my weekly therapy groups was ghosted by a man she had been dating for months. *"He stopped responding to my texts or calls,"* she shared with her group, *"I feel so humiliated."*

The emotional wreckage caused by ghosting

Ghosting is a cruel and cowardly way to dissolve any relationship, a fear-driven choice that causes the ghostee to endure waves of hurt, insecurity, and self-doubt. Rather than confront complicated feelings, the ghoster abandons the relationship and flees like a frightened child. As a result, he remains emotionally immature, preferring to run and hide rather than confront his uncomfortable feelings.

Sadly, many ghosters defend their choices by saying they didn't want to "hurt the other person," a bogus claim since ghosting causes such profound pain. It's downright delusional to think that abandoning someone without an explanation is an act of kindness.

How ghosting hurts you

Emotional maturity in relationships is driven by successfully confronting and resolving frustration. Each time you assert yourself and work through frustration with a partner or friend, intimacy grows, trust strengthens, and the relationship becomes fortified to weather all kinds of challenges.

Ghosting undermines emotional maturation by abandoning frustration rather than confronting it. When people rely on ghosting to avoid conflict, they likely develop a chronic fear of intimacy.

Here are three ways ghosting is hurting you:

1. Ghosting Fosters Emotional Immaturity

It takes a long time to establish healthy intimacy with others. You must work through frustration, miscommunication, misunderstandings, and hurt feelings. You need to develop these communication tools to sustain lasting intimacy.

2. Ghosting Lowers Resilience

The process of getting close is rarely smooth sailing. It requires a degree of emotional resilience to stay connected when the going gets tough. Ghosting weakens connections, resulting in fragile and unstable relationships.

3. Ghosting Damages Self-Esteem

Ghosters are rarely proud of their choices. As they continue to abandon others, their self-worth plummets. They feel guilty and ashamed. As a result, they are more likely to suffer bouts of depression and loneliness.

Five ways to break your ghosting cycle

1. Be honest with yourself

If you feel the urge to ghost someone, identify the feelings that you're having. Trepidation? Irritation? Fear? Tune into those feelings and explore them.

2. Analyze your feelings

Locate the source of these feelings. Are they projections? Are they a result of past trauma or anxiety about the future? Do you have a pattern of fleeing relationships?

3. Share your feelings

Process your feelings with a friend or therapist. If you want to challenge this pattern, group therapy is the best modality for resolving intimacy issues by providing a place to work through the fear and conflicts that emerge in relationships.

4. Be transparent

Once you have gained better self-understanding, instead of fleeing, share your thoughts and feelings with your friend or partner. Be assertive and mindful of emotions, and show respect for the relationship.

5. Avoid being impulsive

Contain the impulse to run—don't act on it! Get comfortable with discomfort and focus on listening and sharing. Learning to process and express complicated feelings directly, strengthens your authentic self and fosters more mature and rewarding relationships.

Why Romantic Relationships Won't Fill Your Emptiness

Depending on romantic relationships to heal you always backfires.

The secret to happy romantic relationships is straightforward: Start by being happy alone.

You may view this as an oversimplification, but I've spent over 25 years as a group psychotherapist, studying how people manage their feelings in relationships and exploring communication styles. I can assure you of this: Nothing predicts the demise of a relationship faster than solely depending on your partner to fill the sense of emptiness you feel inside.

What causes a feeling of emptiness in romantic relationships?

"Emptiness" is often a symptom of unresolved pain. For example, an emotional wound was left unhealed somewhere in your past relationships. Such wounds are often caused by someone intimately close, such as a parent, a sibling, a friend, or a lover.

The delicate process of understanding the source of such pain is challenging. Many people deny it and seek "solutionships," i.e., a partner who will make it disappear. The expectation that a romantic partner will fill the emptiness you feel may provide for an exciting honeymoon period, but the relationship won't endure in the long term.

Unpacking that feeling of emptiness begins with exploring the unresolved pain, investigating what part of your history needs deeper understanding, and working to heal yourself. Ultimately, this is the ideal preparation for any healthy romantic relationship.

Common Mistakes of "Solutionships"

Here are common misfires that many folks make when they expect a romantic relationship to meet all their needs:

1. Confusing "relationship issues" with "self-issues."

If you suffer from anxiety or depression, a new romantic relationship may drive those symptoms into dormancy, but those feelings will eventually resurface. Like a house built on a faulty foundation, the relationship will be unstable when one person in a relationship ignores their emotional issues. Perhaps one of the most common mistakes people make in romantic relationships is blaming their partner for self-issues, i.e., issues that existed before the romantic relationship began.

For example, many people remain in unhealthy relationships because they can't tolerate being alone. To them, loneliness is evidence that they are unloveable. But rather than spend time understanding how to be a better company for themselves, they seek comfort from others and cling to them for relief. This explains why many people may stay in unhealthy relationships (even when they know they deserve better).

2. Weighing down your partner with excessive expectations.

We bring our unmet childhood needs into our romantic relationships. Frequently, we hope that a new partner will fill those needs. Like a small child crying for attention and love, we may demand our partner give us all the attention and love our parents failed to provide. This puts an excessive burden on a romantic partner. With such high expectations, your partner will feel burdened and weighed down by your neediness. They soon feel they can never satisfy you, no matter how hard they try.

3. A chronic need for validation fosters unhealthy dependency.

It's natural for people in romantic relationships to seek validation from each other. We all want to feel understood by those close to us. However, a chronic need for validation is symptomatic of placing too much of your self-worth on a relationship. As Buddhist peace advocate Daisaku Ikeda writes, "Nobody defines your self-worth but you."

An endless need for validation will eventually weigh down your partner and drain the joy out of any romantic relationship. If you want to be blessed with a healthy romantic relationship, start by blessing yourself.

Why Seeking Unconditional Love Can Destroy Relationships

Distrust, anxiety, and even illness.

Friends and family warned you and coworkers and colleagues expressed concern, yet you can't see what they see: the person you're in love with isn't good for you–you refuse to believe it.

How did this happen? How did your vision become so clouded?

A Brief History of Unconditional Love

In human relationships, love is a force like no other; it is the beating heart of our most incredible memories, the glue that binds us to others, the fuel that drives our passions, and the comfort that soothes us.

For most people, the earliest experiences of love are of being held in an all-encompassing embrace. Think of an infant cradled in her mother's arms, completely safe and protected. That unconditional love is intoxicating; it's an emotion like no other.

This is where things get complicated.

Longing for Unconditional Love

Sometimes, we seek to recapture that early feeling of unconditional love in our romantic adult relationships. This may be especially true if you felt deprived of love during childhood.

When you doggedly seek unconditional love, you can start to cling to the desperate notion that if someone loves you unconditionally, your life will be perfect; all needs will be met, and you will feel complete. Unfortunately, the media and popular culture promote this idolized view of love.

As the yearning for unconditional love grows, it pressurizes a relationship and puts it under stress; your vision and judgment become distorted.

When Unconditional Love Becomes an Obsession

Craving unconditional love can destabilize you and flood you with uncertainty and confusion. Soon, you stop thinking clearly and close your eyes to red flags and the warning signals of an unhealthy relationship. In other words, you don't see the person in front of you; you know the person you *want to* see.

The quest for unconditional love springs from primal hunger and projections; for this reason, it nearly always ends badly. Like a house built on a weak foundation, no relationship can withstand the weight of such enormous expectations.

Ultimately, a desperate desire for unconditional love masks a profound lack of self-love.

Why Seeking Unconditional Love Is Bad for Relationships

No relationship is smooth sailing. But when your want of unconditional love is unmet, chances are you will react in the following three ways:

1. **Distrust.** You constantly badger your partner for proof of their love. Yet no matter how they try, you find a reason to distrust them. To manage your fears, you may double down on controlling behaviors, such as tracking or interrogating your partner.

2. **Anxiety.** You continually feel hurt and confused by your partner's choices; you start to doubt your judgment, and soon, your anxiety skyrockets. You feel rejected and abandoned when your partner attempts to set boundaries or asks for space.

3. **Illness.** The quest for unconditional love can make you physically sick. Headaches, backaches, insomnia, and a host of psychosomatic symptoms can result when you feel let down or disappointed in your partner. Such

ongoing emotional strain can damage your mental and physical health.

Breaking Free of the Unconditional Love Dilemma

The best way to find a loving relationship is to start with a loving relationship with yourself. Rather than seeking a partner to complete you, complete yourself by practicing self-care and developing your interests and passions. And if you feel stuck in relationships, group therapy is an excellent choice. All these self-care efforts will strengthen your sense of identity and self-worth so you won't develop an unhealthy dependency on your partner to meet all your emotional needs.

Remember, falling in love is easy; sustaining love is hard. True love takes time and patience to nurture. Demanding unconditional love, particularly too soon in a relationship, is a choice that is bound to end in regret.

Growing Up Without Healthy Emotional Boundaries
Intimacy feels suffocating and terrifying.

No parent sets out to sabotage their child's development. But when a parent fails to provide healthy emotional boundaries, they unwittingly cause lasting damage to their children's ability to trust others and embrace intimacy.

Separation, individuation

As children mature, they naturally seek independence. From the moment they learn to walk, they delight in autonomy. Parents with healthy emotional boundaries become cheerleaders for their children as they strive for independence. They applaud their children's efforts, celebrate their unique voices, and praise their talents.

This process, known as separation-individuation, is vital to a child developing a strong sense of self.

When a parent doesn't support separation, individuation

Unfortunately, many parents who experienced emotional neglect in their childhood are often saddled with unmet emotional needs. Long after childhood, they continue to struggle with feeling incomplete and unappreciated.

Parents may affix their yearning for unconditional love to their children to resolve those gaps in their development. In a strange turn of events, they seek their child's adoration, approval, and affection.

During early childhood, when their child is very young and relies on them, they feel nourished by the child's dependence. However, as their child enters the separation-individuation phase and craves more freedom, such parents start to feel rejected by their child. To quell their anxiety, they discourage their child's efforts toward independence; they want to keep them attached.

Rather than celebrate separation-individuation, such parents see it as a threat. They feel abandoned and betrayed by their child and start to criticize, shame, or guilt their child.

Sadly, their parent's emotional demands crush the joy of independence. The child feels held hostage, burdened, and weighed down. Such children are frequently described by adults as "old souls" when the reality is that their parent's emotional neediness shortened their childhood and caused them to grow up too quickly.

Soon, the child starts to internalize the parent's critical voice and feel ashamed for having their own needs. They're told they're selfish so often that it takes root in their psyche, and they begin to feel guilty for wanting an independent life. Self-doubt plagues them. They develop a profound distrust toward anyone who tries to get close to them. Bouts of depression and social anxiety cling to them.

Such children grow up feeling alone in the world, often preferring to remain isolated rather than taking the risk of getting close to others.

Childhood imprints that endure

Tragically, the parent's critical voice becomes the child's inner voice. The child starts to engage in self-criticism and self-shaming. As an adult, rather than crave intimacy, they reject closeness because it triggers this early traumatic experience with their parents.

Frequently, they accuse their partner of "being needy," undermining or suffocating them. They act destructively in relationships to break free of the "prison of intimacy" they endured in childhood. The phantom of oppression clings to them and undermines their relationships; the closer someone gets to them, the more claustrophobic they feel.

Group Therapy: A Corrective Emotional Experience

In group therapy, a central part of the healing process lies in helping group members learn how to assert and maintain healthy emotional boundaries. The group therapist seeks to foster mature communication between members so that the group relationships can provide a corrective emotional experience. For example, therapists often intervene in the exchanges to provide members with guidance and leadership that they were denied in their childhood.

Group therapy helps members master the central tasks needed to establish healthy emotional boundaries, such as:

1. Dismantling fear-based decision-making.
2. Asserting needs maturely.
3. Respecting their own and their partner's wants.
4. Containing destructive impulses.
5. Engaging emotional communication through better attunement.

As group members internalize healthy emotional boundaries, intimacy is no longer threatening. Relationships feel more rewarding. A gravitational shift occurs in their unconscious; they feel more free and hopeful about their relationships. Instead of feeling trapped, they feel liberated.

Why Narcissists Reject Social Distancing

In the age of COVID-19, Narcissists can be dangerous to your health.

These days, simple tasks have become complicated. Face masks, gloves, and jars of hand sanitizer fill our coat pockets or line our closet shelves. Any discomfort caused by these burdensome new accessories is minor compared to catching or spreading the coronavirus.

With all the information and warnings about preventing the spread of COVID-19, why do some people still blatantly ignore CDC recommendations?

The Narcissist in Your Community

Recently, I was struggling to read my shopping list as I pushed a shopping cart through a crowded grocery store. The mask covering my nose and mouth was hot and itchy, my eyeglasses fogged up, and I was trying my best to practice social distancing in the narrow aisles crammed full of anxious shoppers.

That's when I spotted a classic narcissist coming through the crowd. No nose or mouth covering, mindlessly bumping into other shoppers and shimming between people as he bellowed into his cell phone:

"No, I don't want to see that movie... Al Pacino is too old; it's depressing. We'll talk about it tonight... Everyone is coming over around seven. Whatever you bought me, I hope you didn't wrap it in that gaudy paper that you like so much."

That's right, not only was he ignoring all health recommendations, but he was throwing himself a birthday party as well. So much for quarantining.

Communal Thinking is Impossible for Narcissists

Coronavirus spreads quickly and can be deadly depending on your age and health. We've all had to adjust to new social norms to protect the most vulnerable. We've changed our schedules, adapted our behaviors, modified our lifestyles. By thinking communally, we defend ourselves and each other from COVID-19.

Narcissists never think communally. They lack empathy, have an omnipotent view of themselves, and like to believe that they are exempt from social norms. Is it any surprise that they ignore CDC recommendations?

Narcissists Are Emotionally Immature

No matter how intelligent they are, narcissists remain emotionally immature. Like children or teenagers, they find it difficult to put the needs of others before their own. No matter how many times you try to educate them about the power of empathy or altruism, such lessons never stick. Narcissism is an "insight-free" zone. A therapist who's worked with narcissists will tell you how little progress they make in helping them form healthy relationships.

But narcissists aren't always easy to spot. They can be a lot of fun. They can be charming, have a sense of humor, and be very entertaining. Many celebrities, people in politics, and highly successful business leaders likely meet the criteria for narcissistic personality disorder. So what's the problem?

You don't want to have a narcissist for a close friend, a relative, or a boss. They're more likely to abandon you when you're in need, turn against you when you question or doubt them, and ignore you when you're hurt. When narcissists aren't the center of attention, their warm glow of friendship fades quickly.

The Narcissist Test

After spending time with someone that you suspect is a narcissist, ask yourself:

- *Are they draining my energy and leaving me feeling emotionally fatigued?*
- *Are they self-absorbed, constantly seeking praise and attention?*
- *Are they distorting facts to feed their grandiosity?*
- *Are they obsessed with their image?*
- *Are they only interested in me because they want something?*

If you answered yes to three or more of these questions, there's a good chance you're dealing with a narcissist. Narcissists can be more than just annoying; in the age of the coronavirus, they can also be hazardous to your health.

———————

How to Spot a Bad Friend

Are unhealthy friendships holding you back?

The Friends We Choose

It's a long-held belief of psychotherapists that the friends you choose reflect your innermost feelings about yourself. For example, if you don't value yourself, your friends won't. They won't think twice about standing you up, phoning in last-minute cancellations, or forgetting about you entirely. They don't consider your feelings or needs. But don't blame them: They mirror your low opinion of yourself.

Moreover, if you're self-critical or disparaging, expect unsolicited advice, criticism, and discouraging comments. When it comes to friendships, you get what you believe you're worth.

Why You Put Up with Lame Friends

As long as personal insecurities dominate you, so will unhealthy friendships. The more insecure you are, the more likely you will tolerate bogus friendships.

There are three reasons you may think poor treatment from friends is acceptable:

1. Low Self-Esteem. You excuse your friends' lackluster behavior because you don't believe you deserve better.

2. Fear of Loneliness. You harbor fears of abandonment and isolation, so you accept your friends' shoddy conduct.

3. Being a Caretaker. You tend to service others and neglect yourself; caring for others is the only way you feel valued.

The Friend Test

If you repeatedly leave an encounter with a friend feeling discouraged, it's time to ask, "Why am I still friends with this person?"

Try this simple test: After you meet with a friend, take a quick emotional inventory. Ask yourself:

1. Do I feel lighter?

2. Am I encouraged?

3. Do I feel valued?

If you answered yes to all three questions, that friend is a keeper. Suppose you don't, try it again. Remember that even good friends have bad days; give them a pass now and then. But if a friend consistently leaves you disheartened, disappointed, or depressed, they fail the good friend test. Let's move on.

Friends Who Grow Together, Stay Together

No one likes the idea of a jettisoned friendship, mainly if it's an old friend. Yet, sometimes friendships expire. Priorities transform as you mature. You may no longer be compatible. For instance, a new dad may quickly find that he has little in common with his high-school drinking buddies.

Only when friends evolve and grow together do friendships withstand the test of time. A true friend is a constant source of inspiration, someone you can always turn to for support, someone who will champion you.

So, if your friends are leaving you feeling unappreciated and neglected, put them to the test. Challenging your friends is not a crime, but staying in unhealthy relationships should be.

How to Make Love Last

Love fading too fast? 5 key skills for keeping love fresh.

Why do some couples remain madly in love while others see love fade fast from their relationship?

If you think those couples are lucky, think again. Luck eventually runs out. Short-term love is easy; long-term love requires dedication and commitment. But the benefits are mind-blowing.

For example, loving couples in long-term relationships experience significant health gains. Studies have shown that the happily married (not just married — *happily married*) live longer than single or divorced people, with lower rates of heart disease due to less stress, healthier diets, and improved cancer survival rates.

So before you blame fate or your partner for your loveless love life, here are a few qualities that loving couples share, regardless of how long they have been together.

1. Sex

According to a 2018 report by CBS News, research conducted with 30,000 people in three different studies found that couples who have sex at least once a week score higher on life satisfaction and happiness. Sex scores higher than money in determining mutual happiness. Affection beyond the bedroom and PDA, such as holding hands, hugging, kissing hello and goodbye, and saying "I love you" regularly, also helps couples stay present and feel valued by their partner.

2. Communication

What is the number-one reason for divorce? Poor communication. According to the American Academy of Matrimonial Lawyers, the number-one cause of failed marriage (67.5 percent to be exact) is a breakdown in communication. When communication fails, the relationship follows. Working together to polish your communication ultimately strengthens your identity as a couple and reduces misunderstandings and hurt feelings.

3. Separate Passions

Depending entirely on your partner for happiness isn't recommended or sustainable. Couples with separate passions are less likely to become enmeshed or codependent. They inspire one another, cheerlead each other, celebrate each other's victories, and grieve each other's losses. Separate passions also give couples a break from each other, making time together more special. Plus, your partner has a chance to miss you, which will make them value you more.

4. Equal Rights

Sharing household responsibilities and dividing up chores may seem mundane, but cancerous resentments take root without an equal balance in a household. When this happens, someone becomes a nag or a complainer and feels more like a parent than a partner. This dynamic, left unresolved, will sour any partnership.

5. Arguing Well

Conflict is inevitable in any relationship. Knowing how to argue well means not hitting below the belt, not attacking your partner's character, and not abandoning your partner amid a disagreement. Generally speaking, fear drives most arguments between couples: fear of intimacy, abandonment, and betrayal. Putting these fears into words and sharing your insecurities will defuse arguments quickly and inspire more intimate discussions. Take responsibility for your emotional states; no one will feel blamed or burdened. Couples who can argue well develop a deeper appreciation for their partner — and themselves.

How to Break Free of Unhealthy Romantic Relationships

Who you're attracted to may not be who's best for you.

Popular culture markets a version of romantic love at odds with daily life. Movies and television perpetuate attraction built on "love at first sight" and throw in swelling music and unrestrained passion between naked people who look like Olympic athletes. (*How many of us look like that?*) Too often, this glossy vision of romantic love re-enforces negative relationship patterns. Locking eyes with a sexy stranger from across a crowded room may get your heart racing, but such relationships rarely pan out. Most times, they're disastrous.

The less you know someone, the more you project feelings onto them and imagine them as the person you want them to be. Unconsciously, you close your eyes to red flags and fantasize how they will fulfill your needs. You may think this new person is everything you ever wanted, but chances are they are just an enticing stranger, without more time and honest communication.

Breaking Unhealthy Patterns in Relationships

Frequently, people come to therapy because they're tired of unhealthy relationship patterns. They repeat the same mistakes and cycle through the same dead-end romances. When individual therapy isn't helping, I always recommend one of my therapy groups. Why? Simply put, individual therapy focuses on self-understanding, while group therapy focuses on relationships. You can't beat the power of group to improve the quality of relationships in your life.

In group therapy, you explore the space between you and another person and discover a hidden world of complicated feelings and impulses that most often originate from your history. With a skilled leader's aid, you understand the roots of your attractions and navigate intimate relationships with greater skill and mastery.

How Romantic Illusions Can Doom Relationships

Recently, a young woman in one of the therapy groups realized that she has a history of being attracted to unavailable or emotionally distant men. No matter how "hot and heavy" the relationships began, the men eventually withdrew or "ghosted" her, leaving her confused and abandoned.

As she explored her feelings in group therapy, she became aware that she was raised with a "Prince Charming" view of men. Unconsciously, she believed a man would save her, provide for all her needs, and rescue her from her mundane life. These men, of course, had to be handsome, rich, and passionately devoted to her.

Rather than relate to the man before her, she surveyed his resume and put him through her checklist. As a result, the men she dated felt enormous pressure from her. They didn't feel loved, valued, or understood; they felt the burden of her expectations. Eventually, that burden became too great, and they fled.

As the group helped her come to grips with her unconscious wish to be saved, she realized that her "Prince Charming" philosophy was built on fears and anxieties that she was incomplete without a man, a dependency that devastated her self-esteem. Slowly, as she began to make new choices in relationships, she began to have a more fulfilling romantic life.

Finding the Best Partner for You

Romantic love is a big business. It sells movies, dating apps, music, and books. However, you will have to get real for healthy intimacy and lasting partnerships. Here are five guidelines that will never let you down:

1. **Get to Know the Person First**

   No matter how attractive a person appears, it takes time to get to know someone. Don't rush.

2. **Hold Off on Sex**

   If you're looking for a serious relationship, having sex too soon is a big mistake. Wait, be mindful, and decide whether you want to proceed. Don't be impulsive and regret it later.

3. **Be Your Authentic Self**

   Remember that relationships are hollow without authenticity in a world driven by branding and marketing. Don't accommodate, lie, or hold back your true feelings. Be yourself. If it doesn't work out, it wasn't meant to be. And you won't have sacrificed your integrity.

4. **Lead a Fulfilling Live**

   You take a significant risk if you count on a relationship to deliver meaning and happiness. Bring meaning and joy with you, and you'll have a solid foundation for a healthy relationship.

5. **Stay Present and Grounded**

   Keep your eyes open, listen, and work on communication. When you fall for someone, don't lose yourself in the adrenaline of the moment. Take a deep breath, stay present and focused.

Many successful couples confess to not being initially attracted to their partner. They started as friends or acquaintances. They enjoyed each other's company, had the same sense of humor, and shared values. Gradually, however, romance blossomed. When the quality of the relationship came first, romance followed.

---

3 Reasons Why You Resent Happy Couples

How group therapy can help with resentment.

When you see a happy couple walk down the street, do you feel a rush of resentment? Do such public displays of affection get on your nerves?

Before considering the cause of your resentment, consider this parable I share in my therapy groups that focus on developing healthy relationships. It's about a bird stuck in a cage:

Once upon a time, there was a bird whose cage was in a quiet, shadowy room, the only room the bird had ever known.

Then, one day, the bird's owner, while doing some much-needed house cleaning, decides to move the cage outside.

For the first time, the bird sees other birds flying free. The bird watches them dive through the air, sing and play, wrestle in trees, coo and peck one another. The caged bird immediately feels resentful:

> *"Those birds should be in cages."*

The bird tries to ignore them but finds everything about them vexing.

> *"How shallow and irresponsible they are!"*

Even their lovely singing is torturous to the bird.

> *"I wish they would stop making that noise!"*

Finally, after a long day of cleaning, the owner returns the bird to the dark, shadowy room.

The bird sighs with relief, never questioning the bars or considering the possibility of a life beyond the cage.

When I share this story in group, members always respond incredulously:

- *"The bird doesn't know any better."*

- *"He didn't choose to live in a cage."*
- *"He has no options. It's not his fault."*

True, sometimes we all have cages: schools, jobs, and even our family can sometimes feel like imprisonment. But after we move out into the world, the cages we take with us are of our own making—and the material we use for the bars is fear.

When fear holds us back, we lose passion for life. We bypass the unknown for the familiar, avoid taking chances, and stop exploring new activities or pursuing new dreams. Like the caged bird, we may feel safe, but are we living?

Our cage grows smaller when we vanish into lackluster routines, settle for unfulfilling jobs or unsatisfying relationships, or abandon our dreams. We hunt for scapegoats rather than reflect on our choices and attitudes or consider alternatives. In this way, happy people are always targets for the miserable.

Here are a few confessions I've heard in group therapy sessions:

- *"I hate seeing couples holding hands and smiling."*
- *"When I see couples kissing in the park, I want to kick them."*
- *"I can't stand whenever my friend tells me how much she loves her boyfriend."*

Yes, misery loves company, but why do some resent happy couples so vehemently? Among the top reasons I've observed are:

1. Happy couples represent intimacy that is missing from your life.
2. Happy couples put you in touch with a yearning for a healthy relationship.
3. Happy couples awaken feelings of loneliness.

Though we may gather comfort from judging others, it is a bitter pleasure that never lasts. After nearly 25 years leading therapy groups focused on building healthy relationships, I can tell you this: No one stumbles into a happy relationship without working on themselves. Happiness is something you bring into a relationship, not something bestowed on you by others.

The key is to build a core state of happiness in your life first. It is a painstaking journey, filled with peaks and valleys, but, in the end, only those committed to ongoing growth and self-improvement can savor loving relationships that last.

So next time you find yourself resenting a happy couple, remember the caged bird. Then, push aside your resentment and ask yourself, "How can I get some of that?"

Do You Have a Controlling Personality?

This anxiety-driven defense destroys relationships.

Do you feel betrayed when others don't do what you want? Do you wrestle with trusting people? Have a history of combative relationships?

If you answered yes, you may have a controlling personality. That's right: *You* may be the cause of your biggest interpersonal headaches. But don't worry, *everyone* has some controlling traits. Let's look at their origins and how you can better manage them.

Why We Try to Control Others

High levels of internal anxiety drive the wish to control others. Rather than address those deep-seated fears at their source, controlling people project them onto their relationships, generating emotional pandemonium and instability by making others responsible for their discomfort.

In this way, the impulse to control serves a protective function against feelings of vulnerability, which controlling people associate with powerlessness. This is why they are often vigilant against appearing weak.

All of this makes sustaining intimacy with controlling people challenging because their behavior causes:

1. Escalating conflicts

2. Decreasing trust

3. Ongoing bickering

The Good and Bad News

People with controlling tendencies are frequently successful in their careers. They manage people, meet goals, and are relentlessly goal-driven. In business, they may rise to the top by working hard and surrounding themselves with employees who do their bidding without questioning them.

However, the personal life of a controlling person tends to be a mess. Friendships are volatile, intimacy runs hot and cold, and their relationships are always on trial.

How Do You Develop a Controlling Personality?

Certain parenting styles tend to foster a controlling personality. At the core of these parent-child relationships is a profound lack of attunement. For example:

- Love was conditional and achievement-based. As children, controlling people didn't feel loved until they performed or met their parent's needs.

- Tasks were valued over relationships. The message was that what you produced was more important than who you are.

- Nurturing was unreliable and inconsistent. Children learned to be wary of relying on or trusting others. As a result, they become fiercely independent adults but frequently suffer bouts of intense loneliness.

Driven to Control

Rather than foster cooperation, folks with controlling personalities demand compliance. When denied, they can become punishing and vindictive.

Since they experience relying on others as dangerous, they develop unhealthy defenses against dependency, such as passive-aggressive behavior (guilting, shaming, or withdrawing) and bullying tactics (threats and ultimatums).

Additionally, when conflicts arise, the controlling person may turn paranoid or ruthlessly distort reality to maintain the feeling of being in control.

Controlling Language

Let's take a look at how the controlling person communicates and how it undermines relationships. As you read these statements, pay close attention to the feelings they induce in you.

Controlling statements:

- *"I need you to do this now."*
- *"I didn't ask for your opinion."*
- *"Don't interrupt me."*

These "I-statements" aren't requests; they're *orders*. Orders and imperatives escalate conflict and fuel resistance. Notice that each statement lacks consideration, empathy, and respect.

Here are the same statements with the controlling aspect removed.

Cooperative Statements:

- *"I feel anxious about this. How can we get it done together?"*
- *"I appreciate your opinion. Let's explore the best solution."*
- *"I know you're excited. Let me finish speaking, and then I'd like to hear your ideas."*

The difference between the controlling and cooperative statements is simple: The controlling statements don't value the relationship, while the cooperative statements do. Cooperative statements are built on shared expectations and mutual respect, making people feel recognized and appreciated. Controlling statements make people feel inhibited and resentful.

3 Solutions for the Controlling Personality

If you suspect you have controlling tendencies, here are some tips to consider.

1. *Soften Your Approach.*

   Watch out for whether you're making demands or threats. Explore the situation without blame. Take responsibility for your feelings.

2. *Foster Cooperation.*

   Strive to find common ground. Give and take. Welcome input, and work collaboratively.

3. *Tend to Your Anxiety.*

   Spend time exploring the source of your anxiety without acting on it or projecting it on others. It most likely springs from your history, particularly any trauma related to intimacy or emotional neglect.

   Strive to identify what triggers your wish to control others. Contain the impulse, soothe your anxiety, and you'll find that your relationships will improve dramatically.

How Avoiding Conflict Escalates Conflict in Relationships

Conflict can actually strengthen intimacy.

When faced with a conflict, do you suffer from the Triple As: apologizing, agreeing, and accommodating? Under pressure, are you more likely to compromise or hide your true feelings behind a tense smile or nervous laugh? Afterward, do you find yourself ruminating or losing sleep over the situation?

If you answered yes to any of these questions, conflicts in relationships trigger anxiety in you. You may blank out, feel panic, or be victimized when faced with the slightest disagreement. True intimacy will remain elusive until you learn to work through complicated feelings and accept that differences are healthy in relationships.

What makes conflicts so upsetting? They're messy, stir unwanted feelings, and reawaken old fears and anxieties. For example, when faced with a conflict, your heart may race, and you may tremble or sweat. These bodily

CHAPTER 11: RELATIONSHIPS

reactions often spring from trauma from your past, a dynamic that can make even the most minor conflicts feel paralyzing.

How You Became Conflict-Avoidant

To understand how you became conflict-avoidant, let's take a peek into your past and examine the causes and conditions that foster conflict-avoidant behaviors:

Bullying Parents

When parents are too strict, short-tempered, or practice excessive punishment, they inundate kids with unmanageable anxiety, which leaves emotional scars that don't heal. As adults, conflicts with others reawaken this childhood trauma and can trigger panic reactions such as sweating, shaking, or heart palpitations.

Rather than confront troubling difficulties in your relationships, you turn to childhood defenses such as denial, repression, or depersonalization. To protect yourself, you may remain emotionally distant from others, end relationships abruptly, or abandon friendships without warning. Another extreme reaction is to victimize or demonize others to justify your fears.

Aggressive Peers or Siblings

Antagonistic siblings or peers easily overwhelm vulnerable children. Without an adult to step in and set boundaries, repetitive attacks from siblings or peers cause profound damage to a child's fragile sense of self. As a result, you're more likely to flee from conflict or overreact to it. As a child, you were never given the skills to positively work through conflict with others. Consequently, as an adult, you have few tools at your disposal when relationships get rocky.

An Absent Caretaker

When a loving parent or caretaker isn't available to soothe and calm an anxious child, that child struggles with intimacy and trust. As an adult, when a conflict arises, you're more likely to isolate or retreat. You may appear cold, uncaring, or unreachable, but deep down, you struggle with feelings of emptiness and worthlessness. Few people know the real you because you keep yourself hidden from others.

Working Through Conflicts

Every relationship is bound to hit a few snags. Here are three ways that avoiding conflict causes more conflict in relationships:

1. You hide your true feelings.
2. You store up frustration.
3. You neglect your own needs.

Working through conflict stabilizes your sense of self and boosts your confidence. Most importantly, it brings you closer to others. Here are a few tips to keep in mind:

Speak Up

Commit yourself to speak up when confronted with a conflict or disagreement. Venting to friends via e-mail or posting comments online won't do. You may feel momentary relief, but these options offer little growth and often come off as passive-aggressive. Bring a friend or co-worker if you feel frightened or anxious about confronting someone. Doing everything you can to address the conflict with the person directly is vital.

Make Friends With Conflict

Avoiding conflict cuts off honest communication. Many stress-related illnesses spring from suppressed feelings and bottled-up frustrations. Accept that conflicts and disagreements are inevitable. Be assertive; instead of running from conflicts, run toward them—strive to resolve them in real-time, face to face, rather than ruminating. The more you address conflicts openly with the folks who are frustrating you, the less likely you'll struggle with bouts of depression or loneliness.

Join a Therapy Group

Therapy groups are a great place to improve interpersonal skills, foster greater intimacy with others, and resolve conflicts productively. When it comes to social anxiety or resolving conflict-avoidant tendencies, you can't beat the power of a group.

From Conflict-Avoidant to Conflict-Resilient

The world is a mess because humans don't know how to work through conflicts peacefully. Unlike destructive impulses, which come naturally, the ability to resolve conflicts without resorting to emotional warfare has to be cultivated. Like any skill, it takes work. Learning to talk through conflicts takes courage, but the payoff is worth it: You'll discover new pathways in communication, closeness, and intimacy.

How "Wanting to Be Liked" Get You Rejected

As long as you depend on others for approval, happiness is fleeting.

Do you long to be liked by others? Do you work hard on your friendships, being a good listener, and being understanding and empathic — hoping other people will like you more?

Sadly, when all your energy goes toward pleasing others, you will likely get the opposite in return.

How Approval Seeking Backfires

Rather than being genuine, you labor to create an image you think people will find appealing. In the process, you compromise your authentic self, gradually becoming less honest, less natural, and less "you." The more you hustle for approval, the less others feel at ease with you. They sense something counterfeit in your responses and have trouble trusting you. They may even begin to feel manipulated. All this can make a relationship with you exhausting.

That's why people feel weighed down by approval seekers: their neediness is an energy drain. Sooner or later, they start to avoid you, forget appointments, or not return your phone calls. The very thing you're working so hard for — friendships and close relationships — gets you the opposite. You're left confused and hurt.

Childhood Scars

We all bring our unmet childhood needs into our present-day relationships to heal the emotional wounds we suffered in our past. But our happiness is fleeting as long as we remain dependent on others for approval.

In my psychotherapy practice, I have found that people who long for approval often experience some childhood emotional trauma. They may have suffered verbal abuse, physical abuse, or emotional neglect. Whatever the situation, they didn't feel valued or celebrated for their uniqueness. Instead, they got the message that love was conditional; they had to work hard for it. Being themselves just wasn't enough.

Scratch the surface of approval seekers, and you'll find individuals battling low self-esteem. They don't realize their value, so they seek affirmation from others. Yet whatever comfort they gain doesn't last. No matter how much recognition they receive, soon, they are laboring for validation again.

Healing Emotional Trauma

Taking ownership of your fears and anxieties is the first step toward improving your relationships. Rather than expecting others to heal you, start by healing yourself.

This requires examining the anxiety that fuels your neediness and longing for approval. The more you can deal directly with that anxiety within yourself, rather than trying to work it out through relationships, the more you will begin to heal those old wounds. Unearthing old wounds in individual therapy will help, but it is of little value if you can't apply those lessons in daily life. You're going to need to develop more mindfulness in your interactions.

Start by noticing how you're feeling when relating to others. Ask yourself these five questions:

- Am I genuine?
- Am I working for approval?
- Am I agreeable to avoid conflict?
- Am I reacting genuinely, or am I objectively crafting responses?
- Am I caretaking, or am I responding truthfully?

The more you become aware of the unconscious forces that shape your interactions, the more you can make new choices. This doesn't mean you should start picking fights or spouting self-serving opinions. It means you will begin to speak with your authentic voice. People who are faithful to themselves are far more interesting than approval seekers. Originality is always more attractive and compelling to others.

The Group Therapy Solution

Group therapy is ideal for people struggling with relationship issues because it exposes bad habits more directly than individual therapy. In other words, it empowers your therapist with greater insight into your social dilemmas.

In individual therapy, people report on events, leaving much room for distortion. For example, a person may report feeling victimized but never realize their role in fostering that outcome. Furthermore, therapists may wonder if they are getting an accurate version of events in someone's life when working one-on-one. When an event is reported, there is always the chance for exaggeration or misinterpretation.

In group therapy, therapists get a live demonstration of interpersonal behavior. Group re-creates a social environment, which allows your therapist to see all your bad relationship habits in action.

The golden rule of group therapy is "What happens in group happens in life." In group, negative tendencies that prevent you from having healthy relationships will come to light. Your therapist can then intervene and steer you toward better ways of relating. The thought of joining a therapy group may make you anxious, but when it comes to breaking the approval-seeking habit, it's the express lane to better relationships.

---

3 Questions to Ask Yourself About Every Relationship

3. Do you feel valued by this person?

When personal insecurities dominate you, so will unhealthy relationships. The more insecure you feel about yourself, the more you'll settle for less than you deserve. Three reasons someone may tolerate unhealthy relationships are:

1. **Low self-esteem.** You rationalize a partner's lackluster behavior because you don't believe you deserve better.

2. **Fear of loneliness.** You harbor fears of abandonment and isolation, so you accept friends' shoddy conduct.

3. **You're a caretaker.** You neglect your needs because caring for others is the only way to feel valued.

The Healthy Relationship Test

Try this simple test. After getting together with someone, take this quick three-question emotional inventory:

1. *Do I feel lighter after being with this person?*

2. *Do I feel encouraged?*

3. *Do I feel valued?*

If you can answer yes to all three questions, that relationship is a keeper. Of course, even good friends have bad days; giving them a pass now and then is OK. But it's time to move on if a relationship consistently leaves you feeling disheartened or bogged down with disappointments, dashed expectations, or score-keeping favors.

Friends that Grow Together Stay Together

Only when friends can evolve and grow together will relationships withstand the test of time. A healthy relationship is a constant source of inspiration and a place to always turn to for support—someone who will champion you in a heartbeat.

If a relationship often leaves you feeling unappreciated and neglected, ask yourself how you might be enabling that person's treatment of you. Challenge yourself and speak up. You'll learn that saying "no" to unhealthy relationships opens the door to healthier and more rewarding ones.

———

Craving Love? Improve Your Relationship With Yourself First

Valentine's Day tip: 5 essential traits for healthy intimacy.

One bogus misconception about love—promoted by society, the media, literature, and social media—is that love will solve all your problems. Meet the right person—and poof! You'll find happiness.

Such an idealized view of love as salvation has probably led to more broken hearts than any other.

Love and Relationship Patterns

If you're unhappy in life and expecting romance to save you, chances are:

1. *You're expecting your partner to meet all your needs.*
2. *You're burdening your partner with unrealistic expectations.*
3. *You feel dissatisfied and frequently frustrated by your partner's behavior.*
4. *Your partner feels they can't please you, and you're trying to change them.*
5. *You feel disillusioned and fantasize that a new partner will satisfy you better.*

Seeking romance to cure unhappiness frequently leads to cycling through the same relationship problems with different people. You change partners, but the outcome is the same: You end up alone and disappointed.

The Challenge of Love and Intimacy

Being emotionally intimate with another human being is one of the most challenging tasks in the world. (*If you don't believe me, check the divorce rates.*) What makes intimacy so tricky? Romance is more likely to thrive when each partner demonstrates five essential traits for healthy intimacy:

1. Emotional maturity.
2. Strong communication skills.
3. The capacity to process uncomfortable feelings.

SHORTCUTS TO A HAPPIER LIFE

4. The ability to tolerate frustration without resorting to destructive behavior.

5. A strong sense of self.

What do all these qualities have in common? *You bring them into a relationship.* That means working on yourself and cultivating these traits is one of the best ways to prepare for a healthy and sustainable relationship.

Starting With Self-Love

It's a long-held belief by psychotherapists that your relationships are reflections of your inner life. For example, if you have low self-esteem, your relationships are likely to reflect that. You may avoid conflicts in your relationship and accommodate or neglect your needs.

Why are the five traits for healthy intimacy so crucial? It's because sustaining a relationship with an emotionally immature person is extraordinarily stressful.

Working on yourself—closing the gaps in your maturity, polishing your communication skills, and strengthening your sense of self—is the expressway to improving your relationships.

Developing Strong Relationship Skills

Group therapy is a workout gym for intimacy and closeness. People come to group therapy to learn how to have more satisfying relationships. In group therapy, you learn the language of intimacy, how to express frustration in healthy ways, and how to be more assertive with your wants and needs while maintaining healthy boundaries. As you develop better communication skills and become more emotionally attuned, your relationships in the world also improve.

If you are dissatisfied with your life, invest in yourself instead of swiping left or right—an investment that always pays off.

―――――――――

3 Signs You've Been "Introvert Shamed"

Do you feel like an introvert living in an extrovert's world?

"My whole life, I felt bad about myself. People asked, "Why are you so quiet? Why don't you speak up? Why do you spend so much time alone?" Derek sighed as he spoke to his weekly therapy group.

"My friends said I was boring; my parents called me unmotivated; if there is an unattractive adjective for a quiet person, I was called it."

Derek isn't alone. Introverts are often judged and made to feel ashamed for avoiding the spotlight. Choosing small gatherings or quiet nights over parties shouldn't make anyone feel like a freak. Yet, that's just how introverts are made to feel.

Derek continued: "Being an introvert in an extrovert's world is unfair. Why do people have to be so mean?"

Introverts and extroverts

Unfortunately, the common thinking about introverts and extroverts is overly simplified: Introverts prefer time alone, enjoy quiet self-reflection, and are overwhelmed by large social gatherings. Extroverts despise alone time, avoid self-reflection, and constantly seek social contact for distraction and recharging.

Many of us exhibit qualities of both; sometimes, we feel outgoing and enjoy social contact, choose to seclude ourselves and enjoy being alone. In a perfect world, we would toss aside negative judgments and accept that all people are unique and express ourselves differently.

So why does the introvert remain a social punching bag?

The shaming of introverts

Before we consider why introverts are targeted, here are three signs you've been introvert-shamed by others:

- You were bullied or mocked for being quiet or shy.
- You were guilted into participating in social gatherings.

- You blame yourself for being awkward and different.

The pressure put on introverts to change their behavior always backfires. The pressure only succeeds in causing increased social anxiety.

Why mistreat introverts?

Frequently, extroverts wield social power and crave validation and attention. To them, introverts are downright bizarre; they have such contrasting values. For example, the introvert doesn't seek attention, doesn't crave social validation, and is comfortable being alone, qualities that extroverts find bewildering.

So, what's going on behind the impulse to target an introvert? Here are some possibilities.

People may feel:

- Threatened by the introverts' quietness
- Insecure about their intelligence
- Rejected or ignored by the introvert
- Powerful knowing the introvert won't fight back
- Anxious and uneasy when unvalidated

The power of introverts

The article "The Surprising Benefits of Being an Introvert" outlines some positive qualities introverts possess. Here's a sample of the benefits of being an introvert that the article highlights.

Introverts tend to be:

- Good listeners
- More thoughtful about what they say
- Comfortable observing others
- Good friends
- Loving romantic partners

- Mindful networkers
- Compassionate leaders

Proud to be an introvert

As Derek shared his feelings with his therapy group about being an introvert, other introverts spoke up and shared their feelings as well. They felt less isolated and formed a healing bond by breaking their silence. They began to celebrate the positive qualities of introverts and put to rest the idea that there is a universal standard for social interaction.

CHAPTER 12:
SELF-HELP

The Healing Power of Hate

Is hate ever helpful?

The word "hate" provokes strong responses. Some parents forbid their children from using it; many religions preach against it. But what if hate isn't the problem?

What if the expression of hate can be helpful—and, at times, healing?

Like every complex feeling, it's not "hate" itself that's the problem. What you do with hate determines if its constructive or destructive.

Samantha's Story of Hate Denied

A few years ago, a mother called me and scheduled a therapy session for her daughter, Samantha. She reported that Samatha had fallen into a dark depression.

"She was such a happy-go-lucky child, but since my husband and I divorced, she avoids me and sulks all day in her room."

When Samantha arrived in my office, she sat in stony silence; a dark cloud seemed to float over her head. Samantha's mother was right—she looked miserable.

After a few attempts to engage her, I asked her if her parents' divorce was the cause of her unhappiness. Samantha's mouth stiffened as she jabbed the tip of her sneaker into the carpet. She nodded tensely.

"What do you hate most about it? I promise I won't tell them."

Samantha erupted, "I hate their fighting! I hate that they're yelling! I hate that they expect me to take sides!"

For 40 minutes, hate poured out of her, an endless flow of pure, unfiltered rage. I barely said another word the entire session.

That night, I received an eye-opening phone call from Samantha's mother:

"I don't know what you said to her, but we had the best day in a long time. Samantha was all smiles again. We went shopping, had lunch, and went to the movies together. I can't thank you enough."

The Positive Aspects of Hate

Samantha had every right to feel hateful, but the hate remained inside her until she could express it constructively. It was at the core of her depression. The adage "depression is anger turned against the self" suggests that Samantha's depression wasn't a result of hatred—it was her inability to articulate it.

There are many circumstances in life when hate is an appropriate and necessary response. Civil rights leaders took action because they hated racism and discrimination. The hatred of British oppression drove the American Revolution. The hate of injustice caused nearly every positive social advancement in human society.

Since feelings suppressed or denied become psychic tension seeking release, the goal is not to deny or suppress but to embrace all feelings and convert them into fuel for positive change. In this way, hate is a source of tremendous energy.

Destructive Forms of Hate

The impulse to hate is human; it's impossible to eliminate it. World history is full of tragic stories of people acting savagely on their hate. Perhaps the most damaging forms of hate are scapegoating and discrimination.

Unprocessed hate, bottled up, nearly always grows toxic and erupts in destructive action. Without wisdom and maturity, hatred is hurtful—not only to the person who feels hate but also to those they hate.

The goal is not to oppress hateful feelings but to release them without harming ourselves or others. Psychotherapy welcomes all expressions of emotions; in fact, a significant purpose of therapy is to release trapped feelings that may be causing us discomfort or even mental illness. In this way, love and hate deserve equal attention.

Learning to Love Hate

I had a friend who battled illness his entire life with stoic silence. Recently, I noticed a change in him. He said, "I woke up one morning and decided I hated being sick." He took his hate and waged war against his medical problems. He changed his diet, added exercise and meditation, and took more time off from work. Acknowledging his hatred didn't cure him, but he was more energetic and happier.

So, the next time you feel hate, don't drain your psychic energy by denying it—move toward it. Ask yourself, "What is the root of this hateful feeling?" You may discover the fuel for the change you've been looking for.

Do You Suffer From "Shame Shudder"?

Shame shudder is a sudden feeling of disgust about your past behavior.

You're walking down the street, feeling great; the sun is shining, life is good. Suddenly, you recall something regretful you did. A jab of shame stabs at you; you shake your head and shudder in disbelief.

"Why did that just happen? I was having such a good day!"

You try to push the feeling away. You tell yourself: *"Take a few deep breaths. It was a mistake. It's in the past. Relax."*

Slowly, after much mental effort, you start to recover your good mood.

What is a shame shudder?

Though not a clinical term, many psychotherapy patients report feeling sudden bouts of shame that appear out of nowhere. Shame shudders, sometimes called "shame attacks," can occur randomly and without any clear trigger. Prompted by the sudden recall of a painful memory, the regret attached to the event activates shame. (See "Breaking Free of Self-Shame")

Unlike intrusive thoughts, a well-documented psychological phenomenon that can spring from fantasies or fears, shame shudders originate from regretful moments in your life. The emotional distress from intrusive thoughts and shame shudders is the same: intense feelings of disgust and discomfort.

3 Potential Causes of Shame Shudder

Why dredge up shame to ruin your day? The three most common causes of shame shudders are:

1. Unresolved guilt

To err is human, to forgive is divine. We all make mistakes or have regrets. Maybe you said or did something hurtful to someone you care about. Chances are you haven't forgiven yourself or made amends, so the shame attached to the event remains unresolved.

2. Emotional wounds

When hurt is inflicted on you by someone else, it's difficult to resolve, particularly if you no longer have contact with that person. For example, if you were betrayed by someone close to you, chances are you feel ashamed for trusting that person. In such cases, you may wish you handled the situation better and affix shame to it. (See "7 Hurts That Never Heal")

3. Childhood trauma

Unresolved childhood traumas can shape and haunt us with regret. Many adults still feel shamed when they recall harmful events from their childhood, even though it's likely they were too young to respond differently.

How to reduce shame shudder

To lessen shame shudders, consider the following:

- **Forgive yourself:** Acknowledge the painful event and absolve yourself. Chances are you're not the same person you were back then. Meditation or spiritual practices can be particularly effective in helping with self-forgiveness.

- **Make amends:** Apologizing can offer relief and resolve old regrets. If the person you hurt isn't available, try writing them a letter. Even if you don't send it, the experience of writing it will offer some relief.

- **Push back against shame:** When shame shudders occur, push back. Tell yourself, *"That was in the past."* A short phrase or word will do. One woman who experiences shame shudders once told me that she says out loud, *"Enough!"* and chases the shame away.

———————

3 Toxic Mindsets That May Be Poisoning Your Life

How to break free of repetitive patterns that breed unhappiness.

If you've contacted a therapist, you are likely dissatisfied with your life. Things didn't turn out how you hoped; you may feel angry, misunderstood, or hurt. With your therapist, you pick through your history, examine your friendships, and scrutinize your family, spouse, or society.

In the early stages of therapy, intense feelings are likely to pour out of you, emotions such as rage, hurt, sadness, or despair. Unburdening yourself of these feelings brings a satisfying sense of relief. Someone is finally listening and understanding you; you feel validated.

After relieving yourself of all these pent-up feelings — then what?

Searching for Clues to a Toxic Mindset

Therapists are skilled listeners. They nod quietly, ask questions, and offer you a tissue when you cry. But beneath their calm exteriors, they are studying your every move. How you sit in the chair, the tone of your voice, the way you avoid eye contact or transmit anxiety by tapping your foot or shifting in your seat.

Since most therapists are naturally empathetic, they also study their emotional reactions to you. They notice the feelings that you induced in them. For example, do they feel anxious, threatened, or depressed when they contact you? These empathic inductions are essential to study because they often reflect how people experience you.

Unearthing Toxic Mindset Patterns

After collecting all this data, your therapist has a collection of emotional puzzle pieces to fit together. Soon, patterns start to come into focus. Repetitive experiences, expressions, or emotional tics appear. Power life-shaping toxic mindsets begin to emerge, such as:

- "I'm always an outsider."
- "I have trouble trusting people."
- "Everyone abandons me."

When phrases such as these take root, they can become a toxic mindset that undermines your life. For example:

- "I'm always an outsider." You anticipate rejection in social situations.
- "I have trouble trusting people." You hold yourself at a distance from others, avoid intimacy, or isolate yourself.
- "Everyone always abandons me." You see the potential for hurt in every relationship. Getting close to others will always end badly, so why do it?

Each toxic mindset perpetuates the same unhappy outcome, a phenomenon Sigmond Freud called the "repetition compulsion." In other words, you repeat what is familiar, even if it is unhealthy.

As Buddhist peace advocate and poet Daisaku Ikeda writes in his book, *The Wisdom For Creating Happiness and Peace:* "When we allow ourselves to be ruled by such negative attitudes, we are like a plane that has lost its direction in a heavy fog. We can see nothing clearly."

But here's the good news: What drives that harmful compulsion? The wish to resolve the unhealthy pattern. This wish contains enormous energy for change. A skilled therapist will harness that energy, challenge your toxic mindset, and direct you toward making new choices that will produce different outcomes and end the repetition compulsion cycle.

Individual or Group Therapy?

Though there are dozens of kinds of therapy, the two most common are individual and group therapy. For extreme mood problems, such as overwhelming depression or anxiety, individual therapy is an ideal choice. To learn how to build healthy relationships or overcome struggles with addiction or impulsive behaviors, you can't beat the power of weekly group therapy.

How Your Disowned Feelings Are Hurting You

Banishing unwanted emotions always backfires.

Have you ever heard someone yell, "I'm not angry?" If you have, then you've witnessed a disowned feeling in action.

Disowned feelings are those prickly emotions you attempt to block out of awareness. You tell yourself you're not feeling them and give them the cold shoulder. Unfortunately, ignoring unwanted feelings comes at a high cost.

The energy it takes to push away unwanted feelings frequently leads to:

Psychic tension that fuels mood disorders, such as anxiety or depression.

Psychosomatic symptoms, such as headaches, backaches, and digestive or stomach issues.

A loss of vitality, resulting in chronic exhaustion, inattentiveness, or forgetfulness.

The Top 3 Disowned Feelings

Though all feelings are valuable, some are more popular than others. Disowned feelings are generally unpopular because they create discomfort or distress. The top three disowned feelings that I've noticed in my psychotherapy practice are:

1. Anger

The adage, "depression is anger turned inward," holds. To deny anger is to deny yourself a propitious source of energy. Learning to access and focus your anger can relieve depression and anxiety while producing revitalizing energy and clarity bursts. Learning to process and express your anger productively is a life-changer.

2. Hurt

When your feelings were hurt as a child, you had a good cry and moved on. As an adult, hurt is much more complex. Admitting that you're hurt can feel shameful and humiliating, particularly if you have a history of being bullied. So, you learned to deny hurt to protect yourself from feeling vulnerable. Ironically, anytime someone proclaims, "I'm not hurt" it's very likely that they are. Identifying when you're hurt and verbalizing it frees you from a cycle of shame, strengthens emotional boundaries, and elevates self-respect.

3. Fear

While it's fun to be afraid while watching scary movies or visiting amusement parks, unbridled fear causes escalating anxiety and panic in real life. Few people enjoy being out of control, so when fear strikes, you may want to deny it or bulldoze over it. Unfortunately, denying fear invites poor decision-making, destructive risk-taking, and lapses in judgment.

The Damage Caused by Disowning Feelings

Denying an unwanted feeling doesn't resolve it; it simply drives it out of your consciousness. It is still there but in hiding. Sooner or later, like an annoying relative who drops by unannounced, the feeling pops up again. You find yourself caught in repetitive relationship patterns or miscommunications.

Every time you disown a feeling, you weaken your sense of self. You water down your emotions until you don't know your feelings. The fallout is even more discouraging: identity confusion, unhealthy relationships, poor boundaries, and chronic disappointment, to name just a few.

Unearthing and Honoring Your True Feelings

When feelings are honored and expressed, your core sense of self strengthens; you are more focused and immediate. Since you're better attuned to yourself, you're better attuned to others. Authenticity becomes your guiding light, making navigating emotionally charged situations much more straightforward.

Of course, warming up to all your feelings takes time. It's a process of evolution—not revolution. Here are a few tips to get you going:

1. **Take a deep dive into your feelings.**

   Too often, we move through life on automatic pilot, zoning out for hours in front of a computer or numbing ourselves with substances, mindless television, or social media. To redirect your attention inward, you'll need to set aside time for reflection. Journal writing is a great way to get started. Whenever you jot down your thoughts and feelings, you bring more mindfulness to your daily life. Feelings become less mysterious or frightening; understanding your pure feelings fosters personal enlightenment. Set a timer, write for a few minutes daily, and slowly increase your journaling time.

2. **Work with a professional.**

   There are more therapists in the world than ever before in history. Art therapy, dance therapy, mental health counseling, support groups, child and family therapy, couples counseling, sex therapy ... the list goes on and on. And now, with teletherapy and virtual therapy, you don't have to leave your home. If talking to a professional is too frightening, open up to a good friend and share feelings that you often keep hidden.

3. **Reward yourself**

   Acknowledge your efforts, and celebrate your victories. Changing ingrained behaviors is one of the hardest things in the world. It's a lonely battle. That's why you must make time to reward yourself. I worked with a young woman who suffered crippling social anxiety. As she started to assert herself, she developed many catchphrases to encourage her, such as "You got this," "You'll be glad later," or "What have I got to lose?" As she became a cheerleader for her growth, she made healthier choices and enjoyed more rewarding relationships.

How To Win the Battle With Yourself

Three essential tools to develop self-mastery.

External obstacles are dramatic, the source of great theater. When you fight against something in your environment that's causing you suffering, you have a clear target. You can see what's standing in your way: financial hardship, a health challenge, a problematic relationship, social injustice.

Every time you fight an external obstacle, you discover a strength you never knew. In the process, you find like-minded people who share your concerns; nothing unites individuals more than a common enemy.

But what about those battles that you have to face alone? The quiet wars we wage within ourselves? How do you win those?

Internal obstacles are fuel for self-mastery

Recently, a patient in my psychotherapy practice became furious with me. She was asking for advice, and I hesitated to offer it.

"Why won't you tell me what to do?" she demanded.

She didn't have a good track record of following the advice. Like many of us, she knew what she had to do but couldn't do it. No matter how she tried, she couldn't give herself an order and stick to it. Even worse, she had a history of asking for advice, not following it and blaming the advice giver. She was losing the battle with herself.

"I'm not sure if you're on your own team," I said.

"Of course I am. I'm here in therapy, working on myself. Don't I get credit for that?"

"Certainly, but it's what you do outside of sessions that counts the most."

Why the battle for self-mastery is so difficult

When you set a goal for yourself, self-doubt appears, your mind becomes muddled, and a fog of uncertainty washes over you. Negative internal voices prod you to give up:

> *"This is too hard."*
>
> *"This isn't important to me."*
>
> *"I'll work on this some other day. Now's not the time."*

When you abandon a goal and give up, your self-esteem takes a big hit. You feel like a failure, and happiness is fleeting. You're tossed around in a sea of uncertainty, a victim rather than a victor of your destiny.

There is no self-mastery without challenges

Buddhist peace advocate Daisaku Ikeda suggests that the battle for self-mastery is critical to establishing a strong identity. He writes that we must:

> *"...push open the heavy, groaning doorway of life itself. This is not an easy task. Indeed, it may be the most severely challenging struggle there is. For opening the door to your own life is, in the end, more difficult than opening the door to all the mysteries of the universe."*

Developing self-mastery

Sustainable happiness is only achievable when you win the battle with yourself. Every time you face and overcome your fears, you experience a burst of pride. Cultivating the self-discipline to keep pushing through obstacles is key to winning. Here's how to get started:

1. Set a goal and hold to it.

In the world of self-mastery, victory lies in the effort, not the outcome. Stop being a slave to your feelings. Give yourself an order and follow it.

It doesn't matter what you're feeling—doubt, fear, uncertainty—push through it. There'll be plenty of time to analyze it and reevaluate it later.

Start with smaller, achievable goals, then move on to larger ones. As Emerson advises: "Do your work, and you shall reinforce yourself."

2. Keep your eye on the prize.

Ups and downs are part of the process of developing self-mastery. Like lifting weights, you grow stronger every time you overcome an obstacle. Stumbling or falling along the way is not evidence of your weakness or failure—it's the way to develop resilience and grit.

3. Be of service.

Altruism is an excellent source of self-esteem and is far more empowering than ruminating about your misfortunes or assigning blame. Helping someone's suffering lessens your burdens, boosts your self-worth, and brightens a darkened path.

Self-mastery is formidable, but the rewards are boundless. When you master yourself, you master life and all its challenges.

Are You Self-Awakened?

The 5 empowering qualities of self-awakened people.

Why do some people thrive in the face of obstacles and setbacks while others in more favorable circumstances lack the drive to persevere?

Buddhist scholar and peace activist Daisaku Ikeda suggests:

"Fortune and misfortune are unfathomable. Even if we achieve a win, our joy will not last forever. But a person of self-awakening, even if temporarily defeated, can go on to build a future vaster, broader, deeper, and greater than someone who seems to have won." (World Tribune, June 6, 2020)

Sounds promising. But how does one become "self-awakened?"

The Resilience of the Self-Awakened

Self-awakened persons aren't dependent on their environment to meet their needs. Even in hostile environments, they feel empowered to weed out toxins and find nutrients. Driven by a sense of purpose and undisturbed by the opinions of others, they embrace freedom and independence. Rather than sink into defeat when obstacles appear in their path, they rally their resources and become even more determined to break through. Their superpower: turning obstacles into opportunities to forge and strengthen their will.

The Fragility of the Self-Discouraged

After conducting thousands of individual and group therapy sessions over 25 years, I think the "self-discouraging personality" is the most difficult to heal. Self-discouraging personalities allow their past to define them; they embrace outdated childhood versions of themselves built on distrust and powerlessness. As adults, they carry around negative voices in their heads that stoke fear, shame, and discouragement. When faced with an obstacle, rather than pursuing growth choices, they retreat and blame others for their misfortune.

5 Empowering Qualities of Self-Awaked People

Working in therapy with self-awakened people is a lot of fun. In every session, they arrive eager and ready to work on themselves. They see therapy as a tool for growth and quickly apply what they learn.

Here are the five qualities self-awakened people most frequently demonstrate:

1. **A Drive for Self-Improvement.** The self-awakened are hungry for growth. Rather than accumulate material goods, they put more energy into working on their inner lives; they question, explore, and challenge themselves, processing powerful feelings with a healthy curiosity and eagerness to understand.

2. **A Cultivated Sense of Gratitude.** Rather than grumble about life's difficulties, self-awakened folks find a way to cultivate appreciation even amid struggles. Unfortunately, complaining comes naturally for most people; gratitude doesn't. It requires work, but the rewards are plentiful. For example, a woman in one of my therapy groups noted, "The office culture at my new job is miserable. Everyone

complains about everything!" Rather than join the culture, she viewed it as a challenge. She set the goal of making one positive comment to each co-worker daily. Sure enough, she became the change the office needed to break free of the resentment and dissatisfaction fostering such an unpleasant work environment.

3. **A Yearning for Mentors.** The self-awakened yearn for leadership and guidance from mentors. They are skilled at finding symbolic parents who can give them the approval and encouragement they crave but perhaps never receive. Rather than blaming their upbringing, they set out to create a more reliable self by strengthening their life force and absorbing the skills and expertise of their mentor.

4. **A Spiritual Practice.** A spiritual practice strengthens one's identity by inspiring you to move beyond the mundane and consider the profound. For example, contemplating life's sufferings, such as one's death, is a great way to reevaluate your life choices and let go of petty concerns. A spiritual practice naturally impels you toward self-awakening by causing you to see the bigger picture and embrace a more altruistic way of being.

5. **Healthy Relationships.** Negative relationships are one of the most significant sources of suffering in life. Identifying unhealthy relationships and moving toward more positive people is vital in striving toward a self-awakened life.

Beginning Your Self-Awakened Journey

There are endless tools to help you initiate your journey of self-awakening. Challenging unhealthy habits and exploring new, creative experiences is critical. Psychotherapy or counseling is undoubtedly a great place to start. You may also find the inspiration you need in support groups, classes, lectures, online courses, meditation, and other creative outlets.

Self-awakening begins with — you guessed it — *you*. No one will knock on your door and offer you a new life. When you accept full responsibility for your choices, you take a significant step toward self-empowerment and a new way of being.

Reversing Negative Thinking Through Gratitude

A gratitude journal saved my life and gave me hope when I had none.

Every morning, I woke up with dread. A feeling of heaviness invaded my thoughts, weighed me down during the day, and tortured me at night. I zombied through the world with little hope that life could change. I even questioned the value of living.

A series of irreversible crises hit my family. My wife and I had always been cheerleaders for each other, but we were both knocked down this time. We didn't know how to help ourselves or one another. She felt equally defeated.

"Why me? Why are these things happening?"

My mind searched for relief and only found more hopelessness. All the tools I learned as a psychotherapist failed me. I felt like a fraud.

Then, early one morning, after a sleepless night tormented by my menacing thoughts, I decided I had to do something different. I had no choice. I couldn't go on living demoralized.

On a whim, I pulled an old notebook from a shelf and sat at my kitchen table on a whim. I opened it to a blank page and wrote four words: "I am grateful for..."

Honestly, I didn't know what I was doing. It was a pure impulse. A part of me resisted and mocked the entire exercise. But a healthier part of me pushed me forward, encouraged me to continue writing, and kept trying to list all the good in my life.

The birth of a gratitude journal

Every morning, I re-read my gratitude journal and added to it. I started to carry it with me. I opened it sporadically during the day and wrote. Over time, a genuinely remarkable thing started to happen. The events in my life didn't change, but my attitude did. I felt lighter.

My gratitude journal forced me to look beyond my pain at the moment and see the bigger picture. It challenged my negative thinking and gave me a broader perspective.

Often, pain seduces you into believing it will never end. All pain is personal for me, so the solution had to be too. If I was generating negative thoughts, I had the power to create positive ones as well. Unearthing gratitude opened my mind to new possibilities.

I don't expect you to believe me. I have no scientific proof that a gratitude journal can help you. I have no statistics to quote or studies to share. It made a big difference in my life. It helped me when I thought nothing could.

Starting a gratitude journal

Over time, my gratitude journal evolved. I divided gratitude into three simple groups: people, places, and things:

People

Who do you love? Who are you grateful for in your life? Make a list as detailed as possible. What qualities in that person do you love the most? If the person has passed away, what did they give you?

Places

List places that have filled you with joy. They could be current places or memories. For me, recollections of visiting my grandmother's house were packed with happiness. As I wrote down memories, I found myself smiling. The memories were surprisingly fresh and accessible.

Things

List anything you like: pets, a beloved book, a favorite meal, a song. Nothing is small or insignificant. If it brings you happiness, it matters.

The internet is full of gratitude journal suggestions and prompts. You can use them as a jumping-off point, print them out, or reference suggestions. Or you can find a notebook or piece of paper and start right now. Once you begin writing, don't stop until you fill the page.

You may be surprised to discover that even in the darkest places, you have the power to generate light.

---

5 Reasons Why Meditation Doesn't Work for Everyone

For some, hiking, swimming, or coloring can work just as well.

Meditation is a beautiful tool for fostering self-reflection and peace of mind. But does it work for everyone?

Before we get into the nitty-gritty of why meditation fails some people, let me begin with full disclosure: I've had a meditation practice for 33 years. I start each day with one hour and set aside time to study teachings related to my mindfulness practice.

Daily meditation is my secret source of strength: It clears mental fog, soothes jittery nerves and anxiety, and helps me find meaning in life's inevitable obstacles. It's a "spiritual gym" that never fails to strengthen my life force.

Does that mean mediation is for you? That depends on several factors.

Meditation comes in many forms; any activity that fosters calm, self-reflection, and mindfulness could be considered a form of meditation. For this post, we'll focus on traditional meditation—sitting silently, focusing on breathing, and relaxing your body and mind.

It sounds pretty chill, right? So what's the problem?

Who May Struggle With Meditation

If you suffer from the following chronic conditions, meditation may not be your best option.

1. **Intense anxiety:** Anxiety can turn your inner world into chaos filled with intrusive thoughts, obsessive thinking, rumination, or paranoia. Turning your attention inward could spike an increase in dread and discomfort.

2. **Ongoing depression:** People struggling with depression tend to isolate themselves, withdraw from the world, and spend too much time alone. Meditation could fuel further reclusiveness

3. **Trauma:** Trauma can cause dissociation and panic attacks. When trauma is triggered, the mind tends to fragment, and trying to quiet your thoughts can feel like an insurmountable challenge.

4. **Psychotic episodes:** Psychosis is generally defined as a break in reality testing; this leads to an unstable and fragile sense of self. Meditation could further this break and magnify distortions

5. **Active addiction:** If someone is in the throes of active addiction, it's difficult for any form of meditation or therapy to be effective. Meditation could increase cravings and thoughts of using drugs or alcohol.

As you can see, traditional forms of meditation direct you to turn your thoughts inward. If your inner world is in turmoil, it may initiate a battle of the mind that makes your symptoms worse.

Nontraditional Meditation Practices to Consider

If you find meditation unbearable, consider forms of meditation that draw your focus outside of yourself by giving you a task or activity to focus on. Meditation involving tactile or stimulating sensory experiences will pull you out of yourself and give you a break from internal distress.

For example, I worked with a young man who was traumatized by a life-threatening car accident. He was overwhelmed with anxiety and symptoms of post-traumatic stress disorder. No matter how he tried to meditate, he couldn't quiet his mind. In fact, he felt worse with each attempt, like he was a failure at meditation.

Then one day, while organizing his garage, he found a small piece of fresh-cut pine. He took out his pocket knife, sat on a crate, and quietly whittled away at it. The more he focused on the wood, the calmer he felt.

Whittling and wood carving soon became his meditation. At first, he carved simple household objects, such as forks or spoons, which became gifts to friends and family. Later, he experimented with larger projects and took an art class.

Developing his natural talent for whittling opened the door to the calm he needed in his life. It slowed his heart rate and metabolism, cleared his mind, and gave him something to focus on other than his pain. The objects he created also became symbols of healing.

Finding Your Form of Meditation

Think of quiet tasks you enjoy that replenish your energy and focus your mind, then explore how you feel after engaging in them. You're on the right path if you feel calmer and more grounded.

Some nontraditional forms include walking, hiking, fishing, swimming, surfing, painting, cooking, chanting, exercising, writing, stretching, coloring, crafting, biking, reading, or gardening.

It will take time and experimentation to find your form of meditation. Enjoy the adventure and remember, a meditation practice isn't just calming; it has the power to improve all areas of your life.

CHAPTER 13:
TEENAGERS

Raising Teenagers in the Age of Anxiety

Teens have good reason to be anxious.

Are you mystified by your teenager's behavior? Broken-hearted by the changes you see in him?

It's natural to mourn the loss of the wonder years when your kid becomes a teen.

> *"He was so creative and playful in elementary school."*
>
> *"She was always laughing and had so many friends."*
>
> *"He loved family time. Now he won't come out of his room."*

If you're eager to know what caused your easy-going child to morph into a sullen, irritable, and complicated person—this article's for you.

Adolescence and Anxiety

Massive biological and psychological maturation floods adolescents with feelings of anxiety. Changes in brain chemistry, surging hormones, and a pesky underdeveloped prefrontal cortex destabilize teens, resulting in a fragile sense of self, labile moods, and poor impulse control.

Sounds like fun? It isn't.

Teenagers are overwhelmed with emotions that they don't understand. Uncertainty and insecurity plague them. Add to their struggles a daily dose of social, sexual, and academic tension, and in a single day, teenagers may experience euphoria, crushing hurt, overwhelming anxiety, or deep despair.

No wonder teenagers don't want to get out of bed.

As anxiety builds, so does psychic, physical, and emotional tension. Unfortunately, teenagers have limited emotional vocabulary, causing them to have more feelings than words. Without the ability to express themselves, the pressure builds, giving way to crushing anxiety that erupts in disruptive behaviors such as erratic moods, senseless raging, or impulsive choices.

Look elsewhere if you're looking for your teenager to demonstrate mindfulness, patience, or clear-headed thinking. Holding such high ideals during this challenging period only sets the stage for more conflicts.

The Age of Anxiety

Warren Getler, the author of the novel *PANIC*, which chronicles the emotional peaks and valleys of a young man with panic disorder, uses the term "Age of Anxiety" to describe our times. He certainly has hit a nerve. Researchers note that nearly 20% of the population suffers from anxiety disorders (US News), and according to ADAA (Anxiety and Depression Association of America), 80% of kids with a diagnosable anxiety disorder are not getting treatment.

What's more, the world's turbulent state compounds teenagers' fears. Consider what they have to deal with today that past generations didn't have to contend with:

- School shooters
- Catastrophic global warming predictions
- Ongoing terrorist threats
- The opiate crisis
- Toxic social media outlets
- Skyrocketing college debt
- Competitive standardized testing

- Compulsive technology use

What's more, teens today are bombarded with bad news on their smartphones at a time when they have very few coping skills to manage their emotions.

The Fog of Teen Anxiety

Emotional tension is at the core of teen angst. When teens feel anxious, they can't think, can't regulate their moods or impulses, and have trouble focusing. Perhaps they have difficulty falling asleep or difficulty waking up. Why? Because anxiety disrupts all aspects of their functioning.

How to Lower Anxiety in Teenagers

If you sense your teenager is anxious, take extra care not to drive up their anxiety by becoming reactive and punitive. Losing your temper occasionally is okay, but constant yelling, guilting, blaming, shaming, criticizing, and other aggressive choices will drive your teenager away from you and spike their anxiety to dangerous levels. As anxiety intensifies, so do destructive behaviors such as cutting, eating disorders, hyperactivity, or substance abuse.

Here are five ways to lower anxiety in your teenager:

1. **Model the behaviors you want to see.** Self-mastery is the key to effective parenting. Do your best to model restraint and keep communication flowing. For example, losing it over an unmade bed, at the cost of damaging your relationship, isn't worth it.

2. **De-escalate conflicts.** Teens are impulsive and reactive—adults shouldn't be. Step away from conflict when it gets heated, breathe, and chill out. When you return, address the core feelings driving the conflict rather than repeating a reactive loop.

3. **Hold family meetings.** Don't wait for a problem to emerge to address it. Family meetings are a great time to show appreciation for what your kid did right, plan family vacations or activities, and discuss chores or conflicts. Frequently, parents discuss thorny subjects at the worst time, such as in

the middle of an argument or when everyone is exhausted from a long day. The ultimate role of family meetings is to provide an outlet to foster healthy communication.

4. **Maintain structure, limits, and boundaries.** Structure soothes anxiety. Routines such as family dinners, bedtimes, curfews, etc., help teenagers feel safe and cared for. It's okay to be flexible, but teens soon go off the rails without consistency. Of course, structure, limits, and boundaries can be amended once trust and consistency are established.

5. **Tech detox as a family.** Put down your phone, store the laptop, and take a break from social media. Compulsive technology use is a growing problem with enormous emotional consequences. Look for self-soothing creative outlets, such as music, art, or exercise. And remember to practice self-care. An unhappy or burnt-out parent is a burden to a child at any age. The best way to help your teenager is to help yourself first. If you're overwhelmed or living in a state of anxiety, you can't parent effectively.

Why Therapy Fails Many Teenagers

Techniques that don't work with teens.

I've provided psychotherapy to teenagers for 25 years. I've worked with them individually and in groups, public and private schools, community centers, and private practice. I've always found teenagers remarkably receptive to therapy, primarily group therapy.

So why do so many parents report their kids being unresponsive to therapy?

Specialized training is needed to work with teens. Working with teenagers requires specific training and experience. Many therapists graduate with few clinical tools for working with teens. As a result, they apply adult therapy techniques to adolescents—a guaranteed failure.

Teens lack the emotional maturity of adults. Poor insight, impaired attention, shoddy impulse control, and an unstable sense of identity are typical characteristics of teenagers. Developmentally, they can't participate in the reflective-thinking and insight-oriented work that adults welcome in therapy. Some teenagers may respond, but the vast majority will not. Trying to do adult therapy with a teenager is like forcing teens to speak a language they don't understand.

Therapists are often frustrated by teenagers. Frequently, therapists get frustrated with teenagers and shame them for being unresponsive and not solution-focused. Believe it or not, I've heard inexperienced therapists say to teenagers:

- "You're wasting your parent's money by not talking to me."

- "Your behavior is hurting your family. Don't you want to change?"

- "Your choices are only making life harder for yourself."

Such guilt-giving communications destroy teenagers' trust and confidence. Worse, they encourage teenagers to avoid therapy in the future.

Signs That a Teen's in Therapy with the Wrong Therapist

Here are two classic excuses therapists frequently use when they fail to make progress with a teenager:

1. **"You can't force teenagers into therapy. They have to want to be there."**

   Nearly all teenagers are therapy hostages. Unlike adults, they don't choose to be in therapy; they are forced into therapy by their parents, school officials, or mandated reporters. It's the therapist's job to convert them into willing participants.

2. **"They aren't cooperating in sessions."**

   Of course, they aren't cooperating. Not cooperating is what teenagers do best. To engage teenagers, therapists need to be creative and flexible while relating to them. Sitting passively and listening, or speaking in psychobabble, doesn't cut it.

3 Qualities Therapists Need to Work with Teenagers

1. **Authenticity.** Teenagers can spot a phony. They always reject distant, detached, or guarded therapists. Such emotional coldness can increase teen anxiety or exacerbate depressive symptoms.

2. **Good humor.** Sadly, teenagers frequently spend time with stressed or humorless adults. An adult with a sense of humor is a breath of fresh air and a good role model. Teens are drawn to them.

3. **Playfulness.** A playful spirit requires lighthearted attentiveness and cheerful flexibility. Teenagers love to talk about movies, sports, video games, etc. A therapist who welcomes all their interests and responds with curiosity will be far more successful.

---

7 Things Teenagers Desperately Need Adults to Understand

7 ways to quiet your teen's negative self-talk.

"Every day is a prison, trapped inside this changing body, repeating the same day over and over. My whole life comprises things I *have* to do, not things I *want* to do. Tests, quizzes, reading assignments, papers, group projects — I spend the entire day with people I am forced to be with: teenagers who feel just as messed up as me.

"Sometimes my feelings get hurt at school — by teachers, deans, counselors, but primarily by other students. I don't tell you this because I'm ashamed to feel hurt. I don't want you to know how hurt I feel all the time.

"My whole life has become 'I don't want to...' I don't want to wake up. I don't want to go to bed. I don't want to go to school. I don't want to...I don't want to...I don't want to.

"I can't think of anything I want to do — except sleep. It's the only time I'm not stressing, the only time I'm not worried, the only time I'm not upset.

"Sometimes I hide in my room and binge-watch Netflix, YouTube, or mindless videos over and over because I can't stand to be with my thoughts. I'm distracting myself from me. Does that sound crazy?

"And, yes, I know that my room is a mess. I *like* it that way: It looks how I feel inside. And please don't ask me what's wrong, because I don't *know*. I don't know where these feelings came from.

"I know that you're mad at me. I can't blame you. I stopped talking to you. Sometimes I say such mean things to you, horrible things. I blame you, curse at you, push you away. Sometimes, I break things because I feel broken inside.

"It wasn't always this way. When I look at old photos of me in elementary school, I see a little kid who was always so happy. A little kid who loved to dance and sing, who loved to be silly, who didn't care what people thought.

"I feel like that little kid is dead.

"I'm going to tell you something now that's hard to say. Please listen, because I mean it: *Don't give up on me*. Don't hate me back. I need you to be stronger than me. I need you to be my parent, even though I say I don't want one. I need you to be more patient, understanding, and accepting than I can be. Even when I yell at you and tell you that I hate you, I still need you to love me.

"If I could tell you how to help me, this is what I would say:

1. Give me space.

Don't come into my room, corner me, or make demands. I don't have any answers. When you push me or yell at me, I feel worse. I need to be alone. I need space.

2. Don't yell at me.

The noise in my head is so loud sometimes that I can barely hear my thoughts. I can't stand it. When you yell, I feel worse about myself. I feel unloved. I feel like I am your biggest disappointment.

3. Take my electronics away.

I can't put my phone down; I try, but I just can't. I know it's devouring all my time, but I can't help myself; I can't stop checking it. I need your help. I need you to set limits on technology. Please. I will fight you, but it's what I need. Don't try to reason with me: Just do it.

4. Bring me someplace quiet.

I say I don't want anything to do with you. But if you could bring me somewhere quiet, somewhere we could walk together and not argue, somewhere I can feel the sun and listen to the wind in the trees, somewhere I can breathe and forget about everything that's bothering me, I think I would like that. Even if we don't speak, I will feel comforted.

5. Stop spoiling me.

Stop giving me everything I want. The more you give me, the more I resent you. I *want* to earn things. It helps me feel grown up. I want to learn how to save, spend, and share money. And I will never learn that if you keep giving it to me. I hate being dependent on you; please help me become independent.

6. Find me someone to talk to.

I need someone to look up to who isn't you. I need an adult to admire, someone I want to be like, someone who believes in me, pushes me, and understands me. A mentor, a counselor, a therapist...anyone who can give me hope when I have too little for myself.

7. Tell me that you love me.

I pretend not to care. But I need to hear you say, 'I love you.' Because right now, *I* don't love me. Even though I'm making your life hell, I still need to feel loved, especially by you.

"I guess that's it. I know that being a parent is hard. Sometimes, you probably wonder why you did it. But I'll get better. I promise. I'll get older, and we'll enjoy each other again. Until then, understand that I appreciate you.

"I may not say it often, but still, I love you."

Three Signs Your Teen Needs Therapy

How to tell the difference between teen angst and more serious conditions.

Some kids pass through adolescence swiftly, with little turmoil. For others, puberty detonates like a time bomb; once it goes off, nothing is the same.

As a psychotherapist, I've sat with many brokenhearted parents who agonize over their teen's behavior, mystified by the metamorphosis.

> *"She was such a happy child."*
>
> *"He was so easy."*
>
> *"She used to be so kind-hearted."*

Desperate for answers, parents often get a bad case of the "shoulds."

> *"I should have been stricter."*
>
> *"I should have spent more time at home."*
>
> *"I should have seen this coming."*

Or fault DNA:

> *"He's just like his father."*
>
> *"The men in my family are all alcoholics."*
>
> *"Depression runs in the family."*

Unfortunately, blame is a soothing balm with a short shelf life. Any relief it offers fades, and discomfort returns. Blaming your kids for their behavior is another faulty solution that can make conflicts go from bad to worse.

What's typical teenage angst? How can you tell if your kid needs professional help?

Developmental vs. Atypical Depression in Adolescence

In "The Handbook of Child and Adolescent Group Therapy," I identified two different kinds of adolescent depression: developmental depression vs. atypical depression:

Developmental Depression in Adolescence

Adolescence is frequently accompanied by a grieving period triggered by a sudden awareness of the fragilities of life. As teens enter developmental depression, they engage in disquieting meditations about death, symbolic of their loss of innocence and childhood identity. Realizing mortality, that loved ones and themselves are vulnerable, darkens their outlook.

Though developmental depression causes internal unrest, it also signals a fresh chapter in a teenager's life in which a new sense of self emerges. This unrest is normal and necessary; teenagers cannot forge a cohesive sense of self without sifting through these insecurities and uncertainties. The two key issues of developmental depression—identity and separation-individuation—must be wrestled with. If not, teenagers remain mired in outdated, early childhood behaviors such as temper tantrums or bullying.

The following features of adolescent developmental depression are suggested:

- Mood instability
- Feelings of sadness and melancholy
- Loss of interest in some but not all pleasurable activities
- Social anxiety
- Occasional fatigue, insomnia, or hypersomnia
- Infrequent suicidal or homicidal ideation without intent

Atypical Depression in Adolescence

Conditions that exacerbate developmental depression and create more emotionally severe instabilities result in atypical adolescent depression. Generated by increased levels of emotional distress, atypical depression is often triggered by disruptive forces such as:

- Undiagnosed learning disabilities
- Illness and injury
- Trauma
- Social rejection
- Parental conflicts
- Death of a loved one
- Financial hardship
- Changing homes or schools

Unlike developmental depression, in which teenagers experience tolerable levels of melancholy and mourning, atypical depression overwhelms teens with crushing despair and overpowering psychic tension. Unwelcomed feelings of rage, frustration, hopelessness, or powerlessness flare up, frequently leading to mercurial moods, negativity, or destructive obsessions.

Adolescents experiencing atypical depression are engrossed in a psychic battle to ward off unwanted insecurities and engage in defenses such as denial, projection, or dissociation. While these defenses are helpful and necessary, they require much psychic energy. For this reason, during atypical depression, teenagers may appear persistently fatigued, hypervigilant, or exhausted.

Features of atypical adolescent depression may include:

- Predominantly depressed or irritated mood
- Loss of interest in once enjoyable activities
- Social isolation and panic attacks
- Persistent fatigue, insomnia, or hypersomnia
- Prolonged feelings of hopelessness and indecisiveness
- Severe mood swings
- Persistent suicidal or homicidal ideation

Three Signs That Your Teenager Needs Help

Sometimes it can be difficult to know whether your teenager is suffering from a developmental or atypical depression. Here are three red flags that demand attention:

1. Self-harm

If your teenager is cutting, hitting or hurting him or herself, this is a sign of unbearable emotional turmoil and psychic imbalance. Self-harming behaviors can become habit-forming and escalate over time.

2. Chronic substance abuse

Experimentation with drugs or alcohol may be all too common in adolescence, but if your kid is regularly coming home drunk or high, a serious problem is taking root. Act immediately, particularly if your family has a history of substance abuse. Teens suffering from atypical depression are far more likely to develop substance abuse problems.

3. Suicide ideation or attempts

I'm always shocked when parent don't take threats of suicide or actual attempts seriously. They believe they can manage the situation themselves or their kid is "just being dramatic." With teen suicide rates on the rise, particularly among girls, all attempts or threats demand professional attention.

What to do if your teen suffers from Atypical Depression

When something goes wrong with their kids, asking for help can trigger feelings of failure or shame in parents. But getting help for your child is an act of compassion, not a sign of weakness. More importantly, atypical depression, left untreated, can negatively alter the entire course of your child's life.

In Chapter Eight of When Kids Call The Shots, I outline seven parenting crises that parents face and actions they can take to resolve them. Parents often tell me that they were surprised to discover how much support is available.

For starters, the internet offers endless opportunities to consult with professionals, such as crisis hotlines, support groups, parenting coaches, parenting classes, parenting blogs, books, and articles. Speaking with your kid's guidance counselor is also a great way to reach out and ask for help.

---

3 Rules for Arguing With Teenagers Without Pushing Them Away

How to fight for - not against - your teenager.

We walk in silence now, awkwardness wedged between us. Instead of laughing, we battle. We plot to defeat each other. But there are no winners in our war of words, only scars that ache with loneliness.

You feel like a prisoner in our family. You want more freedom. I get it. I understand that you're upset. But I can't allow all the independence you want. I am your parent, not your friend.

You hate me. You say this with flaming, resentful eyes, and for a second—just a second—I don't recognize you. Suddenly, an old bridge washes away, and we stand on separate shores, a raging bitterness between us.

I am reaching out to you now to find a way back. As your parent, I have to make unpopular decisions. (I don't expect you to understand this.) But maybe with kinder words, we can build a new bridge we can cross.

Your independence will soon arrive, and you'll spread your wings wide and full and break free. And I will cheer with delight as you lift off into the glowing sky.

Until then, let me put away angry words, cast aside my arrogance, and lead us in a better direction. I promise to try harder when we disagree. I will follow these simple rules:

1. No more judging
2. No more blaming
3. No more wanting to win

I pledge to listen more and talk less. I pledge to put my frustration aside and work to understand you. I pledge to be more sensitive and less reactive. I pledge to act out of respect instead of defensiveness.

This will take time. I will stumble and fall back into old habits. But I'll keep trying—I won't give up on us.

And in the future, when harsh moments fade and silence echoes in the emptiness of your room like the strings of your unplayed guitar, I'll take this letter out and, with an open heart, give thanks.

I will be thankful that we learned to fight for each other instead of against each other. And that together, we found the strength, on our journey as parent and child, to step away from stubbornness and lead with love.

Sincerely,

Your Parent

The Truth About Teens and Sex
... and the one factor tied to virginity loss two years earlier than average.

When I lead parenting workshops, I can feel the anxiety in the room spike when the issue of teen sex is raised. Mothers and fathers often get anxious when they see their teenagers—specifically their darling sons or daughters—morph into sexual beings. One mother, in parental panic, blurted out: "How will I know when my kid is having sex? Please tell me."

Unfortunately, my office isn't equipped with a crystal ball. But the following statistics about teenagers should soothe fears and resolve some of the mystery.

According to a recent study by the U.S. Centers for Disease Control, which conducts the National Survey of Family Growth (NSFG), the average age of teenagers in the U.S. when they lose their virginity is 17 years old (16.9 for males, 17.2 for females). Over 80 percent of Americans have had sex by age 20, usually with someone slightly older than them—0.6 years older for males and 1.4 years older for females. (The ages for mutually consensual sexual activity are largely the same among homosexual and heterosexual youth.)

Exposure to Sexually Explicit Materials

Due to relaxed restrictions on film, television, and the internet (that porn empire in your home!), teens have more access to sexually explicit material than ever. One click and they see more, learn more, and be traumatized more by sexually explicit materials than any other youth in history.

Even more troubling, while parents do their best to block and filter access to these materials, tech-savvy teens have an uncanny way of outsmarting them. (See my book, *When Kids Call the Shots*.) Parents, if you're worried that all this exposure has increased sexual activity among teens, you can relax: The age for virginity loss in the U.S. hasn't changed. It has been consistent for years.

Do Female Smokers Have Sex Younger?

Study outcomes can be wacky, but this outcome leaps off the page: The NSFG study showed that female teens who smoke tend to lose their virginity two years earlier than non-smoking female teens.

You may wonder if nicotine becomes an aphrodisiac for teens or if vaping is the new foreplay. The answers are more straightforward than you think. Young smokers tend to be risk-takers, which makes them much more likely to engage in risky behaviors. If you're collecting data on oppositional defiant disorders in youth, teen smokers are more likely to be featured.

Time to Talk About Sex

If you want your teenager to approach their first sexual encounter thoughtfully, then it's time for you to have an awkward conversation. Yes, "the sex talk" is still a must. Sure, you may receive resistance, eye rolls, and gag responses from your kid ("Gross, mom! Seriously!"), but don't let them discourage you.

If you're anxious about having "the talk," a spouse, cousin, or family friend is an acceptable substitute. The more teens know about sex, the less likely they are to be impulsive or engage in risky behavior. According to the NSFG report, 74.4 percent of parents today talk about sex with their kids. But it doesn't necessarily have to be a parent who has the conversation; any trusted adult will do.

Whether it is sex or another major life decision, open and positive communication with your teenager will inspire them to make smart choices. Remember, the best way to keep your kid healthy is to keep your relationship healthy.

Parents Can Be Arrested for Their Kid's House Party

"Host Laws" hold parents accountable, even if they're not home.

Picture this: You and your partner enjoy dinner at your favorite restaurant and savor quality kid-free time together. Meanwhile, your teenager invites friends over, and they bring alcohol, marijuana, or other drugs into your home to share. Perhaps your kid generously opens your liquor cabinet, and they help themselves to your favorite booze.

Believe it or not, according to Host Laws, you are guilty of an unintended crime. Your home is host to underage drinking and drug use. Even though you didn't give permission and weren't home, according to the law, you are guilty. What's more, if your teenager is over 18, they can also be arrested and charged as an adult.

Police Tracking Your Teen's House Party

How do the police know underage drinking or drug use happens in your home, even when you're away? It's easier than you think.

Social Media

Teens are tech-savvy and love to show off. Well, thanks to social media, the police can know without even leaving their desks. Teenagers frequently post announcements or photos of friends drinking and drugging at parties. Most police departments troll for such information, and officers are sent to the address.

Neighborhood Complaints

Partying teenagers aren't known for being discreet. A phone call from a neighbor or a store owner with a noise complaint is all it takes to bring the police to your house to investigate.

Visible Signs of a House Party in Process

Multiple cars in your driveway, blasting music, all your house lights on or your front and back doors open, all broadcast loud and clear that a house party is in progress. The police can shut down the party and wait for you to come home to arrest you.

Legal Consequences of Host Laws

SocialHostLaw.com reports that a father in Connecticut warned his kids about drinking alcohol at a party at his house over Thanksgiving weekend. They didn't listen. When the police arrived, the father was charged with 44 counts of contributing to the delinquency of a minor and received $110,000 in fines. Though the case is still pending, it's a real eye-opener and illustrates the serious legal consequences that parents could face.

Here are five outcomes that could happen when the police arrive at your kid's party when you're not home:

1. You will be cited or arrested with a criminal Social Host charge, likely a misdemeanor.

2. If the teens drink your liquor, you could also be charged with "Endangering the welfare of a child" and "Unlawfully dealing with a child in the first degree."

3. You are charged a count for each teenager, which results in more fees or jail time. A second offense could mean facing up to a year in jail.

4. If any teen is injured or dies on your property, you could face felony charges.

5. Teens and even minors can be charged as Social Hosts, resulting in school suspension and loss of college acceptance or scholarships. If convicted, they could have a permanent criminal record.

CHAPTER 14:
TRAUMA

3 Signs You May Have Suffered Childhood Emotional Incest

As adults, romantic intimacy may feel threatening.

Parents are the first relationships in a child's life. Parents model everything they learn about relationships. Even before developing language, children absorb their parents' feelings and behavior, their moods, their way of communicating, or how they express affection or frustration.

How the Dynamic Develops

It is not a recognized clinical diagnosis and does not refer to inappropriate sexual contact. The term "emotional incest" (also known as "covert incest") is used to describe parents who are unable to maintain healthy boundaries with their children. Such parents may live with mental illness, substance abuse, an unhappy marriage, or divorce. In essence, such parents feel alone and unloved, and rather than seek support from other adults, they turn to their children for intimacy and care. They may burden children with their own needs, constantly seek their validation, become emotionally or physically clingy, or try to control the child.

In seeking comfort from their child, they are asking their child, in a way, to become their parent. While some children may find this exciting, the excitement quickly wears off. The parent's emotional needs become overwhelming; few children caught in such a dynamic can meet all the parent's needs.

How Children Try to Break Free

To break free of this unhealthy dynamic, children attempt to create distance; they pull away from their parents and try to establish healthy boundaries. Unfortunately, parents may feel abandoned and shame or guilt their children, become physically or verbally abusive, slip into depression, or withdraw from their children altogether. They can attempt to make their children feel ashamed for wanting to be separated. They demand that their children stay merged with them, an effort that runs counter to healthy emotional development.

Signs of a Problem in Adulthood

Emotional incest leaves a deep scar on a child's experience of closeness and intimacy; specifically, they struggle in intimate relationships as adults. Signs of enduring this dynamic include:

1. **Difficulty sustaining intimate relationships.** Your romantic relationships start strong and may have great honeymoon periods. But they tend to decline quickly as emotional intimacy grows. You begin to distrust your partner and feel insecure or trapped.

2. **Disassociation, confusion, or taking distance from your romantic partner.** You start to pull away without explanation. Sex becomes unsatisfying, even revolting. You may grow inexplicably cold and critical, quickly finding fault with them, or blame your partner for discomfort.

3. **Panicky responses to intimacy, such as flight or fight.** As fear grows, you may invent a reason to stop seeing a partner or ghost them completely. Sometimes, you initiate fights to get a partner to break up with you. Either way, you are in flight from the relationship.

---

7 Hurts That Never Heal

... and 3 ways to cope.

You wake up with a familiar ache in your heart. Sadly, you can't remember when it wasn't there.

You've done everything you can to help yourself. You started weekly therapy, began journaling, exercising, and watching your diet, and self-help books piled up on your nightstand. And yet, the hurt rarely leaves you. Even if you forget it briefly, it returns soon after, a distressing reminder that nothing has changed.

Empty Promises and Reckless Optimism

Hurts that won't heal are rarely discussed openly and are frequently denied. In our solution-focused world, they are pushed into the shadows or met with empty platitudes:

> *"Everything happens for a reason."*
>
> *"Look on the bright side."*
>
> *"Tomorrow is a better day."*

Such hollow sentiments only deepen your despair by trivializing it and not acknowledging your loss.

Not All Hurts Heal

The reality is this: Some hurts will always be a part of you. And while they don't have to define you, they remain a daily reminder of your unforeseen challenges.

But before we examine how to cope, let's consider the seven most common hurts that won't heal.

1. **Death of a loved one.** Losing a beloved spouse, parent, or child is perhaps the deepest hurt one can experience. When people you love are taken from you, you struggle to go on. Every day, you have the impulse to call them, speak with them, or share something with them—and then you're reminded that they're gone, leaving a space in your heart that may never be filled.

2. **Mental illness.** A patient recently recalled when he realized his brother had schizophrenia, saying, "When the doctor told me, I didn't want to believe he was really sick." Although there are many successful treatments for chronic mental illness, patients often refuse to cooperate: They may drop out of therapy, stop taking meds, or depend on their parents or loved ones to rescue them.

3. **Addiction.** Addiction is a cruel affliction because the person you love is still there but no longer themselves. To make matters worse, someone addicted to substances may become skilled at lying to and exploiting those who love them. Unfortunately, hope is often short-lived as they tend to relapse again and again. Witnessing someone you love descend into addiction is a hurt that is genuinely heart-wrenching.

4. **Chronic illness.** You refuse to believe your doctor tells you about your condition. "It's not possible," you think. No matter how often you ask, "Why?" you can't find an answer. So, you try to get on with your life as you fear that your condition could worsen. For the first time, your life has an expiration date.

5. **Betrayal.** A betrayal by someone close to you cuts deep. You have trouble trusting others and push them away because you don't want to get hurt again. You may isolate or turn away from the world, convincing yourself you're better off alone. Betrayal not only makes you doubt others; it makes you doubt yourself as well.

6. **Permanent injury.** You have to re-learn how to move through the world. Daily tasks that were once simple now take a great deal of effort. People look at you with sorrow or pity, which makes you feel pathetic and small. You want to wish your injury away but must live with it.

7. **Trauma.** Trauma leaves an imprint that endures and can change the course of your life. It may undermine your ability to feel safe, trust others, or move through the world without fear. When trauma is activated, time and space

stop, and you find yourself trapped in the feeling of terror that occurred the moment the trauma took place. That terror may live inside you quietly or overwhelm you at any moment.

How to Cope with Hurt

Hurts that won't heal don't have to define you. When managed well, they deepen your humanity and foster greater empathy and connection to others. Hurts may remind you that life is fragile, but they can also remind you that life is precious. Many patients have reported that such hurts have inspired them to live in the moment and appreciate life more.

No one is exempt from unhealable hurts. Eventually, they appear in every life. No matter how people present themselves on social media, everyone eventually faces hurts that won't heal. The chances are that they are not posting their struggles, which creates a lopsided view of their lives.

3 Ways to Cope

1. **Turn your hurt into a mission.** I've witnessed many patients channel their hurt into a profound sense of mission. For instance, a friend who survived stage-four cancer found new meaning in life when he started volunteering at hospitals and counseling families and cancer patients. "If I can offer them any hope, I've been of value." A woman who was sexually assaulted volunteered for a hotline for young women in crisis. Though she initially struggled, she soon found it empowering: "I discovered that "helping others not only triggers healing in them, but it triggers healing in me as well."

2. **Share your pain.** Isolation is the enemy of healing, so commune with others, particularly those who've suffered similar experiences. A support group or group therapy is a wonderful and safe way to practice opening your heart and letting others get close to you. Prayer and meditation will also help you to find meaning in pain.

3. **Keep growing.** Grieving your hurt is essential. But it doesn't have to dominate your life. Don't give it power over you by playing the victim. Acknowledge it and move forward despite what you're feeling. Be a good parent to yourself by practicing self-care and expanding your creative and social outlets. Though the hurt may never disappear, you can bring its volume down by honoring it, embracing it, and moving forward with your life.